God, Sex, and Politics

God, Sex, and Politics

Homosexuality and Everyday Theologies

Dawne Moon

The University of Chicago Press
Chicago and London

Dawne Moon is assistant professor of sociology at the University of California, Berkeley.

The University of Chicago Press, Chicago 60637
The University of Chicago Press, Ltd., London
© 2004 by The University of Chicago
All rights reserved. Published 2004
Printed in the United States of America
13 12 11 10 09 08 07 06 05 04   5 4 3 2 1

ISBN (cloth): 0-226-53511-8
ISBN (paper): 0-226-53512-6

The Scripture quotations contained herein are from the New Revised Standard Version Bible, copyright 1989, by the Division of Christian Education of the National Council of the Churches of Christ in the U.S.A. Used by permission. All rights reserved.

Library of Congress Cagaloging-in-Publication Data

Moon, Dawne.
    God, sex, and politics : homosexuality and everyday theologies / Dawne Moon.
        p.   cm.
    Includes bibliographical references and index.
    ISBN 0-226-53511-8 (alk. paper) — ISBN 0-226-53512-6 (pbk. : alk. paper)
        1. Homosexuality—Religious aspects—Christianity.   I. Title.
    BR115.H6M66   2004
    306.6'61835766—dc22   2003024282

⊗The paper used in this publication meets the minimum requirements of the American National Standard for Information Sciences—Permanence of Paper for Printed Library Materials, ANSI Z39.48–1992.

Dedicated to
Robin Fogarty, the high school teacher who made me want to
be a scholar. Could this be what he had in mind?
And to the memory of Donna Byers,
the one who definitely saw it coming.

Contents

Acknowledgments

In writing acknowledgments, people often express some kind of surprise that no project is individual, no man is an island, or something like that. I am not the kind of person this surprises. I find myself with countless people to thank for a variety of contributions to this project, without which it would not be what it has become. So many people have helped me in so many ways, and I am overwhelmingly grateful to all.

A grant from the Sexuality Research Fellowship Program of the Social Science Research Council, funded by the Ford Foundation, and a grant from the Charlotte W. Newcombe Foundation, in collaboration with the Woodrow Wilson National Fellowship Foundation, were instrumental in giving me the time and money to conduct my research and write the dissertation version of this book. I am grateful to both programs, especially to the SSRC's Diane di Mauro and Mirja Pitkin for organizing the wonderful fellows conference of 1997. The Committee on Research at Berkeley also granted me some support to revise the dissertation into something more readable.

The University of Chicago community provided me with a rigorous, yet strangely supportive, environment in which to do my project. The faculty and students involved in the Center for Gender Studies and the Lesbian, Gay, and Queer Studies Workshop sustained me intellectually and gave me much of my education. I am forever indebted to those who expended extra personal and professional resources to create these spaces for intellectual inquiry.

I have been privileged to work with a number of scholars and activists who have given me hope as well as personal and intellectual support while I conducted this sometimes very painful study, some of whom are dear friends as well. They include: Anaheed Alani, Susan Allan, Leora Auslander, Matt Baldwin, Pat Carr, David Churchill, Bert Cohler, Eduardo Contreras, Sabrina Craig, Katie Crawford, Anne Eaton, Jeff Edwards, Jessica Fields, John Gagnon, Dave Grazian, Chad Heap, Maria Kefalas, Jeanne Kracher, Anne Lorimer, Cheryl Miller, Joey Mogul, Gina Olson, Jen Pashup, Mary Patten, Moishe Postone, Rosemary Powers, Piper Purcell, Mike Reay, Greta Rensenbrink, Steve Rosenberg, Joe Shepley, Arlene Stein, and Tara Tremmel. Debbie Gould was great in helping me to think not just about the project as it unfolded but also about the political implications of my research.

Through the course of my research, I accrued debts to a number of informed and helpful people who guided me through the workings of church and theology, including Greg Dell, Jade Dell, Greg Eaton, Doug Geyer, Mike Raley, Kent Svendsen, and the staffs of the Reconciling Congregations Program and Transforming Congregations.

I have been sustained through the research and writing by a loving and supportive community of dear friends and family, who inspired me and pulled me through the day-to-day, including Darren Carter, Virginia Chang, Lisa DeBoer, Gawain de Leeuw, Joyce Fitzgerald, Helen Hadley, Sonia Katyal, Matt Moon, J. O'Neill, Kelly Scanlan, and Colman Scanlan-Duro. Especial thanks for enduring me at my worst go to the friends who were around on pretty much a daily basis: Ali Abunimah, John Jasek, John Shamberg, Bil Susinka, and the latecomer who gave me hope and made writing a dissertation and then a book seem not so bad, the lovely and delightful Miss Searah Deysach. And a super-special debt of gratitude and countless other things goes to Becky Sandefur, who contributed almost as much to this project as I did in ways I cannot begin to enumerate. She went way beyond roommate duty.

In the dissertation phase of this project, I was fortunate to have an amazing dissertation committee. Each member demanded something different of me. Andy Abbott saw a spark of potential in me early on, and helped me through the anguish, self-doubt, and transformation of ethnography, and helped me to keep ever in mind an audience outside the literatures I drew from. Leslie Salzinger helped me to think about my role as a feminist, queer theorist, and researcher. George Chauncey was there from the beginning and pushed me to keep my eyes on the big questions. Lauren Berlant was sweetly forthcoming with the Kleenex and gave me a language with which to think about what I observed but struggled to articulate. Beth Povinelli endured my numerous struggles to understand how we are all shaped and constrained by hegemonic discourses, and helped give me a theoretically informed method for analyzing people's shifting ways of thinking and speaking. In short, she showed me how to be a critical and respectful storyteller, and I fear that my tremendous intellectual debt to her does not come through in the text.

While I was at Chicago, Billie Crawford, Alta Goodwine, and Linnea Martin were instrumental in getting me through it all.

Once I was happily settled at Berkeley, Robert Bellah, Michael Burawoy, Nancy Chodorow, Kristen Luker, Jimmy Klausen, Raka Ray, Jonathan VanAntwerpen, and Melissa Wilde provided me with feedback that was helpful, interesting, and encouraging. Jaye Cee Whitehead provided expert research assistance, and John Shamberg came through at the end with the editorial suggestions that made things seem to come together as I prepared the manuscript. Anonymous readers provided me with challenging and engaging feedback, and my editor, Doug Mitchell, and his assistant, Tim McGovern, handled me and the process with charm and skill.

Most important, this project would not exist without the generous support, cooperation, and insights of the members of "Missionary United Methodist Church" and "City United Methodist Church." Both congregations warmly received me and accepted me as one of their own, even as I poked around with my own agenda and failed to get with the program of either place. The love and grace their members showed me made me, in some ways, a different (and hopefully better) person. They may not like or agree with everything I have to say, but I hope my work will bring some light to the heat of the debates, or at least provide one or two useful perspectives.

Blest be the tie that binds our hearts in Christian love;
the fellowship of kindred minds is like to that above.
Before the Father's throne we pour our ardent prayers;
our fears, our hopes, our aims are one, our comforts and our cares.
We share each other's woes, our mutual burdens bear;
and often for each other flows a sympathizing tear.
When we asunder part, it gives us inward pain;
but we shall still be joined in heart and hope to meet again.
—"Blest Be the Tie That Binds," John Fawcett (1782),
The United Methodist Hymnal

Only three times has the Council of Bishops, this governing body of our denomination, split amongst themselves within the denomination, and this is what really put these issues into perspective for me. They split over the issue of racism, over ordaining women, and now over gay and lesbian concerns. A group of fifteen bishops signed a document saying that they don't support [church policy] on this. And so it really seems that when we have these splits is when progress happens. [. . .] As a student, it's interesting to see how social justice comes about. But as a human being, it's painful, to see things be so slow.
—Alex Carter, a seminary intern at City Church

Doing unto Others . . . (A Theoretical Introduction)

C hristianity, in its many historical manifestations and theological adaptations has, like the people that believe in it, a
long history of both propagating social injustice and fostering
social justice. This book explores how members of two Protestant congregations determine what is just and what is unjust,
what is right and what is wrong, what is loving and what is sinful. It is an ethnographic study of congregational debates about
homosexuality and how people construct, in everyday thought
and interaction, their beliefs about God and humanity. I strive
to convey accurately people's beliefs and the logics internal to
beliefs, but more important, I strive to make sense of these conflicting logics.

As sociology, this study examines the socially contingent aspects of things members of a group take for granted as timeless
and natural. As a sociologist *of religion*, I explore the socially
contingent aspects of those things many members of the religious groups I study take for granted as timeless, God-ordained
truths (Berger 1969). And as a *critical* sociologist, I seek to uncover how people's taken-for-granted assumptions can reproduce forms of power, even when they intend otherwise (Fraser
1989; Scott 1999). In doing so, I examine the ways members
of two United Methodist congregations struggled to negotiate
a conflict so explosive it threatens, to this day, to split their denomination. I examine the languages they used to negotiate their
profound disagreements and to make sense of debates about homosexuality in everyday thought and interaction.

I examine the social component of religious beliefs, exploring how members' perspectives are *naturalized*. That is to say, I explore how, by using particular languages, people make their beliefs feel timeless, natural, unquestionable, things to be taken for granted. It is on the foundation of taken-for-granted beliefs, of common sense, that people build our sense of the world and our places in it. In particular, I look at languages of emotion, especially how a language of *pain* worked to naturalize certain positions and shape these debates' outcomes. Finally, I reflect on how members naturalized their own views by opposing them to the almost universally demonized category of *politics*. Although I was struck at first by the extent to which congregation members repudiated politics, I came to realize that politics worked as a code word for things that threatened to *de*naturalize people's foundational assumptions, to expose them as "not universally true." I suggest, in the end, that this demonization of politics pervades most forms of debate in contemporary American society, be it in secular political culture, in personal narrative, or in church.

Homosexuality has been an explosive public issue during the last three decades. It foments conflict by revealing underlying social tensions in religious groups, in schools, in government, and in civil society at large. When I began this project, I wanted to know how people who saw themselves largely as regular middle-Americans were motivated to engage so vocally and so emotionally in debates about homosexuality. To find out what propelled these debates, I would need to talk to people whose engagement with these issues ran more deeply than just voting for a particular ballot initiative or candidate. I needed to find people participating in these debates face-to-face with others, people who *had* to engage each other sincerely, maybe even try to hear each other, and articulate their viewpoints at a more nuanced level than just being superficially "pro" or "anti." I quickly determined that some of the best places to find the middle-Americans so engaged were in Protestant congregations.

Very early in the project, as luck would have it, I was invited to a day-long seminar for members of United Methodist congregations in my region. Organizers of the seminar worked with the gay-affirming Reconciling Congregations Program of the United Methodist Church, called the RCP.[1] The seminar focused on how participants could move their congregations toward joining the RCP. At that seminar I learned that, to a far greater extent than in many forums in our society, members of congregations took each other's opposing views seriously and engaged with each other. In a congregation, members could not dismiss each other as readily as they might dismiss strangers (or even neighbors) with whom they disagreed about an important community issue. True, their debates certainly generated ill-will and hurt feelings at times, and even drove some members away. However, members tended to share the conviction that they all believed in the same God and needed to discern what God demanded of them, and they tended to share a commitment to their congregations and love for fellow members.[2] These shared feelings and ideals kept people from giving up on each other as quickly as secular neighbors might give up on each other about, say, a state ballot initiative.

As I observed and thought about my two United Methodist congregations—one theologically liberal, which I call City Church, and one more theologically conservative and evangelical, which I call Missionary Church—I began to learn that debates about homosexuality were about far more than homosexuality. As members debated homosexuality, they simultaneously debated the meanings of concepts such as equality, community, sin, and love. In spite of these differences, members largely agreed about one thing: their disdain for what they considered "politics." Although they disagreed about what might fit into the category, I was struck in my observations by the extent to which they agreed that to be "political" was contrary to church ideals. Furthermore, they expressed differing definitions of the term "politics" itself. To understand these wider ramifications, we must first understand the debates themselves—as debates within congregations, and as debates about homosexuality.

These debates were so volatile because they pointed to the socially contingent nature of the things members thought of as essential, natural, or divinely true. In these congregations, and within the church environments of which they were part, these debates threatened to highlight the very differences people most wanted to avoid noticing—not only different relations of power, or different anxieties about sexuality, but different beliefs about God. In a monotheistic religion such as this, the commitment to a single god created tension when members had such widely variant beliefs about what the divine was and what the divine expected of them. In effect, much of what we will see in these pages revolves around members' attempts to reconcile this central theological difference.

A Critical Ethnography of Beliefs

In my approach to religion, I draw from a vast tradition of ethnographic research examining how, in and through social processes, people make sense of the world and their places in it.[3] I ask, given that members of these congregations believe in God, what do they do with that belief? How is it that

members can purport to believe in the same God and yet have such very different theologies? In doing so, I treat church as both similar to and different
from the rest of life. For many of the members I heard from in my research,
church was not separate from secular life, but a place where people went, in
part, to learn how to be better persons in the secular world.

For theological liberals among Methodists and other Protestants the relationship between the church and the secular world meant "bringing about
the kingdom of God on earth," for instance, by making the world more just
and loving. For evangelicals the goal was to interact with the world from
their place of faith, to be "in the world but not of it," to show the world
by example the difference Jesus Christ made in their lives. In either case,
many members would hesitate to advertise their faith out in the world to
the point of alienating nonbelievers. But members of both congregations
drew judiciously from secular life to learn about God, and saw their faith
as guiding their understanding of how the secular world should be and what
they should do in it, whether that meant participating in a quiet pro-life
demonstration away from the fracas of abortion clinic blockades, building
houses for low-income families, or raising money for AIDS or breast cancer
research in a walkathon. Among members of both the evangelical and the
liberal congregations, a highly porous boundary separated their church and
secular lives.

Considering how many Americans attend worship services regularly
(44 percent of American adults attend worship *weekly*, making it the industrial nation with the highest percentage of weekly churchgoers), it stands
to reason that religious views would inform secular debates and vice versa.[4]
The sociologists N. J. Demerath and Rhys Williams (1992), for instance,
explore the relationships between civic religion and the separation of church
and state and find that religious and secular ideals inform each other to
a far greater extent than American ideals would have us believe. Arlene
Stein (2001) studied debates over homosexuality surrounding state- and
municipal-level ballot initiatives in a small town in Oregon and found religious beliefs and church groups informing both sides of the debate. Like
me, she observed both sides of the debate; however, the people she studied,
as in many hot debates, became split and ended up highly factionalized, two
opposing camps facing off in a "culture war."[5] By focusing on congregations, I limit my study to a group of people firmly committed to the same
doctrine and firmly committed to one another. Unlike civic debates, where
people easily become closed to each other's arguments, in church debates I
found people committed to articulating their beliefs, to seeking shared moral
ground—much more so than in many secular debates. By articulating to one

another their logics, members reveal their grounding assumptions, allowing us to refine our understanding of what is at stake in such debates.

Specifically, as members struggled to make sense of these debates and to understand what God intends for the world, they revealed the broad range of everyday sources from which they drew and naturalized their understandings of God and what God requires. As they articulated their everyday theologies, they articulated the categories they used to think about the world. With the many sources available to them, they could select from various assumptions, which led to competing conclusions about what is "timeless." In effect, the sheer number of different sources people used to naturalize their beliefs could risk *de*naturalizing them all, exposing their social contingency. To avoid this instability, members needed *something* they could all take as given, and that pillar was their nearly ubiquitous disdain for "politics."

In group discussions or privately with me, again and again members invoked the "political." The category emerged as a default negative category, the opposite of whatever the speaker held as ideal. People on all sides of these debates distanced themselves from this category of politics, and saw political motivations among those with whom they disagreed. Strikingly, this occurred even among those who were activists. Even among those activists who in one-on-one conversations would say that they saw some political work as righteous and necessary, I observed a public stance in line with the assumption that "political" meant "bad."

I argue that debates about homosexuality have proven so explosive because they bring to light the political issues, the earthly negotiations and hierarchies of power and privilege, which often tacitly inhere in congregational life. I show that members of these two very different United Methodist congregations all saw "the church"—it was often unclear whether they meant their own congregation or the larger "body of Christ," Christianity—as a place to connect with God, the transcendent and universal, and to connect with other people more deeply than was often possible in secular life. Any conflict, but perhaps especially debates about homosexuality, brought to light the social nature of this realm where members sought a haven from social debates and hierarchies. In the end, I draw from other sociologists' similar findings from secular arenas to suggest that while the commitment of church members to one another is unusual among most voluntary organizations, the disdain for the category of politics might not be particular to religious contexts, especially in the most religious of industrialized nations.

To understand people's beliefs about religion and politics, it helps to see firsthand how people develop and apply them, a task suited to ethnographic methods. One school of ethnography maintains that ideally an ethnographer should live among those she studies and strive to see the world from their perspective. Participant-observation and cultural immersion are at its core. Few maintain that it is possible to adopt another's worldview completely. Many maintain that an ethnographer should challenge her own fundamental beliefs as she studies another group, either to observe them "objectively" or to learn to think like them and to portray their worldview.[6] If this is the task of ethnography, I am only partially successful.

I made, and make, no pretense of being an "objective" or neutral observer, because I, too, am a social creature. I did indeed change in the course of this research; my understandings of various forms of Christianity and Methodism changed, and the people I spoke with brought me down their paths to an extent I never would have thought possible before. But I did not become a Christian. Furthermore, although I do seek to illustrate the different ways of thinking among the people I observed, I do not stop there. To simply "show" what happened is neither possible (it is, after all, my own representation) nor, in my opinion, desirable. What is the point of sociological observation if not to analyze the social processes we observe?

I thus agree with the school of thought that maintains that the purpose of ethnography is to have a conversation.[7] I entered these congregations as myself, asking people to converse with me about their worldviews, sometimes pushing them on points that did not make sense to me from my outsider perspective. Some people no doubt spoke to me with the hope that they could touch my heart with the truth as they knew it, to sow the seeds of conversion. They may feel betrayed that my heart was not open enough to them for me to see the world as they saw it, but I could hardly adopt each of the many conflicting and opposing worldviews I encountered. People from many different perspectives did touch my heart—the most deeply held core of my worldview and sense of self—and bring me partway down their respective paths.

Of course, I could not be a sociologist and abandon my worldview entirely, for each night I went home to my books, my music and TV, my loved ones, my retro-kitsch décor, and my journal, to try to keep a sense of myself as a person interested in understanding, critiquing, and, yes, changing the subtle and effective workings of power. Similarly, readers can approach the reading of this book as part of a conversation, asking not how to generalize from these two congregations but how to expand our own formal and everyday theories about conflict and community, power and identity. We expand these theories when we make them account for things they did not or could not previously explain. What theories I seek to expand upon, and how, becomes clear below.

To understand where different participants in these debates were coming from, I needed to have a conversation with church members. In doing so, I gave them an opportunity to help me to understand their differing perspectives, what they saw as being at stake in these debates, how they negotiated conflicting beliefs, and what religious life has in common with secular America. To set up these conversations, I relied predominantly on two ethnographic methods: participant-observation and interviews. In what follows, I lay out members' conversations with me, with each other, with themselves, and with their God. I approach these debates from a perspective of critical theory.

The political theorist Nancy Fraser defines a critical theory as one that "frames its research program and its conceptual framework with an eye to the aims and activities of those oppositional social movements with which it has a partisan, though not uncritical, identification" (Fraser 1989, 113). A critical theory, according to Fraser, must demystify approaches that obfuscate or rationalize the relations of power under critique. I take this approach to my own work, but while Fraser can aim her critique at a rival, I do not have that luxury. As an ethnographer, I cannot see the people I observe as my rivals; ethnography thus lends itself to a more refined understanding of critique. The purpose of my critique is not to prove people wrong, or to show them how to be more like me. Rather, my purpose is to attend to the ways people can reproduce power, often the very forms of power they, or we, seek to escape or redress. Thus, an ethnography should not simply adopt people's own analyses of a situation. As the sociologist Dorothy Smith points out, we do ethnography to understand how people see the world, but not by simply parroting their analyses of it. She comments, "It is essential that the everyday world be seen as organized by social relations not observable within it" (Smith 1987, 89).

In some circles, it might seem especially disrespectful to critique and denaturalize religious views. Religion, where people explicitly encounter their understandings of the sacred, is sacred itself, untouchable, and often not a proper ground for critical examination. But sociology of religion must observe not only how social processes work in religious groups as well as secular groups but how groups of people come to develop their collective beliefs. As the anthropologist Clifford Geertz pointed out in 1973, and as the sociologists Mary Jo Neitz and James V. Spickard (1990) echo, there has been a recurrent trend in social scientific studies of religion to focus on the institutional dynamics of religion and to neglect religious meanings. Many recent ethnographies of American religious life look at how religious bodies work and weather conflict, why people join them or not, how their members engage the nonreligious world, how they challenge scholars' prejudices about religion.[8] These studies are important, for, by highlighting the social and institutional aspects of religion, many of them tend to demystify aspects of religion that have been needlessly mystified. Furthermore, they counter social critics' tendency to characterize contemporary life as hollow and meaningless.

Although beliefs are not ignored by such institutional studies of religion, they tend to be treated as given or else subsumed under sweeping social changes. Some sociologists of religion look at specific conflicting beliefs within religious bodies, and Penny Edgell Becker (1998, 1999) goes so far as to consider how people's beliefs adapt as they seek to resolve conflicts; but she and others do not examine how people develop particular beliefs in the first place.[9] Robert Wuthnow (1988, 1998) examines how large-scale trends in belief change in the context of sweeping changes in the economy and politics over decades. Similarly, Robert Bellah (1970, 1992) looks at a broad range of societies to see how belief systems contend with the world-historical processes of modernization.

In other projects, Bellah and colleagues (1985, 1991) examine beliefs at the individual level, interviewing hundreds of Americans about their views on a variety of topics, including religion. Similarly, one of Bellah's collaborators, Steven Tipton (1982), looks at how social class affected the ways particular individuals' beliefs and institutional affiliations changed as they left the 1960s counterculture and had to deal with the large-scale social and ideological upheaval in the 1970s and 1980s. Like the others, these studies still focus on the important question of how individuals' beliefs were shaped by larger social trends, but they leave relatively untheorized the question of how individuals developed their particular beliefs.

These approaches provide important corrections to a mystifying image of religion as distinct from social processes, but, as Geertz points out, by neglecting the social construction of religious meanings, they can effectively "[take] for granted what most needs to be elucidated" (Geertz 1973, 125). And if we accept that social power works through beliefs, through people's deeply held understandings of the world, then it is all the more crucial to examine how people develop and legitimate these beliefs and to analyze their effects on people.

Language and Power

To explore how people's beliefs can have material consequences, we must attend to the relationship between language and power. In doing so, we can develop an understanding of how socially informed ways of looking at the world can come to seem natural and timeless, and how this appearance of timelessness can guide and foreclose possibilities. Philosopher and social theorist Michel Foucault spent much of his career—and influenced a wide range of contemporary scholarship—looking at changing beliefs about the nature of truth and selfhood in modern society. My method of analysis draws from Foucault's (1977, 1978, 1980) move to see languages and culture as themselves transmitting social power in ways they did not before roughly the mid-nineteenth century.[10] For Foucault, and others like him, people's identities and possibilities are limited because a very real social power works through knowledge itself. This power works not only in prohibitions but in assumptions about what simply *is*. In teaching people what it means to be part of society and what it means to be human, power works through knowledge to produce people's very identities, desires, and dispositions. This power works not only in hierarchies but in the micro-level interactions between people, in what sociologists call socialization, in the capillaries of the social body.

Drawing from Foucault's concept of *discourse,* I define a language as a set of categories people use to organize their world, and in our society there are many languages available to people at any given time.[11] In the debates I examine here, we see people speaking the languages of sin, of emotion, of organizational rationality, of child rearing, of legality, of personal choice and responsibility, of health, and so on. Each different language limits the ways a speaker can think about a topic. For instance, we often treat a rule-breaker differently if we see her transgression as willful rebellion as opposed to something she cannot help. Which language we use—one of choice versus one of compulsion, or one of righteous struggle versus one of complacency—shapes how we see her and how we respond to her rule breaking.

These languages are similar to what sociologists call "frames," in that they shape the choices people perceive as available to them to deal with a given situation.[12] Members of the two congregations studied here often seemed intentional about their framing of the issue of homosexuality, for instance, about whether to frame it as an innate quality or as a choice. In this sense, their strategic actions lined up with frame theory. However, I wish to stress that I see languages as not only something people can use intentionally, as tools, but more importantly as the system of categories that shape our minds, our fundamental ways of understanding the world and ourselves in it.[13]

Because we think in language, language creates the realm of what we can even think possible. The languages available to us shape our deeply held understanding of the world as well as our deeply felt knowledge of our place in it, our identities. Post-structuralism adds to this view a theory of power. In the post-structuralism I associate with Foucault, power works not only through some people's conscious efforts to repress others but also by producing people and relationships. It is most effective when it is least visible. Which languages are available and legitimate, what they lead us to think possible, how we know to act without even thinking about it, and what is obscured from our consideration all have to do with the way social power works in and through language.

Each language is based on a set of unspoken assumptions that people must agree upon if they are to use that language effectively to communicate with one another. The fact that these assumptions are often unspoken and invisible makes them seem to be timeless, natural facts rather than the contingent, unnatural artifacts they are. To maintain a sense that the socially constructed world is relatively orderly and materially coherent around us, we need for certain things to just *be*, to be unquestionable. For instance, many people who were raised with Western medicine have trouble believing that other kinds of medicine, such as acupuncture, can even work. The fact that acupuncture has worked for centuries in Asia does not matter to those who believe solely in the Western model. That many Westerners are resistant to acupuncture has everything to do with their need to let their understanding of how bodies work seem unquestionable and "natural." This unquestionable, naturalized truth can include unspoken assumptions about how to measure and envision bodily processes and deeply held beliefs that "modern Western" knowledge is *true* while "ancient Eastern" knowledge is *superstitious.*

Similarly, Americans, like many others, assume things about sex, gender, love, God (regardless of what or whether we believe), and what it is to be human. Often these assumptions provide us with a basis for our own identities, our understandings of who we are and how we relate to others. For example, Foucault (1978) articulates the perspective that sex—sexual thoughts, feelings, and acts—has come to seem a source of truth, that contemporary ways of categorizing and identifying with sex seem natural because of the power at work through the languages people use to speak about it. He was not the first to observe that categories of sexuality seem natural and timeless in spite of great variation through time and across cultures. A number of scholars have called our attention to the sociological work on sexuality and identity that had been done before the publication and popularization of the first volume of Foucault's *History of Sexuality.*[14] But Foucault echoed these key sociological insights while expanding on them to theorize sexuality as a central artifact of power and to articulate the link between power and personality. Since then, other scholars have examined how our understandings of sexuality, including heterosexuality, both naturalize and are naturalized by our understandings of other aspects of the social world, such as race, economy, and our definition of humanity.[15]

God, Sex, and Politics draws from these observations, examining how congregation members, more or less effectively, used particular languages to make the world around them seem stable and sensible while naturalizing their grounding assumptions. It explores how, during my observations, assumptions about such central concepts as nature, God, and sexuality worked to naturalize each other.[16] Yet precisely because these languages naturalized *each other*, because no singular language served as an anchor, their mutual dependence risked exposing the social contingency of people's beliefs, thus denaturalizing them. It can disturb us greatly when someone questions the things we assume are inevitable and unquestionable, too obvious to need mentioning. But when we let these assumptions go unquestioned, power works on us and through us in ways we might not intend, by producing our understandings of ourselves, each other, and what is possible. As we will see, congregation members responded to this risk by calling attention to something all seemed to agree was less natural, less timeless, less true, and less ideal than anything else: the repudiated category of politics.

In the ways people have written and thought about Foucault, they often focus on pieces of his theoretical framework. Some scholars draw from his theme of disciplinary power—the power that works through language and which people internalize without necessarily knowing.[17] Other scholars focus on Foucault's idea that power works in micro-level interactions and not only in hierarchies; often, these scholar-activists critique Foucault for what they see as his weakness in accounting for those forms of hierarchical, oppressive power that dominate many people's lives, such as sexism and racism.[18] We can, however, look at capillary, everyday power not in terms of people overtly policing one another's behavior, comportment, or language but in terms of how, in everyday thought and interactions, people produce linguistic categories (such as those of sex, race, health, or righteousness) and systems of meaning that affect what is possible and what is simply unthinkable, which in turn produces actual people.

Foucault and many of the post-structuralist thinkers who follow him, even sociologists, tend to focus their inquiries on texts.[19] These inquiries are important and useful for understanding how power works through certain systems of thought, but I see a paradox in attempting to look for a nonhierarchical form of power in something that bears and reproduces authority by virtue of being published or archived. Furthermore, if we want to look at how people go about reproducing power in the capillaries of everyday thought and interaction, there is also a paradox in looking at something so fixed as a text. In the way I do ethnography, I add to Foucault's theory of power from a perspective that more closely reflects his theory, by examining the micro-level interactions in which he sees power inhering.[20]

Ethnographers can examine and analyze people's living, everyday reflections as they change and develop. We can also see a little more closely how that capillary power Foucault describes might work—how systems of power grow ever more rooted (or become uprooted) in people's everyday thoughts, theologies, interactions, and practices and come to be seen simply as the natural, God-given, really real, fabric of the world. It is in this sense that my ethnography is "post-structural"; I start from the post-structural assumption that as people produce systems of meaning, they exert productive, capillary power.

Although I maintain that methods of textual analysis can help us to understand the everyday production of beliefs and power, I would not say that I understand people's "true thoughts."[21] First, by interviewing people or even speaking to them as an outsider, a naïve, or an ethnographer, I must have encouraged at least some people to speak more authoritatively or unambiguously than they might in their own minds; our thoughts and feelings are often more ambiguous than the words we use for them, even if we do not feel that we need to speak with authority and clarity.[22] Second, by freezing people's words in time and transcribing them in a book, I risk reifying their constantly developing thoughts as texts themselves, treating their developing thought processes as fixed things. However, we can look at these excerpts as snapshots to see a model of how we might think about and engage our own thoughts and interactions and those we observe.

Everyday Theologies

I respect and take seriously the people whose comments I draw from here. For me that means engaging their beliefs and looking at how social processes shaped their understandings of what they saw as God's eternal truth. With this will to scrutinize beliefs instead of taking them for granted, I challenge an assumption that pervades much sociology of religion, as well as common sense: the assumption that church doctrine unproblematically represents what members believe. We tend to think of religious beliefs as simply dictated by scripture or doctrine. As the sociologist Michele Dillon (1999) points out, this view posits believers as more or less automatons, believing whatever their churches tell them to believe, or else as static and fixed consumers, searching for a church whose beliefs mirror their own.[23] Neither view acknowledges something the members of the two congregations I examine took very seriously, their ability and mandate to learn and grow in faith.

The eminent sociologist of religion Peter Berger (1969) points out that society and culture come from people, which nonetheless seem to act on people as an objective reality wholly alien to human creation. Berger implies that from a sociological perspective religious beliefs depend on each individual member to reproduce them, and thus individuals have a role in changing them. As Dillon (1999) demonstrates in her exploration of Roman Catholics working to change church doctrines on women and sexuality, seeing beliefs as dictated by doctrine denies that members are thinking and communicating people who learn from a variety of sources, including one another. Furthermore, as sociologist Mark Chaves (1997) demonstrates, seeing doctrine as representative of belief renders us incapable of accounting for doctrinal change.

When we talk face to face with people about their beliefs, questioning or even challenging them—or when we observe them questioning and challenging each other—we cannot help but notice the mismatch between beliefs and doctrine. Scripture and tradition are very important to the people in these two congregations, but they cite a wide range of scriptural interpretations and an even wider range of traditions when talking about God and what they believe God expects or demands.

Furthermore, beliefs about what God expects cannot always come directly from Scripture or tradition. Few members of these congregations accepted at face value the scriptural pronouncements that women must keep their heads covered and cannot teach men; none believed that slavery is a righteous and godly social order.[24] Indeed, in these rapidly changing times, people ran into problems and other experiences that even their parents could not have imagined for them, ones that they themselves would not have imagined twenty or thirty—or sometimes even five—years earlier. The quandaries that people find themselves in today are sometimes novel, and it took the church members I met a great deal of prayer, study, reflection, and discussion to determine what their God expected of them, to determine the right thing to do—and they often came up with very different answers. This study traces a number of different paths to show how people developed the answers they did.

People develop everyday theologies not just when they worship and read Scripture but as they reflect on a wide range of inspirational texts, conversations, personal experiences, and understandings of their God. They think about these things every day—as they deal with bosses or coworkers, as they drive around town, as they wash the dishes or get their kids ready for school. Members of these congregations produced understandings of what is right and what God demands every day as they worked to make sense of a changing world in terms of what they already knew as God's truth. These truths were shaped by how they understood such key themes as sacred versus profane, community versus politics, spirit versus body, and love versus selfishness. And, as critical thinkers, we must ask when and how, in determining these truths, people can reproduce various kinds of power.

Religious truths are not, by any means, the only truths that reproduce power—all forms of knowledge have that potential and most live up to it. However, congregations are a good place to look at the production of power through language, because church members are clear and largely unambivalent about seeking eternal truth and talking about it. They provide a clear model of the various truths we all produce and reproduce as we seek to make sense of the world. By looking at church members, we can see how people come to various understandings of God. But we can also see how people in secular contexts come to other foundational understandings about how the world should work, what is essential, what simply "has to be." To paraphrase what Berger put forth so convincingly, people need to make sense of the world, and we do it in a lot of different ways.

To understand what is happening in debates about homosexuality, and other major debates in the United States today, we must attend to everyday theologies. But that is not the end of the story. Important scholars of religion have pointed out that religion, and culture more generally, are the means by which people order their worlds.[25] People order the world through language; language comprises the sets of categories and oppositions by which we make sense of the world and organize everything around us.[26] More recently, scholars have come to see how this ordering is not an apolitical process but involves creating and reproducing certain hierarchies. Drawing from Jacques Derrida, the literary critic Eve Kosofsky Sedgwick (1990) observes that oppositions tend to be set up in hierarchies: us/them, strong/weak, good/evil, healthy/sick, sacred/profane, light/dark. Complicated but undeniable sets of values attach to the same categories by which we make sense of the world. Furthermore, depending on how a person is categorized, she or he has a particular authority or lack thereof to assign categories and values to other people and things.[27] Once a person has been labeled insane, for instance, it is difficult indeed for her to convince the sane that she is really one of them.

Once a person has been labeled a genius, people give his thoughts a great deal more credence than they give to the idiot next to him.

As people think about and share collective knowledge about right and wrong, godly and sinful, natural and unnatural, and healthy and sick—in seeking to make sense of the world—they also reproduce the power that works through language. Sociologists such as Orville Lee (1998) and Nina Eliasoph (1999) point out that linguistic forms of power do not reside only in the realm of the symbolic but have actual material consequences. The philosopher Judith Butler (1993) takes this one step further by positing that power and knowledge actually create, moment to moment, what we perceive to be material, natural reality. She adapts sociolinguistic theory to describe how power works through language to produce the realities we think of as natural, such as bodily sexual differences. As history has shown repeatedly, whether and how a person fits into our categories—what kind of person we deem someone to be—has not only psychological or social effects but consequences for the material conditions of a person's life.[28]

Although this production of truths is political, by which I mean that it is based in and reproduces hierarchies of power and privilege, it is not explicitly so. It creates and legitimates these hierarchies, but the people we shall hear from here define truth as the opposite of politics. For many of the congregation members, even political activists, the category of "politics" serves as a code for self-interest, cynicism, and worldliness in contrast to the love, community, and timelessness of godly truth.[29] By defining certain things as "political" even political activists (on all sides) can, symbolically and with material consequences, cast them out of the realm of the legitimate.

I have not come to this approach alone. There is a field of inquiry that attends to how people produce power in their everyday lives as they produce and reproduce their ideas about truth, selfhood, and what is normal and right. Butler (1990, 1993) looks at how the language of gender can produce coercive and racially inflected gender norms that shape how normal society views and values different people's lives. Sociologist Paul Gilroy (1991) examines how antiracist programs in the United Kingdom in the 1980s reproduced racist power. Anthropologist Elizabeth Povinelli (1997, 2000) shows how the liberal Australian government's attempts to return stolen land to Aboriginal people can place the would-be beneficiaries in an impossible position, hemmed in by contradictory liberal imaginings of what or who is legitimately "traditional." The point of such critical studies is not to say that people with power are bad or mean, as such a view itself would posit power as a property of individuals rather than a social production. The point of such studies is to show how we all fit into systems of power that might be beyond our own intentions.

These studies look at how systems of power envelop people and shape their relationships, and how these systems are produced—generally in texts, in government or institutional policies, and sometimes in events. A few studies look at the processes by which individuals collectively produce forms of power in their daily lives; for instance, Nina Eliasoph (1999) and Penny Becker (1998) look at how people unintentionally reproduce racism in daily interaction, even when seeking to challenge it. Similarly, here I will look at the thought processes by which, in attempting to determine what is right and what God demands of them to live their lives in communities of love and care, people can, contrary to their own intentions, produce relations of power in their everyday lives.

Many of those who look at the role of language in the production of power focus on the role of unexamined or unspoken assumptions. *God, Sex, and Politics* analyzes the languages people use in an effort to locate unspoken assumptions. This does not involve mind reading or somehow knowing what others are "really" thinking. It's not the speakers but the languages that I scrutinize—where they might lead, where they keep people from going, what an audience might hear in them. I do not analyze people's experiences to determine whether they were real or not but, rather, to see what those experiences can tell us about the conditions that made them possible.[30] In other words, people's experiences of what they consider politics can suggest to us broader trends in the American political culture they inhabit.

I assume from the outset that languages constrain and shape everyone, in that languages are the terms in which we think, in which we make sense of the world and our place in it. I do not point to inconsistencies in people's arguments to show that these people are illogical. The difference between myself as an ethnographer and those whose comments I look at here, like the differences among members from different sides of these debates, are simply differences in stakes. As an outsider, I have a stake in different things than most of these church members have stakes in; different things shape my sense of the world and my place in it. This difference, and not any place outside of language, gives me a vantage point from which to analyze their debates and their statements of what they believe.

Although I am something of an outsider to church debates, and to church life in general, I too produce and am produced by systems of language, identity, and power. When beliefs about homosexuality, or the contemporary system of sexual categories, attach to people's senses of our own places and roles within that order, and our senses of comfort and peace, then something or someone who challenges these beliefs can threaten, at least temporarily, these bigger senses. This happens in church debates, and it happened in my encounters with members. When I first began this project, for instance, I found myself profoundly shaken by the daylong Reconciling Congregations Program seminar I mentioned earlier. At this seminar, I realized that my beliefs in the fundamental goodness of sexual and other human variety and fluidity, and my goals of justice, were not, in fact, antithetical to Christianity. I realized that while I had thought I had simply dismissed the United Methodist religion of my childhood, in fact I had built myself an identity in opposition to it.

The beliefs around which I organized my life, built my sustaining relationships, and by which I felt I had a place in the world, had included an opposition to Christianity that the seminar's participants shattered before my eyes. In the closing service, at the end of a long day, the presiding pastor invited those congregated to communion with the thought: "It never fails to amaze me that Jesus was sharing this most important meal with the people he loved most in the world. He knew they would betray him within a couple of days but he shared it with them anyway."[31] By the time she finished her remark, I found myself sobbing uncontrollably and spent days trying to reestablish my sense of place in the world.

Later in the course of my research, I was similarly shaken by a discussion I had with Andy Gilmartin, the director of an ex-gay organization, who showed me how the belief that homosexuality was sinful in no way needed to derive from an unsophisticated reading of the Bible or a knee-jerk belief that homosexuality is the opposite of all that is godly or good.[32] He, and later others, showed me that, contrary to my unexamined assumption, one could be a thoughtful and reflective person, not overtly afraid of or threatened by homosexuality, and still believe that study of God's word reveals a divine intention that all people find wholeness in either chastity or heterosexual marriage. In these moments, I felt my sense of how the world was organized being threatened as the oppositions I had maintained—queer versus Christian, gay versus antigay—were shaken, and with them my sense of a place within them.

As these oppositions shaped my worldview and identity, other oppositions similarly shape those of the people who speak in this book. My task as an analyst, then, is to locate the systems of categories members use to order their worlds and to trace when those sets of categories fail to account for the world around them, as mine did. If, before I attended that RCP seminar, someone had asked me about the relationship between Christianity, on the one hand, and queer critiques of heterosexism, on the other, they might have analyzed the languages I used to see how my unspoken assumptions were shaped by the then fairly current language of queer nationalism. If they had asked me to account for church groups that worked for a radical change in the organization of society, they might have been able to analyze my answers to reveal my own unspoken assumptions about religion, and my stakes in those assumptions. What had been at stake for me—my identity as a queer activist and as part of a sustaining community of friends who idealized love, freedom, and justice in the face of coercive heterosexuality—was shaped by the languages and oppositions I used to make sense of my place in the world. My stakes in maintaining those oppositions were given by the categories that gave me an identity. I did not invent those categories, but I had made them my own. Similarly, these congregation members' stakes are shaped by the categories they come to employ.

This suggests that when members show one another what terms to use in engaging in these debates, they exercise a power to shape one another's identities and to give them a personal stake in maintaining a particular worldview as truth. Language is bigger than any small group of people— we are all shaped by it—and even as old sets of terms fail new ones take their place. Which terms fail and succeed has everything to do with people's ongoing struggles with and for social power. In one sense, who has the authority to interpret and define what counts as sinful, right, wrong, or equal and to have those definitions stick has authority over those with whom they disagree. In another sense, power is not just something people have over others in a hierarchical way, it is also exerted among equals as we tell and show one another what is ideal and what is even possible. When we examine how people struggle with one another and with themselves to define their situations, we can highlight what assumptions lie unspoken amid the swirls of language and power around us, what is at stake in preserving the invisibility of those assumptions, and how those assumptions limit people.

chapter ONE

Debating Homosexuality

In 1996, when rooms full of clergy and lay delegates wrote and revised the policy on human sexuality in a series of quadrennial General Conferences of the United Methodist Church (UMC), the mood was often tense. The delegates came together with widely divergent views, not only about sexuality and its place in Christian teaching, but about who God is and what God demands of people, and the tensions dividing them were codified in the following passage from the *Book of Discipline of the United Methodist Church* (often called simply the *Discipline*):

> We recognize that sexuality is God's good gift to all persons. We believe persons may be fully human only when that gift is acknowledged and affirmed by themselves, the church, and society. We call all persons to the disciplined, responsible fulfillment of themselves, others, and society in the stewardship of this gift. We also recognize our limited understanding of this complex gift and encourage the medical, theological, and social science disciplines to combine in a determined effort to understand human sexuality more completely. We call the Church to take the leadership role in bringing together these disciplines to address this most complex issue. Further, within the context of our understanding of this gift of God, we recognize that God challenges us to find responsible, committed, and loving forms of expression.
>
> Although all persons are sexual beings whether or not they are married, sexual relations are only clearly affirmed

in the marriage bond. Sex may become exploitative within as well as outside marriage. We reject all sexual expressions that damage or destroy the humanity God has given us as birthright, and we affirm only that sexual expression which enhances that same humanity. We believe that sexual relations where one or both partners are exploitative, abusive, or promiscuous are beyond the parameters of acceptable Christian behavior and are ultimately destructive to individuals, families, and the social order.

We deplore all forms of the commercialization and exploitation of sex, with their consequent cheapening and degradation of human personality. We call for strict enforcement of laws prohibiting the sexual exploitation or use of children by adults. We call for the establishment of adequate protective services, guidance, and counseling opportunities for children thus abused. We insist that all persons, regardless of age, gender, marital status, or sexual orientation, are entitled to have their human and civil rights ensured. . . .

Homosexual persons no less than heterosexual persons are individuals of sacred worth. All persons need the ministry and guidance of the church in their struggles for human fulfillment, as well as the spiritual and emotional care of a fellowship that enables reconciling relationships with God, with others, and with self. Although we do not condone the practice of homosexuality and consider this practice incompatible with Christian teaching, we affirm that God's grace is available to all. We commit ourselves to be in ministry for and with all persons.[1]

This passage, known as paragraph 65G of the Social Principles section of the *Discipline*, reflects the UMC membership's ambivalence about sexuality. On one hand, the authors maintain that "sexuality is God's good gift to all persons," a gift that the church, society, and individuals themselves must affirm for persons to be "fully human." In this way, sexuality is timeless and good. On the other hand, the authors also clearly fear sex's destructive potential. They call on scientists to unpack its mysteries and find the hidden truth of this complex gift. They believe that it is a *challenge* for human beings to "find responsible, committed, and loving forms of expression," recognizing that even when affirmed in Christian marriage, sex can be "exploitative, abusive, or promiscuous." Such sex has, in their view, the power to destroy "humanity" as well as "individuals, families, and the social order."[2]

In spite of the divergent views of sexuality that are the subject of this study, the authors of ¶65G nonetheless agree to define and delimit sexuality by setting it up as a foil to their concept of humanity. In this passage, humanity comes with intrinsic natural rights on which sexuality may encroach, and humanity is itself a timeless "God-given birthright," which may be destroyed or affirmed by sexual expression. They see full humanity as requiring "fulfillment," which requires fellowship as well as affirmation. Fellowship is deemed necessary so that people may have "reconciling relationships with God, with others, and with self." These reconciling relationships must include the affirmation of the gift of sexuality. However, not all "sexuality" is equally affirmed—along with exploitative and abusive sexuality, undefined "promiscuous" sex and homosexuality are seen as "beyond the parameters of acceptable Christian behavior" and "incompatible with Christian teaching." Sexuality serves as a foil for natural and timeless "humanity," as a dangerous threat.

The passage contains another potential contradiction. In stating that "homosexual persons no less than heterosexual persons are individuals of sacred worth," the authors divide the category of persons into two clearly defined types: heterosexuals and homosexuals.[3] As part of a passage that asserts that full humanity can only be achieved when individuals find fulfillment, which requires the affirmation of their sexuality, this divide plants in the passage a seed of internal conflict. Some readers no doubt read the sentence "Homosexual persons no less than heterosexual persons are individuals of sacred worth" to mean that homosexuals are a distinct kind of person, that homosexuality is parallel to heterosexuality. If homosexuals are a kind of person—rather than a group of potential heterosexuals damaged by sexual abuse, exploitation, and commercialization—then the statement mandates that persons who are of that kind must, no less than any other kind, have their sexuality affirmed by the church. This potential may seem dangerous to those who believe homosexuality to be contrary to God's plan for humanity.

For members of the church, a number of other tensions are embedded in this passage. Notably, the categories of heterosexual and homosexual are made to seem as the fixed, timeless forms of human sexuality; human sexuality is not understood as many theorists of sexuality have understood it, as fluid and contingent on social forces.[4] In fact, by positing "humanity" itself on the God-given gift of sexuality and people's acknowledgement of it, this assertion of categories reproduces what Foucault (1978) observed as emerging in the late nineteenth century: two distinct sexual species of human beings, naturalized in their reference to nature. In the world portrayed in the Discipline, there is no room to imagine the fluid and organic daily lived practice of sexual behaviors, desires, and gender identities. For the UMC, the possibility of a valid nonheterosexual mode of being has called into question

the universality and timelessness of heterosexuality. By attempting to include homosexual desire within the range of human experience, the authors
attempt in this passage to naturalize an expanded notion of sexuality with
two (instead of one) fixed variants, but end up excluding other categories.

There is another notable tension, particularly for those who wish to open
the doors of the UMC to gay men and lesbians: if the church is to offer
fellowship and guidance as members seek to give "proper stewardship to this
gift" of sexuality while maintaining that homosexuality is "incompatible
with Christian teaching," how can it minister to those who feel that God
desires and demands that they be gay or lesbian, or something else? Such
tensions emerge partly as a result of the collaboration between groups with
very different understandings of God and sexuality. But these tensions and
obscurities exist not only in the official policy of the denomination but in
what I call the everyday theologies of UMC members.

Is Homosexuality a Moral Question?

God, Sex, and Politics examines the far-ranging effects of what we might
call a middle-American desire to avoid conflict. One of the first things one
notices about debates about homosexuality throughout the United States
today and in recent years is that contenders rarely address each other in the
same terms. To illustrate, I'll draw from a story from my field notes.

Late in 1996, City United Methodist Church—a large, diverse downtown congregation with a theologically liberal pastoral staff—reopened the
debates, closed two years before, about whether the congregation should
publicly and officially welcome gay men, bisexuals, and lesbians and affirm
that homosexuality is part of God's good gift of sexuality. Members of the
congregation had organized a series of meetings for members to talk about
their concerns about this move, or about homosexuality in general. One
meeting was particularly heated. At this meeting, Mark Montero, an attor-
ney in his late thirties, presented the viewpoint that the people of God must
stand against the practice of homosexuality, both to promote God's will and
to preserve social order.[5] He was confronted chiefly by Marsha Zimmerman,
a woman in her mid-forties who had a college-aged lesbian daughter.

A third participant remarked on what he described as the church's homophobia, to which Mark replied:

> Is someone homophobic if they think homosexuality is contrary to God's
> teachings? There's a reason not to think homosexuality is okay, and it's
> not a phobia, it has to do with social order. Is the idea that homosexual

relationships will be seen as comparable to, or as good as, heterosexual relationships?

Marsha: Excuse me, but do you think they have a choice? It seems like you're saying that they must have a choice. Now, I can tell you as the mother of three daughters, all about the same age, all with the same father—two of them are heterosexual, and the youngest one, well, since she was a year and a half old, I knew she was different. I didn't have a name for it back then, but she is a hom—. . . homosexual. And she did not choose it; in fact, she tried very hard to not be. She tried to fight it, and she was afraid to tell us [getting upset]. Are you saying that she chose that? Because she didn't choose it, and having two heterosexual sisters, all about the same age, with the same father . . .

Mark: Well, if you want to make a genetic argument . . .

Marsha: But how could she have chosen it? She fought it. Do you know gay people?

Mark: Sure, I mean, maybe they haven't been my best friends, but . . . yeah.

Marsha: But you think they chose it?

In this conversation, we see a dynamic that would continue throughout the discussion and which, in fact, permeated many of the disagreements I observed over whether homosexuality was sinful. When Mark Montero began by stating that homosexuality is sinful because it undermines the social order—not because the church is phobic—Marsha Zimmerman could have responded by saying that homosexuality is *not* a threat to social order. But she did not. Rather, she began her naturalizing argument against him from the standpoint of "choice," claiming that homosexuals do not have a choice about being homosexual. She cited her experience and expertise as a mother to support her claim that homosexuality is not a choice and that her lesbian daughter had fought against it. Rather than answer Mark's claims in the language of morality and social order, Marsha argued her position in a language of choice, and homosexuals' lack thereof.

As the conversation wore on, members took on Mark's claim about social order by arguing that gay people did not choose to be gay, that church members should love everyone, that to call homosexuality sinful is insensitive to gay people, and that love is not harmful. Yet they did not address Mark's central argument on its own terms. Mark maintained that homosexuality is sinful because Christians must follow certain codes God has laid out to mark themselves as people of God. Most of the people I spoke with in these two congregations, but especially pro-gay liberal members of City

Church, did not maintain that definition of sin and righteousness.[6] Yet no one challenged Mark's theology in those terms.

Regardless of whether or not these members were theologically correct, they failed to address Mark's moral concerns. At one point, when Mark asked whether their idea was "that homosexual relationships will be seen as comparable to, or as good as, heterosexual relationships," no one could just say yes. Mark left the meeting more convinced than ever that the pro-gay church members had abandoned God and God's laws.

Pro-gay members repeatedly found themselves unable to respond to their detractors within the language of morality. There is a reason for this particular silence. To respond to a moral claim with an opposing moral claim would highlight the very large differences that exist within the church—differences that members strove to leave unnoticed. In these two congregations, pro-gay members and those who believed homosexuality to be sinful had a great deal in common, but they could define sin very differently, and they could even have radically different understandings of God. But to discuss openly and publicly the very different theologies and moralities that separated members of the United Methodist Church, in general, as well as these two particular congregations, would be to force the United Methodist Church into a fundamental conflict about God and risk splitting the denomination. Either way, members would lose what they strove to maintain most of all: the church, Christian life, as a haven from struggle and politics.

It may seem strange to say that members wanted the church to be free from politics, when they clearly engaged in debates about homosexuality and many other things all the time, and when many engaged in secular political debates as well. This puzzle is solved when we understand that secular engagements could be based in members' foundational beliefs about what was timeless and true, while debates about homosexuality threatened to denaturalize these foundational assumptions by highlighting members' different understandings of them. Members sought to transcend feelings of isolation by coming together in church, yet to perceive themselves as a community they needed to avoid discussing the factors of social power and privilege that separated them. Rather than discuss *politics*, issues had to be discussed, and experienced, in the naturalizing language of *feelings*. Paradoxically, although feelings are supposed to be a transcendent language that all can understand, the language of feelings can make people address concerns as the troubles of isolated individuals rather than the concerns of a community. In short, members wanted to overcome the isolation of contemporary American life, but they sometimes reproduced it instead.

These members could not find clear answers in the Scriptures or in church doctrine. Not even what is codified provides a simple answer to conflicts over homosexuality or other controversial issues. Church members do not simply believe what church leaders, doctrine, or even Scripture says. Alongside the doctrinal beliefs of their congregations, which members may not even know, many members see their spiritual life as a growing or maturing in faith—learning more about God and God's will through prayer, Bible study, books, religious and secular radio programs, casual discussions, and everyday experiences.[7] They did not see the church as separate from the rest of life, in that they believed that God is everywhere and that their duty was to be Christian in the world, not just in church. In response, members developed their own evolving everyday theologies as they sought a deeper understanding of God. And because people had had a wide range of different experiences, their understandings of God varied widely, even within the same congregation.

As members strove every day to discern what God demands of people, what church and a life of righteousness are about, they constituted these ideals—such as care, love, and justice—as the opposite of "politics," which they often defined as worldly, selfish, and inhumane. These members' everyday theologies are informed by a notion that seems to dominate American political culture: the repudiation of politics.

Sociologists have shown how Americans struggle to create a sense of community within a world that many find competitive and isolating.[8] Whereas political action has sometimes been seen as a way to overcome isolation and competition, these interviews and observations suggest that the word *politics* has come to stand for these immiserating tendencies. Repeatedly, I heard people demonize political thinking and scapegoat consciously political actors, while seeing individual emotions as true, as natural, as transcendent, as uniquely *human*. Despite their efforts to create community, they found less truth in collective action and more truth in isolated individuals' emotions.

A number of scholars, coming from different approaches, also see contemporary American political culture as dominated by the avoidance of politics. The sociologist Nina Eliasoph (1998) looks at several volunteer and social service groups, all of which run across political issues at one time or another. She shows how members' political and even communitarian views can only legitimately be expressed in private. In public, members must voice their concerns in terms of self-interest. Literary critic Lauren Berlant (1997, introduction) found that popular media expresses an exhaustion with politics, a recurrent desire among those at the top of hierarchies to be un-marked by race, class, sexuality, and gender and thus to remain "innocent" of politics. And in a study of congregational conflicts, sociologist Penny Becker (1998) finds that racial integration is more easily achieved in a congregation where it is not posited as a political issue, because congregation members view church as not the place for politics. These studies all point to an ex-perience and definition of politics as divisive, exhausting, mean, or worldly rather than humane and conducive to building community. In short, peo-ple experience "politics" as destabilizing and denaturalizing, and it works the other way around as well: experiencing those feelings causes people to categorize their causes as "politics."

We will see such definitions at work in the debates examined here. These debates tell a story about a political culture wherein people want desperately to transcend a world they see as heartless. They have sound, culturally log-ical reasons to see the contemporary world as heartless. Yet their desire for transcendence can lead to particular forms of isolation. Their anxieties about politics lead members at times to ignore, rather than to address, the mate-rial conditions and inequalities that prevented people from living out their ideals. But despite the unintended effects of their actions, members wanted the church to be a place where they could transcend these earthly conditions and pursue what they saw as the up side of being human—the lofty, the spiritual, the part of being human that allows human beings to know God.

Searching for a Haven: Theologies of Dwelling and Seeking

From one perspective, this avoidance of or distancing oneself and one's com-munity from politics might be seen as a search for a "haven in a heartless world." The two congregations differed in their theologies—one liberal and the other more conservative and evangelical—but members of both seemed nearly unanimous in their belief that political questions were distinct, and distant, from spirituality. Members felt that church, at its best, should be a place for believers to commune with God, to find a home where they could seek spiritual sustenance and transcend the terrors, anxieties, and depres-sions of everyday secular life. This desire for such a haven is hardly new. The sociologist of religion Robert Wuthnow (1998) sees the theology of a haven as one of two enduring trends in spirituality throughout history. In his view, during times of social and economic stability, people associate their spirituality with places. They feel at home in their world, they feel at home with the sacred, and they associate the sacred with such places as their home and religious buildings—churches, mosques, synagogues, and temples.

For a brief period after World War II, imagined as a golden age of industrial modernity, the world did feel stable in the white American collective imaginary. For unprecedented numbers, wages were high enough that a single income was enough to support a nuclear family. Although this period was aberrant in history, many Americans maintain it as the ideal, believing, apparently, that until recently life had always been (or should have always been) organized the way it was in this idealized 1950s. They imagine this time as a modern Garden of Eden. Wuthnow sees white middle-Americans' faith as having been centered in religious *places:* church buildings and synagogues. To live a spiritual and righteous life meant to attend services and other activities at one's church or synagogue each week, to focus one's charitable contributions of time and money there, to make that place a second home. In this worldview, dwelling among the righteous and avoiding places that were deemed unrighteous were the keys to maintaining a righteous heart.

On the other hand, Wuthnow sees another kind of theology recurring throughout history—the spirituality of the quest, the pilgrimage. In times of change and uncertainty, he argues, people have trouble believing that the divine sits still. In the spirituality of the pilgrimage, people search for glimpses of the sacred, for moments of transcendence. In recent American history, Wuthnow sees this trend as emerging in the spiritual revivals of the 1960s, going through many permutations, and expressing itself in the 1990s through such diverse forms as belief in angels, the occult, Nature, and the ritual practices of many different peoples, often those outside their immediate culture. With a rapidly changing economy and technology, with the harsh and ever intractable realities of violence, Wuthnow argues, it is hard for many people to associate God's presence with one particular place, especially a traditional church or synagogue.[9] Rather, they experience the sacred and supernatural as fleeting, or else as located solely within themselves.

For Wuthnow, even members of traditional churches and synagogues are oriented toward seeking rather than dwelling. Rather than seeing the act of entering the place of worship as spiritual in itself, these members search to deepen their understandings of God through reading inspirational books, listening to inspirational speakers, and praying on their own. These members see the religion of the 1950s generation as shallow and superficial. The people we hear from here, members of two long-established congregations in a mainline denomination, are reflected in Wuthnow's description. Those who were in their fifties or younger, who were raised in the 1950s or since, were willing to shop for congregations, to meet different needs in different religious groups, to learn about God from a variety of sources.[10] They tended to see their elders, those who adhered to a sterile 1950s model of churchgoing, as lacking touch with the Holy Spirit. Among those I encountered, this younger set tended to look for congregations and other groups they found "spirit filled."

In distinguishing between theologies of dwelling and seeking, however, Wuthnow misses something very important about contemporary church members. It could be that in seeking to create two ideal types, Wuthnow focuses on those whose spiritual experience is more "extreme," whereas I focus intentionally on those who might be said to reflect something more of the "middle." These members experience everyday life in much the way Wuthnow describes, confronting realities of drugs, violence, unstable jobs, and the like. But the people I encountered *wanted* a haven, and had the means to produce that haven in their ritual experiences. Unstable times lead not only to the spirituality of the quest that Wuthnow describes, to constantly seeking peace in an eclectic range of places; they can also steer many on a quest for stability and community. There are ways and times in which these members looked to themselves for the answers, but they also looked for a haven and sought to create it together. To many, the freedom of the quest meant the freedom to search for a community and security in God.

As they sought that sense of transcendent truth, however, in assembling their everyday theologies, various factors threatened to denaturalize that truth, to reveal its social qualities and negotiability. In ritual, members came together searching to be part of something greater, to feel the Holy Spirit's presence, to be part of something so vast and timeless as to make the concerns of everyday life seem petty or irrelevant. Even seekers, those Wuthnow describes as not participating in the religious practices of their upbringings—such as non-Lakotas seeking spirituality or God in Lakota sweat lodges; Christians or Jews who find it in Zen meditation, in the trees they jog past, or simply within themselves—might seek to transcend the cynicism, selfishness, and violence of the world. They, too, might be seeking a haven in what seems to them as "timeless" and "natural."[11]

The people we hear from in these pages affirm that church membership has come to be a place for people to seek a personally meaningful sense of security and happiness through God. In contrast to the dichotomy Wuthnow presents, they combine the spiritualities of the quest and the haven. This hybrid ideal shapes members' everyday theologies. A number of members told me that God does not intend for people to be miserable in this world but to enjoy life and be happy. Yet members could not achieve this happiness in isolation. In their quest for happiness and security, members came together and found one another. But not all of them found a haven.

Debates over Homosexuality in Two Congregations

This study is primarily based on my participation in two United Methodist congregations and loosely structured interviews with their members. The United Methodist Church (UMC), whose more than nine million members make it the second largest Protestant denomination in the United States,[12] resembles many other major Protestant denominations split over issues related to homosexuality. The Methodists have a history of division over social justice issues, having split in the nineteenth century over abolition. The denomination's democratic structure and range of theological beliefs make it seem liberal to many Protestants and conservative to others. The policy-making General Conference meets every four years, and each time it is contentiously divided over these issues as the members negotiate to revise official policy as stated in the *Discipline*. We have seen that the Social Principles that were current in the *Discipline* during this time stated both that "the practice of homosexuality is incompatible with Christian teaching" and that "sexuality is God's gift to all people." The 1996 (and subsequent 2000) *Discipline* also came out strongly against both the ordination of "self-avowed practicing homosexuals" and the blessing of same-sex covenants or same-sex marriages, even though both rules were frequently broken (*Discipline*, ¶304.3; ¶65C; ¶65G).[13]

Members of the UMC and several other Protestant denominations have formed movements around the issue of homosexuality.[14] The Reconciling Congregations Program was formed in 1984 to encourage United Methodist congregations to explicitly affirm gay men, lesbians, and bisexuals and welcome them into the church. RCP proponents saw the church's history of excluding such people from the church as overtly anti-Christian, in that Jesus' own ministry was based on loving the despised and disempowered members of society.

Organized in response to the RCP in 1987, the Transforming Congregations movement agrees that the church should welcome all people, yet unlike the RCP they see the numerous biblical injunctions against homosexuality as unquestionable proof that it is contrary to Christian teaching. These congregations support the ex-gay movement, based on the belief that God can heal and transform people living as homosexuals, helping them to become ex-gays.[15] When proponents of the Reconciling Congregations movement counter that those scriptural passages perceived as antigay are often mistranslated and taken out of context, the two sides reach a deadlock. Each side, Reconciling and Transforming, gains support as the issue of homosexuality confronts more and more congregations.[16]

The two congregations in this study do not reflect the so-called extremes of this debate, as members maintained a wide range of views and struggled with and displayed ambivalence about the issue as they sought to know and do God's will. I spent fourteen months, from November 1996 to January 1998, at City Church, a large, theologically liberal metropolitan congregation that prided itself on its diversity. During my time there, the congregation debated joining the RCP but the process was held back because a number of vocal members maintained that homosexuality was sinful. I spent the following seven months (March–October 1998) attending the more evangelical Missionary Church, located in the small city of Johnsonville, about seventy miles from City Church. Missionary Church's primary mission was to offer a spiritual home to growing numbers of people, but an active subset in the congregation participated in denominational politics, including mobilizing letter-writing campaigns and resolutions for the regional-level Annual Conference in opposition to the goals of the RCP and in alliance with the Transforming movement.[17] We will look at these congregations in greater depth in chapter 2 and beyond.

Throughout the book, I use pseudonyms for the congregations, places, church members, and pastors, though I refer to public figures by their own names (as noted in the text). I have striven to make pseudonyms reflect the ethnic makeup of the respondents, but they do not necessarily reflect the ethnicity of the speaker's real name. At times, to protect members' identities, I have created composite or otherwise fictionalized personae. I use pseudonyms not only to protect members' confidentiality but to reflect my awareness that by writing about what people said at one moment in time, by extracting their remarks from the context in which they were said, and by translating their spoken comments into a more readable written language, I have created fictional characters. These characters are of course based on the people I spoke to, but while characters are frozen into a text, I would be surprised if the people I spoke to in 1996–1998 had not grown and changed. In the spring of 2000, on completion of the dissertation version of this project, I gave the people I have quoted an opportunity to review the quotes I used from them and received several responses, to which I adapted the manuscript. Regardless of their approval at that time, people may have said things then far different from what they might say now or at some point in the future.

In keeping with what appeared to be the custom at both congregations, after introducing members by first and last name, I generally refer to them by their first names, as I did in person. Even though many members of City Church sometimes referred to clergy by their first names alone, when

I describe interactions between clergy and laity, I have at times elected to refer to the clergy by title to maintain the distinction that is present even when unspoken in these interactions. Those at City Church who favored formal titles referred to the pastors by their last names, so the Reverend Fred Hershey was called either "Fred" or "Reverend Hershey." This custom was unlike that at Missionary Church, where the Reverend Richard Voxmann was commonly referred to as Pastor Richard.

I attempt throughout this book to reflect the languages members employed within these debates, to show how they organized their worlds with respect to sexualities. Although RCP supporters tended to see these debates as being about "gay people," "gay men and lesbians," or the more awkward "gay and lesbian people," they more rarely included bisexuals and transgenderists as having the same interests and concerns as gay men and lesbians, and I never heard, heard about, or read any discussion of the needs of these members as separate from the needs of gay men and lesbians.

Even though members did not generally use this term, throughout the book I use the term "pro-gay" to refer to the move among some members to see being gay or lesbian in nonclinical ways—that is, to see being attracted to and loving people of one's same sex, or challenging traditional sex and gender norms, as fully in keeping with God's plan for people. I do not mean to imply that those who oppose this move are "antigay," as many would eschew such a label and its implications.

I found both of my congregations by asking local pastors involved in the debates if they knew of congregations that might be good for my study. I then secured permission from the senior pastor of each congregation, informing them that I was a sociologist interested in changing meanings of family, marriage, and sexuality, interested particularly in people's views about homosexuality in these debates. Each pastor gave me permission, with the caveat that I not disrupt the normal flow of church life. For that reason, I was not formally introduced, but left to introduce myself to individuals and groups as any newcomer would.

I began at each congregation by attending meetings specifically on the topic of homosexuality. When inviting people to be interviewed, and when meeting people and speaking to them for any length of time, I informed them that I was a sociology student doing a project on the United Methodist Church's debates about homosexuality. Given my view that ethnography is a conversation, I participated in group meetings and discussions in a way that seemed appropriate to the context, speaking of my own life when the time came, asking questions as they occurred to me in the course of a discussion, though as will become apparent, different expectations led me to present (and experience) myself differently among different groups of people within and across congregations.

With each congregation, I first entered with little idea of who the members were and little idea how I could best present myself as an unthreatening researcher studying debates about homosexuality. In each congregation, I picked up on what seemed most appropriate. Among the Young Adults group members or the reconciling congregations task force at City Church, it would not have been appropriate to conceal my sexual identity, while in other circles at City Church, as at Missionary Church, it would not be locally appropriate for someone who was gay to, as they would think, "flaunt" it. On the other hand, the Young Adults' openness to gayness did not necessarily mean it was appropriate for me to share my disagreement with people's beliefs or to point out what I perceived as their inconsistencies. In retrospect, my willingness to mostly play by the local rules at the conservative Missionary Church, more so than I did at the liberal City Church, contributed to my recurrent but conflicted desires to fit in. The differences in these experiences showed me the roles that conflict and its suppression can play in constructing the church space as a haven from the heartless worlds of work and politics.

When I first began my research, I thought a great deal about what I should say when people asked about my sexual orientation. In fact, following the general etiquette (and, perhaps, assumptions) of heterosexual society, very few people asked. In groups where hiding one's gay, lesbian, queer, or bisexual identity would be inappropriate—that is, in groups that had openly gay members and where it was not considered an issue—I was as open about my own sexual identity as I am in the rest of my life. In groups where nonnormative sexual identities were considered "private" or taboo, I behaved normatively by being quiet about my own life.

Of far greater interest to church members was my own religious experience. When members asked whether I were "saved" or "Christian," or what my religious background was, I informed them that I had been raised in the United Methodist Church but left it by the time I started college. This is a common experience among church members, as are the occasional questions about the nature and existence of God that I posed from time to time. Thus I was understood to be much like many members who leave the church for a while in young adulthood but then are drawn back for one reason or another later in life. That it was research that drew me back made little difference to many members. I was there to learn about their beliefs, so I spent as little time as possible discussing my own. The questions I asked about faith and reason were questions central to many members' spiritual lives, and thus, in spite of my own lack of religious belief, I was an engaged participant.

My own lack of belief in God made so little difference to some members (or, perhaps, was so unconvincing) that an assistant pastor at City Church once asked me to take over facilitating his adult Sunday School class for a few weeks when he could not make it. I objected that I should be the last person to teach a Sunday School class, but he repeatedly assured me that it wouldn't be difficult; he had picked out the book and we could just discuss a chapter a week. People would be interested in discussing it, and as a teacher myself, I could ask some questions to get discussion going. Finally I broke down and said, "Ricardo, I can't teach this class. I am an atheist!" Nonsense, he replied, "You are a seeker. That is what we all are doing; seeking the truth." I couldn't argue with that, so I taught the class.

At the evangelical Missionary Church, as well, even though they knew I was doing sociological research, members understood me as a seeker, drawn to their congregation by God rather than coincidence. The members closest to me treated me as a spiritual apprentice, seeking to usher me along in my understanding of God in much the way they felt others had ushered them. I was more reticent about my sexual identity in this church, where people frequently said (or implied) that gay people were welcome if they didn't make it public. I found out later that my friends in the congregation had thought I might be gay all along—why else would I be studying debates about homosexuality? My closest friend in the congregation assumed I might be gay, as she informed me later, but never asked outright; my soul was of far greater interest.

Throughout my research, I often spent the larger part of the day at the church, jotting key words from the service on the Sunday bulletin or taking notes on a class or meeting in my notebook. I wrote detailed notes as soon as I could afterward. In telling my story, I often use quotes that I reconstructed days after the event from my detailed notes, and I signal that after the remark with the phrase "reconstructed from notes." Unless otherwise indicated, the quotations come from tape-recorded interviews. Quotes have been edited for readability.

Along with participant-observation, I also conducted interviews with members involved in the broader discussions in their congregations, to find out about their spiritual life and reasoning. I only interviewed people who expressed a willingness to be interviewed. This method of selection suited my desire to respect people, and my desire not to obtain a representative sample but insight into people's reasoning when they had thought a great deal about the questions at hand. With their permission, I tape-recorded the interviews and transcribed them later. On the rare occasions when a member did not wish to be tape-recorded, I carried on our interview as a regular conversation, and made subsequent notes as I would for any other fieldwork. Following a general outline, I asked them to elaborate on what they knew about God, the church, homosexuality, marriage, or current events that had been discussed in church. The formality of the tape-recorder aside, I strove to make the interview feel more like a conversation than a survey, and allowed them to set the tone and tell me what was on their minds.

How we look at groups of people shapes what we can know about them. Specifically, by analyzing participant-observation and interview transcripts the way a literary critic might analyze particular texts, we can see how members developed their own everyday theologies in their everyday lives. Their understandings of God were shaped by what they knew of Scripture, doctrine, and the teachings of their clergy, but they were shaped as well by outside readings, radio and TV, daily interactions, and experiences of current events. Through all of these experiences, most of the people in this study sought to glean God's timeless truth and set it apart from what they saw as the "fallen," human component of life, everyday sin.

Chapters 2 and 3 introduce the two congregations that form the base of this study. In chapter 2, I describe a Sunday service at each and show how each congregation's rituals produced, as social scientists from Emile Durkheim to Victor Turner and Peter Berger have suggested, a feeling of transcendence, of connection among members and connection to God. In chapter 3, I introduce members' widely ranging belief systems about God and homosexuality. In doing so, I show how these belief systems were not simply handed down to members and accepted at face value but came out of their own everyday experiences with God, including their widely differing readings of Scripture. Given that members' individual experiences can lead to very different theologies, it is not surprising that members would have been in conflict over an issue as loaded as homosexuality. Because differing views of what it means to be Christian bred the potential for conflict, chapter 4 explores the very different ways these two congregations understood and dealt with dissent.

Conflict disrupted members' experiencing their congregations and spiritual lives as transcendent. Thus, it is not surprising that members should often have seen conflict as the very opposite of what they held as ideal. What might seem more surprising is the frequency with which members defined the opposite of goodness, care, community, God, and transcendence as "political." Chapter 5 looks at how members came to define certain things as political and how these definitions helped them see their church as timeless in its selflessness and transcendence—in contrast to homosexuality, which could figure as selfish, worldly, and divisive. Chapter 6 explores in greater depth how homosexuality differed from other potentially debatable topics by exploring this distinction between body and spirit, showing how pro-gay advocates inadvertently placed gays on the bodily, nonchurch side of that distinction by insisting that homosexuality was a scientific issue rather than a moral one.

Given the system of oppositions that structured these congregational discussions of homosexuality, chapter 7 turns once again to the question, introduced earlier, of how members formed their everyday theologies, how they came to know God's will: if Scripture's objective existence gave members something to disagree about, then a truth of God that transcends human squabbles must, by the logic of conflict-avoidance, come from a less debatable source, that is, from emotions. Chapter 8 shows how this emotional knowledge could itself limit the possibilities for gay and lesbian members seeking equality in church membership. In the end, I place these congregational debates in the context of a broader American culture of political avoidance and explore the question of what it means for a society to collectively define politics as the opposite of the good, rather than as a means to its realization. Such a negative view of politics can lead people to create greater isolation even though many church members and sociologists hope for greater care and community.[18]

These chapters all look at how members of these congregations, in their day-to-day lives, built and maintained church as a space of ideal, unmarked personhood, a zone free from the perpetually conflicting interests that confronted them as they negotiated their worlds of work, government, neighborhood, and family in constant dialogue with popular ideals of tolerance and diversity. Some members believed that God's love could and should change homosexuals, and others believed that God's love could be expressed in homosexuality. These views reflected sometimes profoundly different understandings of God and Christian life. In avoiding conflict, in speaking past each other, in using languages of personal emotion—and especially, in defining their category of politics—members protected themselves from the knowledge that they and the people down the pew from them might worship very different Gods.[19]

chapter TWO

Feeling the Spirit in Two Congregations

Joy is the by-product of our walk with God, a sense that our little lives are part of the larger purpose of God's saving activity in the world.

—William H. Willimon, *Why I Am A United Methodist*

I'm going to tell a story, or rather, several stories. The stories have a plot and subplots, character development, plenty of conflict—in fact, conflict, and avoiding it, are precisely the things on everyone's mind in the stories. I have many roles at various points in the stories' unfolding: a somewhat detached participant, an outsider looking in, an initiate reporting an ever-incomplete conversion narrative, and an intellectual seeker on a journey of the spirit. One thing I was not was an impartial observer, as there is no such thing. I could not pretend to be neutral or to have no groundings of my own.

Although I expressed different parts of myself in different settings, I needed to be present as a person with questions, fears, confusions, and loves. It was only in this way that I could experience what the church members struggling with these debates experience as they try to sort out their conflicting ideals. In fact, as the languages of emotion has become an important ways for people to articulate their experiences of such things as church, sexuality, and marriage, to refrain from speaking that language would have excluded me from much of the substance of these contemporary debates.

In a certain sense, then, I went into "the field" aware of my own theories as well as my own political goals; I went to have a conversation.[1] My goal was to understand people in their everyday lives, to understand what was at stake for them in church debates about homosexuality. In getting to know these new people, I learned how my own beliefs, perspective, and modes of operating were very much shaped by the world I inhabited. When I completed this fieldwork, I returned to doing the things I enjoyed doing and thinking in ways more comfortable to me, but some things had changed about me. Attending church services regularly and trying to listen carefully and engage the people there showed me how one could experience an entirely different persona and way of looking at the world. Here I set forth an argument to be supported throughout this book, that the members I heard from, regardless of what else their church participation may have meant to them, ultimately sought a feeling of closeness to God, of transcending the earthly realm and all its problems.

The Role of a Researcher and the Significance of *Communitas*

This is a study of conflict, of politics and religion, of a heartless world and a transcendent haven from it. It is a story of deeply held beliefs and loving people who disagree with one another but who all feel they understand at least the gist of God's will for people. This is not a story about me, but I will begin with stories about me, hoping that when I later generalize about emotions, politics, and the structure of contemporary life in the United States, it will be clear what is at stake for people in church debates about homosexuality. It is important to clarify where my theorizing finds its grounding. I also hope to show that the anxieties other people express are in no way hysterical responses to undesired social change, as some might be tempted to think. Rather, these anxieties are real products of a particular set of institutionalized social interactions.

I initially decided to study the same-sex marriage debates in congregations in order to understand why homosexuality had proven to be so volatile an issue. I thought of the church as a place where people would really engage one another, push one another's thinking, and not be as quick to avoid debate as in most other settings. Where else do nonqueer people grapple with issues like sexuality and marriage on an ongoing basis? It was a few months before I realized (as we said back in third grade, "Duh!") that to talk about people in churches, I would have to talk about religion, God, salvation, sin, and the meaning of life.

Not just talk about them, but think about them. Having publicly identified myself as queer for a dozen years and a declared atheist for a decade, I thought I knew where I stood in relation to Christianity and the divine, and where it stood in relation to me. I was unprepared to meet people whose views on sexuality (and life in general) were so like mine and yet who believed the church was a place for them as persons. I was also unprepared to find myself in a gathering of Christians where my belonging was so unquestioned that I would for the first time in my life find a degree of communion with a group of self-identified Christians.

Most of all, however, I was unprepared to meet people whose views were so different from mine and yet who showed me a genuine hospitality, warmth, and great love. I was not prepared to meet people whose views on religion made so much sense, in a way, and whose philosophy on homosexuality was so opposed to mine. I tried to set aside my beliefs and politics to experience the world of these two congregations. In so doing, I was shocked to find my atheistic, delightedly queer self questioning at points whether, perhaps, God really did intend for us all to be in heterosexual relationships. More than once I left a long day of fieldwork in the evangelical church wishing to make my life as unproblematic as their lives seemed to be—to marry a man with a well-paying job, to move to (and decorate!) a big house in Johnsonville, to be a member of Missionary Church, to really belong with my friends there.[2]

I expected to find great differences between these two congregations. It is standard sociological practice to pick two cases that have many things in common but differ along one main axis, to measure the effect of these differences. I chose one liberal and one conservative congregation. The most important difference between these congregations was the extent to which clergy and members in general believed in the centrality of one-man-one-woman marriage. At Missionary Church, this traditional view of sexuality was virtually unquestioned. At City Church, many members agreed with that view, but others saw one-man-one-woman marriage as a human, flawed institution. At both congregations, involvement in social and political issues was secondary to and stemmed from the mandate to love.

A later chapter will highlight the differences between these congregations, but we cannot see these two congregations as polar opposites. Although they were dominated by very different understandings of God and what it meant to be Christian, members of each might be surprised to find how much they had in common with members of the other. Within each of these congregations, members had widely diverging theological and social views. Each congregation had members who would describe themselves as traditional or evangelical and who believed that homosexuality was sinful. In each congregation there were members who did not believe homosexuality to be sinful. Furthermore, in each congregation, many members expressed a commitment to social justice, to an end to racism, to a more godly, inclusive, and welcoming church. We have much to learn from the similarities not just between the congregations but between their members who also seem, on the surface, to have opposite theologies.

Demonstrating the polarization that members experience in the religious divide between liberal and evangelical, members of each congregation sometimes wondered if a place like my other congregation could truly be a spiritual place. But both showed me the importance of "communitas" that threads throughout this project. Anthropologist Victor Turner (1969) defines *communitas* as a sense of unbounded connection to or communion with humanity. In spite of my own awareness that such a feeling can be a tool of social control, in both of these congregations I experienced a feeling of unbounded connection to humanity that helped me to feel that I *belonged* in these congregations, that I was not a stranger. But, more important, it gave me, and those I spoke with during the course of this research, a timeless—and natural—feeling of truth, order, and meaning, that I in my uniqueness and they in theirs are part of something larger that we cannot even begin to understand from our own insular perspectives. It helped me to see the profound good in community, the evil in things that are anticommunal (such as corporations and war), within a framework that felt coherent and sensible. And it made all of us feel that we were part of something greater, part of something that transcended our own insular lives. In this sense, the ritual process worked as a naturalizing force, making my own foundational assumptions feel like an external, timeless truth.

Most of the members said they went to church primarily to worship and draw closer to God. For many that feeling of drawing closer to God, that feeling of transcendence, is closely related to the feeling of innocence and a sense of being away from the divisions and conflicts of everyday life. For now, I will show how the rituals of Sunday service at each church could engender that feeling of transcendence.

City United Methodist Church

You can walk by City United Methodist Church (City Church) every day and not know it is there. Nestled among government and corporate buildings, it is one among many downtown skyscrapers surrounded by the large public sculptures that contribute to the city's identity. Its presence in a major metropolitan downtown contributes to its mission of social justice. During the week the senior pastor might run across the street to discuss matters such as children's or workers' rights with state and municipal officials.

City Church's engagement with politics is one trait shaped by its location; another is its generalized understanding of "diversity" as a cornerstone of God's Creation. Members often mention the diversity as something they like about their congregation, and it boasts of its diversity in the weekly bulletin, where the regular member and casual visitor alike can learn that the congregation "embrace[es] members from every ZIP code in the city as well as eighty suburbs. We are 60% single, 60% female, 18% African-American, 18% Asian-American and 5% Latino." During my time there, the bulletin also stated:

> We welcome all people to the life of this congregation. We believe that we
> are all in need of God's love and grace and that God, through Jesus Christ,
> intends the church to be a community which incarnates love, grace,
> and justice for all people. Holding true to that belief, we welcome and
> encourage all persons, including gay men, lesbian women and bisexual
> persons in all aspects of our Christian life together.

Holding true to their ideals of diversity, the congregation was economically diverse as well, with a few "heavy hitters" (people who could afford to donate large chunks of the congregation's budget out of their own resources), a wide range from throughout the urban and suburban middle classes, and a relatively small set of urban poor members and participants. Occupationally, the congregation included enough lawyers to figure as a running joke (the pastors had their work cut out for them, trying to get *that* crowd into heaven), while most of the other members I encountered were in other white-collar professions at various levels.

On any given Sunday morning, to help visitors find this diverse and social justice-motivated congregation, a sandwich-board sign sits on the sidewalk outside, directing visitors in. As a visitor, you may arrive by bus or subway, as many members do, or you may park in the bank parking lot down the street at a reduced rate. You go through the brass doors, through the elevator lobby, and in to the narthex (the vestibule just outside the doors of the sanctuary), where you will be greeted by the day's official greeters, another member serving at the coffee-and-muffin table, and a volunteer staffing the social concerns table. At this last table, depending on the salient issues of the week or month, one could sign a petition about removing land mines from Bosnia or one to end U.S. sanctions on Cuba; buy coffee grown on cooperative farms in Central America; and buy lapel pins to support domestic violence intervention.

Two sets of glass doors lead to the sanctuary, whose main floor could seat perhaps a thousand; the balcony could seat around three hundred more. The church itself occupies the basement, the first and second and parts of the third and fourth floors of a larger building. The entire building is the property of the regional conference of the UMC, which rents space to law firms and the like on the other floors. Because the congregation's building expenses are paid for by the others' rent, all of the offering money goes toward other church expenses, including social concerns and its relatively large annual dues to the denomination. Compared to many other churches, the congregation's facilities border on lavish.

Ushers, men and women of various ages, smile as they greet you and offer you your choice of seating in the large sanctuary, which no longer fills up completely except on Easter or Christmas Eve. Three to four hundred people attend an average Sunday late service. The organist will play a quiet prelude on the enormous pipe organ, usually classical Christian music, until the service begins. As you listen to the music, you might look around and notice the expertly homemade banners hanging in the front of the sanctuary and the enormous stained glass windows lining both sides. On the chancel, the traditional altar, lectern, and pulpit stand before the choir's pews. The wood-paneled walls and soaring, carved beams lead your eyes to carved angels adorning the ceiling beams. You wonder how they have managed to hide this enormous, ornate sanctuary in this building, whose sidewalk-level windows only reveal a bank and a store selling antique collectibles.

As you look around before the popular 10:30 A.M. service, you will see a sanctuary filling with many people who are over fifty, almost as many in their late thirties and forties, and a few in their twenties. Occasionally during the service a baby will cry, and Senior Pastor Fred Hershey will remind the congregation that babies crying in church are something to be thankful for, because that means the church is growing. On any given Sunday morning, between 40 to 80 percent of the people assembled will be white, and there will be a sizable number of Asians, slightly fewer African Americans, and a few Latinos and Latinas. As long as you are conducting a head count, you are likely to notice several interracial couples, some who live close by, others who come from some distance, attracted by the congregation's diversity.

As the service begins, the choir sings an introit from the narthex, then they process in as they and the congregation sing the first hymn found in the hymnal provided in the pew racks. The choir processes up the two aisles, which create a wide central row of pews and a row of shorter ones along each side. As the pastors follow the choir and take their places in front of the choir loft on the chancel, you notice some racial and gender variety in the pastoral staff, which includes interns and student pastors, the minister of Christian education, and the senior and assistant pastors. There can be as many as seven clergy on staff at City Church at any one time, and they rotate Sundays leading worship, so usually three or four appear at the front of the sanctuary, each wearing his or her unique robe and stole.

The pastors rotate in leading parts of the traditional liturgy: the Opening Prayer, the Prayer of Confession, and the Prayer of Pardon and Assurance; the Scripture readings, which are usually done by a lay member; the sermon; the Affirmation of Faith, which could come from a variety of traditional and modern sources; the Pastoral Prayer, the Offering Prayer and blessing of the offering, and the Benediction. Communion is served at least once a month at the popular 10:30 a.m. service, weekly at the early service and at the Wednesday noon service. During the 10:30 service, the congregation usually sings three hymns, all from the traditional *United Methodist Hymnal.*

In addition to the spoken parts of the liturgy, each week the Sunday services feature a choral anthem or special music. The choir has eight paid section leaders for four sections; in addition, the music committee organizes special musical events, such as monthly Sunday afternoon concerts in the sanctuary and professional guest musicians for special days in the Christian calendar, including a New Orleans–style band that accompanied all of the music in the All Saints' Sunday service. Along with the spoken liturgy and the silent prayer and meditation time, the music contributes to the spiritual uplift of the service as a whole.

The overwhelming sense you get from attending your first or second service could be one of, well, polish. The furniture shines, the brass gleams, the stained glass sparkles, the clergy and choir are robed, and the liturgy is highly structured. The aesthetic does not dehumanize the service, however. The clergy often joke with one another during announcements; pastors might misplace their index cards or forget to announce an important upcoming event, requiring someone to yell a reminder to them. Communion servers greet each participant by name as he or she approaches to take a piece of bread and dip it in the grape juice. A soloist or the choir will sing a particularly rousing piece and the sanctuary will fill with applause.

The joking and applause contribute to the performance and the ritual, which, like the services in many congregations, seems designed to create a sense of communitas, a sense of direct, fundamental connection between human beings unmarked by status divisions. As long as one is included enough to understand a joke, if one has been made, one can feel that sense of unbounded connection. On some occasions, a ritual can even create that sense for someone who is not a Methodist or even a Christian. On a few occasions, I experienced that sense myself.

One such occasion took place on All Saints' Sunday, the day on the Christian calendar, in early November, when many Protestants remember their dead. That day, rather than sitting alone in the back, as I usually did, I sat toward the front of the sanctuary with people I knew from my participation with the congregation's Young Adults Ministry, or, as they called themselves, the YAMs. Even with my queerness, my atheism, and my persistent ethnographic questioning, they had accepted and included me as one of them.

Toward the end of the service the time came for the ritual of communion. In this ritual as it is observed by the traditionally temperate United Methodist Church, participants share bread and "unfermented wine" (grape juice) as the symbol of God's continual presence in their lives, their continued belonging to the universal church. Communion exists as a supreme symbol of the church's communitas, and Turner even defines the two terms as synonymous (1969, 96). In the UMC, all Christians, regardless of their age, denominational background, or any other characteristic, are invited to participate. At City Church, the senior pastor takes this very seriously and explicitly invites everyone seated in the sanctuary to partake each time communion is served.

Throughout the course of my research I made it a policy not to take communion (as it is a ritual reserved for those who accept Jesus Christ as their savior), but on this day I was almost moved to do so. Hundreds of congregants passed me in the aisles to my right and to my left, heading up to the front where clergy and lay members served the bread and grape juice, the symbolic body and blood of Jesus, with the organist playing quiet music in the background and people singing along quietly. I reflected on the funeral I had attended earlier in the year, on the tremendous sadness I had experienced, and felt a bond with the others there in the congregation at City Church that day. I thought of us all sharing that sadness, sharing in the experience of death. My feeling of connection to those in attendance built until I felt nearly overwhelmed by the sense of belonging. I felt communitas, a sense of formal social distinctions falling away, replaced by egalitarian, direct bonds between myself and all the other people there. No differences in opinion or politics or walk of life mattered in that moment; what mattered was that we were all undifferentiated, connected, human. I felt my eyes growing a little teary. In the experience of communitas I felt a sense of greater truth, in that the social structural forces dividing me from others seemed to fall away, if only for a moment.

Next to me sat Keith Appleton, a thirtyish white male policy analyst whom I had gotten to know fairly well through our lunch interview and various group activities. It is customary not to talk during communion, but I noticed that Keith's eyes also looked a little moist, so I smiled at him. He leaned over and whispered to me:

> My father is an atheist. He goes to church every Sunday [to a small church in a small town]. He sings in the choir. He says he sits there every week; he knows who cheats on their wife, who steals, who does all this stuff, there's all these people who do all these awful things, and he says he just sits there and thinks, "I love these people." That's how I feel right now, and I don't even know these people. I just feel like I love them. (Reconstructed from notes)

I leaned back to him and whispered, "That's funny, because I was just feeling that too." We both had tears in our eyes.

I tell this story to highlight the emotional and social experiences created by the ritual practices of the congregations I examine here. This emotional and social state of literally communing with others, of communitas, is a goal and reward of church attendance. For Turner "communitas" is opposed to what he defines as social "structure." He defines structure as the formal bonds and distinctions between people, while "the bonds of communitas are anti-structural in that they are undifferentiated, equalitarian, direct, nonrational (though not *irrational*)" (1974, 46–47). In that ritual moment, people feel a sense of transcendence, a sense of belonging to something bigger, a sense of life having a meaning beyond what people often perceive as the cynicism, power, and hierarchies of secular life in late-capitalist America.[3]

Turner sees communitas as emerging where social structure, and its accompanying conflicts, are not present (1969, 126). Although I agree with him in many ways, I believe that communitas and structure exist in the realm of individuals' perceptions rather than as actual collective experiences. Because the congregations in this study maintain pervasive unspoken hierarchies, those who see themselves at the bottoms of those hierarchies may see and struggle with a fundamental disconnection between themselves and those who have power or privileges over them, at the same moment that people at the top are experiencing communitas.

But at this moment, even those hierarchies of which I knew I was at the bottom stopped mattering to me. I was sitting with people who I knew and who knew me, who knew my less-guarded personality, who knew me as queer and as an atheist, and who shared with me their belief that God loved *me*. Participating in the ritual in these circumstances, even I, a nonbeliever, could experience a sense of intimate connection to other people, as well as to that which a believer might well call "God." The prayers spoke to me as someone who had shared in the common human experience of another's death, and I experienced them as part of a group of other people who knew me and made me feel welcome among them as I was. In that moment, I felt deeply connected to all of the people present at the service through this human experience. For many churchgoers I spoke with, that's what church is about; that feeling indicates the presence of God.[4]

My overall experience at City Church fundamentally shaped this book in many ways. Methodologically, I learned that I would never be accepted as a "participant" if I did not participate. When others shared their feelings, I shared my feelings. The Young Adult Ministry's biweekly Wednesday meetings were devoted to discussing the issues confronting members in their daily lives—conflicts with parents and siblings, concerns about finding rewarding work (many did freelance or clerical work they found unrewarding), worries about finding marriage or life partners, or the problems arising in such relationships. The YAMs were not alone in their focus on articulating feelings and negotiating modern secular lives; the rest of the congregation participated in these activities as well, especially in the debates about homosexuality. However, it was with the young adults that I experienced firsthand the power of a language of personal emotions to shape a debate, and it was among them that I first noticed the anxieties provoked in many people by the contemporary economy, which many members experienced as workers in the growing sector of temporary and consulting jobs that were replacing more stable employment.

Likewise, it was among the YAMs that I came to understand the importance of belonging for experiencing communitas. I came to understand that in spite of our differences, and there were many, members could believe that I was loved by God. To them, my being "gay" was not even in the running as a disqualifying characteristic—the group had two gay members already. My constant questioning, my frankness about my nonreligiousness, my political views, the impatience I sometimes expressed—these did a lot more to separate me from the group. Even though I was different in many ways, a feeling persisted in me that I belonged with these people. There were sides of myself that had rarely come out before—patience, understanding—that being with them brought out.

My experiences with the YAMs did not convince me to profess Christianity, but they helped me better understand the other Christians I encountered; they helped me to understand the fears, anxieties, and faith questions I encountered among other members of both congregations. They also helped me to understand some of the joy and love members might feel in being

Christian. In trying to think of affirmations (anonymous affirming statements written for a specific person) to write for the others during an exercise at a summer weekend out of town with the group, I took another step
in learning to speak their language without misrepresenting my beliefs. I
came to understand how religious language can be used to express collective
sentiment, communitas, and transcendence.[5]

I was in conversation with them, but I was also allowing them to influence my own theoretical preconceptions. I started to translate my own beliefs
in a future of justice created by people collectively standing up to the oppressive forces of capital, of racism, of gender and sexual ideologies; I was starting
to hear such calls for justice in the Scriptures I had heretofore only heard as
apologies for oppression and opiates of the masses. Jesus' explanation of the
greatest commandment, to love God and to love others as yourself, came to
echo in my head as the story of a God known only in community, rather
than in selective individualism.[6] It thus naturalized the beliefs I had come in
with, while allowing me to think about them in a new light.

Ironically, my own intellectual distance from the religious project led
me to find a transcendent meaning in it, to hear in some church teachings
the truths around which I organized my life. And as one of the Young Adults
wrote to me in an affirmation, "I just wanted to tell you that God is truth
and don't believe any of that rubbish from the past. Seek truth. I see Jesus
in you." At many moments, I felt a sense of truth.

As for many people, the truth I found did not radically transform my
life; it was in keeping with the understanding of the world I had brought in
with me. Many believers will no doubt see my understanding of the Scriptures and church teachings as cynical and secularizing attempts to diminish
and/or disobey God. In response I would point out a central point in this
book—that religious beliefs help people to address their anxieties about the
contemporary world by helping to blend the beliefs about the world they
take for granted with a story of redemption and a better future.

To a believer who understands that her beliefs come from God, rather
than from herself or society, my argument that beliefs are shaped by one's
own needs and the surrounding world might seem cynical. In the extreme,
it might even seem that I am arguing that there is no God at all, that it is all
"society." But as Berger (1969) points out, one can believe in God and still
ask about the social aspects of religion—one can take as given the existence
of God and God's truth and still want to examine what people do with that
truth when they get their hands on it. People in the same denomination,
the same congregation even, can see themselves as faithful believers while

they nonetheless disagree fundamentally about God's truth. My purpose as a sociologist is to look at the people doing the arguing about God. What do they bring with them to these arguments? What social and material effects on the world do people have, intentionally or otherwise, when they attribute particular beliefs to God? I hope that this project may help people on different sides in these battles to understand one another, and perhaps themselves, better.[7]

Missionary United Methodist Church

Drive out sixty miles along the expressway from City Church, past the suburban sprawl, beyond the outlet malls, through what remains of the prairie; then head twelve miles down the road and you'll wind up right by Missionary United Methodist Church. Located in the small city of Johnsonville, this congregation does not boast a rainbow of diverse nationalities and zip codes, but it too is interested in welcoming all people. Johnsonville has the economic diversity of a small city. It has a lower median income than that of nearby municipalities and the United States overall; however, members of the congregation come from surrounding towns as well as from Johnsonville. Many engineers, lawyers, and other professionals belong to the congregation along with a population of stay-at-home mothers who were more visible than at City Church, where more women were active in their professions. The congregation was growing rapidly, with many people drawn to it by the charisma and preaching style of the youthful senior pastor, Richard Voxmann. Voxmann's vision was to combine new and traditional ministerial styles, which he hoped would eventually triple the congregation's size. His sensitivity and compassion, and his focus on people's spiritual needs, all contributed to drawing and keeping new members.

The iconic church building is made from soft gray stone, was built in the middle of the nineteenth century, and it looks, well, like a church—with a sloped roof, stained glass windows, pointed-arch doorways, and a steeple. As you walk in through the heavy wooden double door, a large bin stands to one side to receive donations of clothes or food for the church's homeless outreach program, and in front of you a few linoleum-tiled steps lead to the main floor narthex. There, small tables contain racks of pamphlets about Christian programs that may be of interest to parents with problem children, married couples, alcoholics, or people wanting to go on a retreat; there are cassette tapes of previous weeks' sermons; copies of the church newsletter and directory; and information and sign-up sheets about upcoming church social events, such as a high school retreat or an upcoming Promise Keepers' event. A bulletin board contains information about ongoing mission activities and letters from missionaries supported by the congregation.

Just as City Church was not officially a pro-gay Reconciling Congregation, Missionary Church did not officially participate in the Transforming Congregations movement to help homosexuals to stop living as homosexual. As a congregation, it had had less experience with gay people than City Church, as no one who attended professed to be gay or ex-gay. There was no literature about the Transforming Congregations program in the narthex, but the church newsletter often contained updates about the United Methodists' debate over homosexuality at the regional level. Although few members of City Church had ever heard of the Transforming Congregations movement, virtually everyone at Missionary knew about the Reconciling movement. This was in part because the Annual Conference for Johnsonville's region had recently declared itself "a Reconciling Annual Conference," provoking outrage among several congregations. A pastoral staff member at Missionary Church served as an active organizer of another movement, the Annual Conference-level organization of the Confessing Movement, which supports the goals of Transforming Congregations but deals with a broader social and political agenda. Other members of the congregation took part in these activities and worked to gather support from the congregation for conferencewide efforts.

At Missionary, the Sunday late service begins after Sunday School, as at City Church. Here, the ushers are almost always men with special markers over the breast pockets of their sport coats; they lead you from a packed narthex full of children and parents scurrying after each other, as well as a good proportion of older people whose children are grown and have moved away. The usher will cheerfully take you to a pew and give you a bulletin with the order of the service and announcements, as they do at City Church, but they also provide a "sermon notes" sheet—an outline of the sermon with spaces left for congregants to fill in key words as Pastor Richard preaches. As you look around the sanctuary you will see many families with children filing in down the center or side aisles; junior high and high school students tend to sit together in the balcony. As at City Church, the sanctuary is rectangular with a high, tapered ceiling and heavy wooden beams and ornate rafters. An altar, lectern, and pulpit are arranged in similar traditional fashion on the chancel in front of the choir loft. The sanctuary seats maybe half as many people as City Church's and is always nearly full for the late service.

Where City Church is heavy on liturgy, Missionary Church's services are heavier on participation. On some Sundays, an overhead projector will shine the words to contemporary and upbeat songs of praise on a screen so that people can lift their voices as they sing together. One or a few members of the congregation will lead the congregation in singing and clapping to these songs. Then, still before the official beginning of the service, one song leader will ask the congregation to pray with him or her. She or he will offer a more or less stream-of-consciousness prayer, praying for the pastors who will lead the service and giving thanks for the day, the week, particular things of significance that have happened, or for each other, whatever comes to the lips of the person leading the prayer. This form of prayer, led aloud by one or more persons, improvised from a written list of prayer requests or a mental list of themes to cover, appeared in almost every church-related event at Missionary Church and stood out to me as central to membership in the congregation.

The order of worship varies from week to week, as Pastor Richard likes to keep the services down to an hour and a half and knows his sermons can get a little long sometimes. Each month, a representative from the congregation's selected "Mission of the Month"—a school in the Dominican Republic, a group that travels to Ecuador, or the local city homeless outreach, for instance—will give a presentation about the work that the church's prayers, gifts, and service have done in the world to help people in need and to show others the love of the Lord.

The choir sings on special occasions, led by the husband-and-wife team who play the piano and organ together for each service. At other times there will be a soloist from the congregation, sharing his or her gifts in worship, such as nine-year-old Chelsea Li on the violin, retiree and church leader Dick Buchman on the saxophone, or any of a number of singers, accompanied by either the pianist or a recorded background tape of the song. The congregation also has a "Human Video troupe," a group of teenagers who lip-synch and dramatize contemporary Christian songs, often very powerfully. Occasionally the congregation might sing a hymn from the *United Methodist Book of Hymns*, but often the songs will be more contemporary, with words printed in an insert in the bulletin. If it is an especially new song, Pastor Richard may introduce it or lead it more actively.

Pastor Richard, always in a beautifully tailored suit and wearing no clerical vestments, tends to give the sermons, while other parts of the service will be led by lay members or the other ministerial staff. Many newer members cite his sermons as their reason for staying after their first visit to Missionary Church. In this respect, he is similar to Fred Hershey, the senior pastor of City Church. Both pastors give sermons that effectively connect scriptural teaching to daily life, thereby helping to foster listeners' sense of themselves as part of a bigger story whose beginning and end extend far beyond but include the particularities of the life of each individual listening to it. Both pastors provide intelligent analyses and profound wisdom, while never making the story so complicated as to lose the message.

Within the first few weeks that I showed up for Sunday School, Pastor Richard informed me of a variety of adult Sunday School classes I might find useful, and when I picked the New Horizons class, he ushered me into the room and introduced me to the class and teacher. The class welcomed me warmly and immediately passed around a box of name tags so we could quickly learn one another's names. The class members were mostly parents in their thirties and early forties, although there were a few younger people. They were working through a book on authenticity in one's Christian life, which included negotiating personal relationships, especially with spouses, coworkers, and non-Christians. The teacher, Tina Harrison, was a delightful former English teacher who quickly befriended me and would become one of my closest friends in the congregation.

At the first service I attended, I was similarly welcomed. Charles and Renée Li, an interracial couple in their thirties, he a psychiatrist and she a part-time social worker, sat in the pew with me and introduced themselves. Later, Charles introduced me to the congregation's system of Bible studies, known as Tender Loving Care (TLC) groups, and invited me to attend the one regularly led by himself and Renée. The group met at Tina and George Harrison's house, and many of the same people from the New Horizons class attended their TLC group as well.

The TLC groups followed a published Bible study program that guided them in reading the entire Bible from Genesis to Revelation in one year. Pastor Richard followed the study's schedule in his sermons, preaching on each week's TLC reading instead of following the traditional UMC three-year calendar of suggested Scripture readings. While studying the Bible, the TLCs also brought up their concerns and prayed for one another at each meeting.

For many of the first several meetings, Charles Li asked the TLC group to pray for their friend Rob, who he had met and befriended through work and who suffered from an incurable cancer. Charles had had lunch with Rob weekly and started bringing him to the TLC group on Sunday evenings. Other members of the group came to know and love Rob as well, and he eventually met with Pastor Richard and they prayed together for the Lord to come into Rob's heart. Rob was saved. By the time I had started attending the TLC group, Rob had become too ill to care for himself and had moved back to his home state to live with his mother. The group remembered him in prayer weekly, and members individually prayed for him at other times during the week.

In the middle of the summer, Charles told us that Rob had died. Members of the group were sad, but they were also happy that his pain was over, that he was now with God. People became choked up thinking about him. They had spoken earlier in the meeting about the difference one person can make with God behind them, which led Tina to think about the great difference Charles and Renée had made in Rob's life; what would have happened to Rob if they had not befriended him, if he had never met any of them, if he had never met Pastor Richard.

Earlier in that meeting, Charles asked for prayer requests and included me by name in the invitation. I tried to shake my head noncommittally, and he suggested they might pray for me in working on my dissertation, the very big project I had undertaken. I smiled sheepishly and tried to shrug in a noncommittal way again. As he led the prayer, he prayed for me personally, for God's guidance and strength in my dissertation, and that I might find my way with the Lord. On other days, a prayer leader would mention me as well; Tina would thank God for bringing me to spend the afternoon with her and her family; Maureen McConnelly would pray for my safe travel back home. (My rusty car made some people nervous.)

This style of praying was far less common at City Church; indeed, some City Church members did not feel comfortable with it. Some found it coercive and distancing, unlike silent, individual prayer, which they believed would bring them closer to God. The prayers of the Missionary Church members made me feel uncomfortable. In one sense, it was the discomfort of an unfamiliar and slightly coercive ritual, but in another it was the discomfort of being given a gift I could not return. I felt sad. At the meeting in which we talked about Rob's salvation and where Charles prayed that I would find my way in the Lord, I felt a tremendous pressure to be saved, to join them, to be able to share in their prayers.

Between Sunday services and evening TLC, I often spent the afternoon with George and Tina Harrison and their kids Katie and Kurt, and, eventually, newborn Kelly. We would take naps, play with the kids, do a little work on the lawn, and have a casual dinner. Other afternoons I spent with Charles and Renée and their daughter, Chelsea, reading, sharing recipes, talking about books. I came to know these families and other individuals through interviews or casual chats, through attendance at New Horizons, and later the Cross Bearers, Sunday School classes, and through participation in the TLC, led by the Lis or Pastor Richard.

I conducted myself as a researcher much differently at Missionary

Church than at City Church. At Missionary Church, even more than at City Church, I suppressed my own opinions (for example, political beliefs), and I found that I shared even fewer concepts and assumptions with Missionary members than I did with City members. This meant that I had to do more work to communicate my ideas in their terms and to understand what their terms meant to them. In spite of these differences, and the exhaustion that accompanied them, a part of me felt it belonged there. Even as I grumbled about getting up early on Sunday morning to make the long drive, in some sense I looked forward to Sunday services, to the energy, clarity, and feelings of communitas that came from singing the upbeat and heartfelt gathering songs. I enjoyed hearing Pastor Richard's message and spending the afternoon with my friends in Johnsonville. Their graciousness and kindness, their humor and ease, made me feel welcome and a part of the church community. I enjoyed thinking about the questions they asked me, and I enjoyed learning about their view of the world and about their faith.

In an interview with one member, I found out that some of her beliefs differed significantly from those of most of the members of the congregation. For instance, she did not believe that homosexuality was sinful; her brother was gay, and she knew that was "just how he always was." She did not think that he should change, and she and her husband and kids would visit with him and his partner often. She did not share this with her friends from the congregation, as she was afraid they might not understand and would pray for him to be healed of his homosexuality. He also had AIDS, and it seemed that her reticence with her church friends became especially difficult during the times he was unwell, when she could only bring him up as a prayer concern in the vaguest way.

One day after the Sunday service, I asked her about his health, and she told me he was doing pretty well, getting better but still a little weak. I told her I understood, that I knew it was a drag; I listened attentively as she apparently tried to sort out her feelings and to articulate how he was doing. That conversation moved me profoundly. I felt grief because of her brother's illness, but I also felt a kinship with her as a member of this congregation who, nonetheless, felt a need to hide part of her life. It was not the only time I felt that way, but it was one of the strongest moments I had, as I drove away from the church that day, of wanting to leave my home, move to this city, and become a member of this congregation. I had the fantasy that I could live here, get married, take care of my house, and maybe work on a book or something in my free time. Marry a liberal, iconoclastic guy. We could be the weird couple, with our wackily furnished house. I could gradually stop having to do this constant self-translating and show these friends of mine *my* truth, that homosexuality is necessary for some people to live an authentic life—the same kind of authenticity they strive for! I would not have to fight all the time. Eventually, I could be one of the group, a regular person.

After I was eleven miles down the road I slapped myself in the head to snap out of it, but I was shocked by the extent to which I could succumb to the temptations of this life, the power of normalcy, the desire to trade in all the love that has made my life so meaningful and worth fighting for—to trade it all in for the love of these people who believed they had so much figured out. While many of my grounding assumptions seemed so debatable, theirs seemed perpetually naturalized.

For people such as my friends Tina and Charles, God's plan is—not entirely but in large part—about helping people to be happy, to lead lives that function smoothly and shelter them from the bitter parts of secular America's sweeping economic and social changes. God can give you some tough challenges as well, but these challenges can help you to be closer to God, to mature in your faith. After reading a draft of this chapter, Tina said to me:

> God allows trials to happen in our lives, but mostly God just calls us to
> walk closely with him, to walk through circumstances with him. Then
> there's more joy in life, because no matter what happens, the creator of
> the universe is there for *you*. In everything. (Reconstructed from notes)

The participants in these debates attribute the kind of pull I felt with them to the Holy Spirit, who many see as present only in certain types of congregations, those doctrinally similar to theirs. However, I felt the same kind of pull in both groups of Christians, those that were pro-gay and those that believed homosexuality is sinful.

Only once before had I felt such a strong pull toward Christianity as I felt after talking to the woman with the gay brother. When I was studying City Church, I had attended the national convocation of the Reconciling Congregations Program. Like the services at Missionary Church, the daily worship services at the RCP "convo" were participatory and what many of the Christians I met might call spirit-filled. Gathering songs got us on our feet, clapping, singing in harmony, moving to the music. Bible study lectures, led by two dynamic speakers, challenged my thinking and showed me new ways of understanding the Scriptures; they showed me how the Scriptures could be seen as stories of redemption from humanity's oppressiveness, a move toward the ideals of radical equality and connection. That feeling of the spirit, and that gentle coercion into Christian life, are clearly not the exclusive province of the politically more conservative churches.

Indeed, an experience I had at the national convocation in my small, assigned "covenant" group demonstrates the power of inclusion. Some of the members of this group were suspicious of me when I said I was a researcher. I explained to them my own history, which had led to my leaving the UMC late in high school. When I revealed my own feelings, they came to see me as belonging, as trustworthy, and as not disruptive to the task of the group, which was to share personal concerns. At this convocation I shared in the ritual of communion for the only time in my adult life.

Communitas is hardly what members claim to seek in church. After reading a draft of this chapter, Missionary Church member Tina Harrison pointed out to me that it was not the *people* who made me feel welcome and drawn to Missionary Church, it was the Holy Spirit working *through* them. But would the Holy Spirit have been working through them, or would I have perceived it, if members had treated me coldly, or if there were no language of shared humanity? Two other Missionary Church members once asked me about City Church; as I described it to them, they wondered how such a church could be driven by the Holy Spirit. Would they have felt the presence of the Spirit had they gone to a service there, been invited to sign a petition to extend Medicaid benefits, heard the senior pastor announce a regional Reconciling Congregations event taking place in the sanctuary that afternoon? Perhaps, or perhaps not. My point is that worshipful, transcendent connection to God is what the members I spoke with said they sought, and they did not necessarily experience it the same way in each congregation.[8] People connect to God in the presence, at least the mental presence, of other people; religion is, for its participants, at least to some extent, a social experience.

When I say that members of these congregations, perhaps of religious groups more generally, experience transcendence, I mean that they seek to be part of a reality that is beyond the material realities and conflicts of everyday life in contemporary America, a truer reality, a timeless reality. In this view, recent decades are seen as times of sweeping social changes, changes that can make all the rules that they had thought organized society seem to disintegrate at the moments they are most needed. In such a time, they struggle to maintain their distinctions between the public and private, profane and sacred, political and transcendent spheres. And as Wuthnow (1998) has pointed out, the sacred can present itself as something people must seek rather than as something that inhabits a particular place.[9] The members of these congregations sought the sacred within their congregations, and they found it together. But they did not find it together automatically. When conflicts emerged, or threatened to, it was harder for people to experience the church as transcendent and communitarian.

chapter THREE

Scripture and Everyday Theologies

C hurch members may have felt transcendent in communion with other members, but as Protestants—whose individual relationships with God are a central tenet of their faith—they experienced their closeness to God as individuals. This chapter explores individuals' understandings of Scripture and God. Maureen McConnelly, a high school teacher from Missionary Church, elaborated on the importance of showing Christian love to those she knew to be in sin, saying:

> I could have a lot of empathy for people. I mean, I can really
> see why they are where they are, and how they got there.
> And then I think it's my responsibility to pray and lift them
> up, and say, "Lord, use me to let them know that they are
> loved and cared for, that I am not judgmental, and, if there's
> any way you want to use me; and I lift them up so that they
> will have a strong, growing, personal relationship with you.
> One that won't condemn them, and say, 'Oh, I'm bad and
> I can't do this.' " I say it because that's the most free and
> releasing thing we can have, that personal relationship with
> the Lord, because then, no matter who likes us or dislikes
> us, if you know that God loves you, that's a *pretty secure
> feeling*. I've been in situations where I wasn't appreciated at
> work or in a personal relationship, but it's like I knew God
> appreciated me.

For Maureen, homosexuality was sinful and homosexuals needed members of the church to show them Christian love. Christian love meant praying for people, lifting them up to the Lord so that they could know what she knew—that they are loved and cared for, and that God's way is the best way. In her prayers she sought to not condemn people, to not idly label them "bad" and exclude them from the possibility of relating to God. In effect, she suggested that sin alone should not be the determining factor in one's relationship, or lack thereof, with God. Rather, she wanted them to experience the freedom and release of a personal relationship with the Lord. In her experience, Christian love shows people the love of God, which gives people a sense a security and strength. Knowing God loves you can bring about a feeling of security, freedom, and release—transcendence.

In her comments, we see a theme that is present in the words of many members of both congregations who are active in debates about homosexuality. Maureen's statement would not spark much controversy among church members, that praying for people can help them to know the secure feeling of God's love. She based this remark on a certain kind of knowledge. Experience showed her that the most freeing and releasing thing she could do for gay men and lesbians was to pray for them so that they might know God loves them. Maureen did not quote Scripture, nor did she cite her pastor, even though both of those authorities might have contributed to her thinking. Instead, the most compelling reason she had was her own experience of the divine. It is this powerful experience of God that shaped many members' thinking on homosexuality, as well as many other things. This chapter explores the ways that personal experience shaped understandings of homosexuality and a proper Christian response to it.

Many members attended church to worship God, to feel close to God, to commune with each other in the Holy Spirit. The church was certainly one place where people learn about God, but for members of both congregations, as for many Protestants, the concept of "priesthood of the believer" meant that each individual could have her own unmediated conversation with God. Thus, many members experienced God and learned about God's truth not only in church teachings and in Scripture but in their daily lives. Given what they had been shown by others and what they experienced in their own lives, members developed their own everyday theologies.[1]

Attending church could create a sense of transcendence through ritual, but there is more to religion than going to church. As the members involved in debates about homosexuality sought to reconcile new social conditions with what they had always known to be true about sex, religion, and life in general, they worked out their individual understandings of God while they interacted with others and dealt with the world around them. In thinking about homosexuality, church members reproduced, and produced anew, what they knew about God's will, God's Creation, God's role in life, and God's demands of people. What would make sense to them about God would depend on what they knew about God already and what they knew about humanity.[2]

Although members of the two congregations all saw the Bible as sacred and containing God's timeless truth, they saw it doing so in different ways. Members had widely different understandings of Scripture, God, and sin.

Heterosexuality, Scripture, and Experience

If a man lies with a male as with a woman, both of them have committed an abomination;
they shall be put to death; their blood is upon them.   —Leviticus 20:13

Although members often saw their beliefs about homosexuality as following from their theologies, in fact beliefs about and experiences with homosexuality, lesbians and gay men, often shaped people's understandings about who God is and what God intends for people. These beliefs and experiences could even shape how members understood Scripture. Given the wide range of possible beliefs about homosexuality, church members often go back to their main textual source, the Bible, to figure out what God expects or teaches. It is clear to many Christians (and non-Christians) that the Bible plainly forbids sex between two men or two women. There are injunctions against homosexual behavior in both the Old and New Testaments, starting with Genesis 19:1–29 and carrying through to I Corinthians 6:9–11 and beyond.[3] Because the Bible refers to homosexual acts as abominable or unnatural in at least six places, it is plain to many that that is how it is. They may assume this view to be timeless and universal, so long as it is not challenged by others around them.

To other Christians, however, biblical injunctions against homosexuality are not the simple truth. A variety of pro-gay theological interpretations abound, including the arguments that homosexuality as we know it today is different from the idolatrous temple prostitution and unequal master/slave sex of Old Testament times; that there is no Eleventh Commandment against homosexuality; that Jesus himself never mentioned homosexuality; that words such as *homosexuality, sodomy,* and *perversion* exist in English translations of the Bible more as a result of the biases of the translators rather than from the intent of the Bible's writers or God; and that injunctions against homosexuality are carryovers from Old Testament purity codes that were overruled with the coming of Jesus.[4] The question for us is not which view is correct but how these different viewpoints develop and are shaped by church debates about homosexuality.

Given the very different approaches to Scripture, many participants in these debates assume that the difference between believing homosexuality is sinful and being pro-gay reflects a simple difference between biblical literalists, who believe the Bible is the inerrant word of God, and contextualists, who believe the Bible is only useful when interpreted with an understanding of the intentions of its authors and the contexts in which the Scriptures were written and codified. In fact, this is not what distinguishes members with regard to homosexuality; anyone who uses Scripture as a guide for life uses both "literal" and "contextual" readings to some extent.[5] The difference, in fact, seems to come from the experiences that shape members' everyday theologies.

Missionary Church's Tina Harrison offered an interpretation with reference to Paul's exhortation to slaves to obey their masters, as well as the Old Testament support for slavery and Noah's creation of slavery in cursing Canaan:[6]

> Oprah Winfrey [the television talk-show host] says that the Bible is for slavery. But it's never for slavery. I have especially watched for this since she said this. When the Pharisees were trying to trap Jesus all the time they said, "Why did Moses permit man to divorce his wife," and Jesus said, "Because people are hard-hearted. God was being easy on you. But God's way is for you not to divorce your wife. It is to love her. Because that's the self-sacrificial thing to do."
>
> God gave certain rules about the way you should treat your slave, but that doesn't mean he approved of it. And back then, people often went into slavery because they were in debt, they would sell themselves. Never anywhere in the Bible does it explicitly condone slavery, yet the Ku Klux Klan would be for slavery, and they would use the Bible to justify it. All sorts of deceitful people will use the Bible to say whatever they want.

For Tina Harrison, the fact that the God of the Old Testament allowed slavery was no indicator that God approves of slavery.[7] For one thing, the different historical context meant that the passage could not be interpreted literally. Second, Tina could interpret the overall message of Scripture to mean that self-sacrifice and love should prevail. In her view, if Christians were less "Bible-ignorant," they would not be so easily fooled by what Paul called people's "deceitful scheming,"[8] believing that the Bible endorses racism or slavery.

With homosexuality, however, Tina saw no exceptions and no analogies to explain away the prohibition. When I asked her to comment on the argument that homosexuality is like the case of women speaking in church, that the passages must be understood in context, she continued:

> I don't see any exceptions to the rule in the entire Bible. I've read it all
> through and I'm reading it through again. With women speaking in
> church, there are exceptions. You see Deborah, the prophetess, you see
> Lydia—I can't remember if her name was Lydia—you see Priscilla. I
> think it was Priscilla and Aquila. Paul writes to them, "Please, don't argue
> and fight. Keep the church whole." You see nobody telling them not to
> speak. But homosexuality, every time it's addressed in the Bible it's an
> evil thing in the Lord's eyes.

When I pressed her further about possible contextual ways that pro-gay members might interpret the injunctions on homosexuality, she stated what was for her the ultimate rule of thumb for Christians: "The number-one thing if you're Christian, you have to remember: God never changes. He's the same yesterday, today, and tomorrow. And I think one thing a lot of people do is to take the Bible and only take certain parts out of it."

Here, Tina stated a rule: God never changes. He is the same yesterday, today, and tomorrow. Some people "want to take the Bible and only take certain parts out of it," by, for instance, leaving aside the injunctions against homosexuality. In Tina's view, women are allowed to speak in church because examples abound in the Bible of women who were great leaders. Slavery was only allowed because God was being easy on people whom he knew to be hard-hearted (though apparently he wasn't being so easy on the slaves).

Homosexuality, however, in her view, is forbidden throughout the Old and New Testaments. She saw no exceptions and no later revisions. In this view, it is irrelevant that in the historical context at the time of the encoding of the law, same-sex sexual activity may have referred to the worship of competing gods in temple prostitution. In Tina's reading, homosexuality was forbidden, and God will never change that. Those parts of the Bible may not be forgotten.

Tina analyzed the Bible contextually to make sense of those parts that she thought needed some explaining. Why did God allow people to have slaves, and why did Paul tell slaves to obey their masters? Why did Paul say that women should not speak in church? To understand God's word, members like Tina can use their extensive knowledge of Scripture, aided by a historical understanding of the time in which it was written, to develop a coherent understanding of God's will. With regard to prohibitions on homosexuality, such analyses are unnecessary. The truth is plain, and it *makes sense* to Tina and people of like mind that God prohibits homosexuality. Tina saw no need to analyze those passages historically, or to reconcile them with any other passages, because, to her, unlike to proponents of pro-gay interpretations of Scripture, these prohibitions did not conflict with passages about the primacy of love, the command not to judge others, or the goodness of all creation.

Such denunciations of homosexuality did not make as much sense to Jackie Richards, Tina's fellow Missionary Church member. Jackie shared her fellow church member's view of Scripture and her understanding of faith, but she did not believe homosexuality to be sinful. She wrestled with the text of the Bible in order to reconcile her belief in Scripture with her beliefs about homosexuality and her experiences with gay people.

About homosexuality, Jackie said:

> I'm not really convinced it's sin. I think the Bible was written in an
> era where everything was a sin because nobody knew anything about
> *anything*. They certainly didn't have scientists then, and I'm sure they
> believed that leprosy was there because the Devil was in that person.
> You know what I mean? And let's face it, not every leper back then was
> a Devil worshipper or was inhabited by the Devil. I don't believe that. I
> believe that some of those people were genuinely, really just sick!

Jackie conveyed an understanding of God's ultimate truth as something that can be discovered; she believed that science can reveal to people new aspects of God's truth, including the truth about what is sinful. Before science, she claimed, people thought illnesses were caused by demons and were a sign of people's sin; now, we know that sometimes people just get sick. She continued:

> And they were probably really good Christians. You know what I mean?
> Back when the Bible was written anybody that was a little out of the
> norm was wrong, was a sinner. It's hard, I struggle with it myself, but I
> guess I don't really firmly believe it's a sin. I know it's written like it's a
> sin, but there are other places where it says to love one another, and God
> loves all people, and God loves all of us, and we're all his children, and I

kind of believe that. In biblical times, what people didn't know about they were afraid of and they usually thought it was wrong, and so that's where some of it started, and . . . [trails off and sighs].

Here, Jackie revealed her working definition of sin. On the one hand, she knew it was written that homosexuality is sinful, but "there are other places where it says to love one another and God loves all people." Jackie seemed to define sin as something that causes a withdrawal of other people's love and God's love. This definition might follow from the premise that when people commit sin, they cause God to pull away. Her reasoning seemed to be that if God loves everyone equally, then that must include gay people as much as straight people and therefore being gay cannot be sinful.

Jackie wrestled further with Scripture, saying:

But, it doesn't say in the Ten Commandments that you shouldn't drink. Okay? Elsewhere it says you shouldn't be a drunkard. Okay. So it doesn't say alcohol is wrong. It says being a drunkard is wrong. And, it doesn't say, in the Ten Commandments, that you shouldn't have sex with a man if you're a man. Now, elsewhere it says that, but I kind of have to interpret it to mean just promiscuous sex with men, that it's just not right. And it's not. Just like men and women, just to have sex is not right.

So, I think that, I guess in a way I think that. My understanding is that maybe it's okay, as long as you're not doing it in excess, like drinking wine in excess. Just like men and women shouldn't just have sex for sex, men and men shouldn't just have sex for sex. And I think maybe that's kind of where it's coming from, but I don't know that, and I do struggle with it. [. . .] I'm not totally convinced it's a sin. Okay?

Jackie set up an analogy between drinking alcohol and having sex. The Ten Commandments, which she saw as the most important guidelines of God's do's and don'ts, do not say "Do not drink alcohol" or "Do not have sex with a man if you are man." Just as the Bible says not to be a drunkard, Jackie used the analogy to infer that non-Commandment references to sex between men should refer to the sexual equivalent of drunkenness, or having sex just for its own sake, being promiscuous. This reasoning resembles the analogy Tina Harrison set up between Old Testament allowances for divorce and slavery, except that Tina understood homosexuality to be sinful, while Jackie began from the assumption that it is not.

I asked Jackie if something happened to give her the opinions she had, or if she had always believed what she did about homosexuality. She replied:

I have a brother who's gay. I'm sure that's obviously colored all of my views. But, I don't know how long before I even knew about it or his situation. I'm not a judgmental type of person. I guess in some ways I am, my husband would say I am. Deep down I've just always been caring and cared about people, and I don't believe you should judge others. I never have believed that. I've always felt like I have to reach out to others that may be perceived as an underdog. Obviously, I don't know, because I've known about my brother for years and years, and had that not come into play, who knows?

My gut feeling is that I'd still be pretty liberally minded, as far as this issue goes, just because of the way I look at other things. For instance, even when I was growing up in a mostly white town, I always saw racial minorities as people; they were my friends. It's just how I am. That's obviously why I know as much as I do, and I haven't gotten personally involved in it here, and knowing what I knew, it's just laughable when I think of my brother, like, having a choice or whatever. It's just laughable. So, that's probably where I come from.

Jackie implied that if she did believe homosexuality to be sinful, she might lack the qualities of being caring and nonjudgmental and reaching out to the underdog. Tina, too, saw herself as a white opponent of racism. Yet whereas the Bible's apparent injunctions against homosexuality made sense and required no further study for Tina, Jackie's life experience led her to search for different answers, just as Tina did for questions about slavery and women. With Jackie's own brother being gay, the idea that God would draw away from a man just for having sex with another man did not *make sense*.

Jackie and Tina provide two examples of everyday theologies. Everyday theologies are not simply the outcome of extreme individualism, but rather are how individuals, as parts of communities and societies, come to make sense of their world and its sacred aspects. These theologies are formed in communities and can help people to experience religion as truthful and transcendent rather than as hollow human tradition. People's experiences teach them about life and shape what makes sense to them. In this way, members' understandings of Scripture are shaped by their life experience. Although sociologists of religion tend to focus on how beliefs are altered by massive social structural changes, it is clear that people experience these changes in their everyday lives and must interpret them. For instance, Jackie and her brother would not have been able to understand his homosexuality in the way they did were it not for the economic, social, technological, and demographic changes that have made gay identities possible since World War II.[9]

The concept of everyday theology helps us to understand the process by which Jackie could make sense of this development in her life, and reconcile it with her faith.

Just as everyday experiences shape what members know about God, so do the experiences they have in their congregations. Congregations form a part of members' everyday realities, a part where they can come together and teach one another about their understandings and experiences of Scripture and God. For members I observed on many different sides, it was impossible for them to believe things about Scripture that went against what they already knew about God and life—interpretations of Scripture had to *make sense*. As members sought to understand God's will, they sought to make a coherent picture of their own experiences with God, including what they knew to be true about sexual morality, love, and compassion.

Love the Sinner, Hate the Sin

Christianity has a long tradition of teaching that believers are to love their neighbor and their enemy alike. It also has a long history of uncompassionate or unloving policies and behaviors that people have enacted in its name, which many church members recite in the course of debates about homosexuality: its support for slavery, its denial of women's rights and potential, the differential treatment of members based on their wealth, its support for racial segregation.[10] In the course of my research, I spoke with church members who were involved in the Civil Rights movement in the 1950s and 1960s and who recalled white ushers physically barring black people from entering segregated church buildings, as well as clergy who had been and still are discriminated against in the church hierarchy for their race or sex. Similarly, groups such as the Ku Klux Klan have, in the name of white, Protestant Christianity, espoused violence against people of color, Roman Catholics, and Jews.[11] Just about everyone I spoke to in either church would characterize these moments in the church's history (and its present) as, to some extent, what the apostle Paul called people's craftiness and deceitful scheming (Ephesians 4:14). Many members understand that the church is made up of necessarily fallen creatures in a fallen world, whose earthly desires and subjective views have sometimes outweighed God's truth. The problem for all Christians is to know which beliefs are rooted in people's subjective desires and which are rooted in God's timeless truth.

Throughout its history, Christianity has at times also extended its intolerance to sexual outsiders, including gay men, lesbians, and bisexuals; divorced people; people who are known to have sex outside of marriage; and those who marry or date people of a different race, ethnicity, or religion. This history is documented, but more important, it is widely known. Some members recalled stories of being told by church officials not to marry people of different races. Similarly, many of the gay men and lesbians I talked to, and the clergy and friends of gay people, recounted stories of gays being asked to leave congregations, being told homosexuals were not welcome, or being preached to about the especially damnable sin of sodomy. When Americans in the 1990s and 2000s think of the Christian response to homosexuality, many think of the spectacularly hateful image of the Reverend Fred Phelps picketing the funeral of Matthew Shepard, a young gay man who was brutally beaten and burned, tied to a fence, and left for dead outside of Laramie, Wyoming, in the fall of 1998. When Shepard eventually died from his injuries, Phelps and some of his followers and family members picketed the funeral with signs reading "No Fags in Heaven" and "No Tears for Queers" (Crowder 1998; Kurson 1998).

Members of the congregations I spoke with all rejected such pronouncements as unchristian and hateful. They all struggled against that kind of spectacle, wanting to distance Christianity from such judgment. In 1984, when the original Reconciling Congregations Program activists began to point out that the United Methodist Church was being anti-Christian to the extent that it ever asked *anyone* to leave, they started to make a highly significant intervention in the UMC. Although earlier it might have been more acceptable to assume that homosexuals had no business in church, the RCP's intervention highlighted the fact that barring *anyone* from the church, for *any* reason, went against the heart of the Christian mission to bring ever more people into the church for redemption from sin (however defined). Transforming Congregations, and congregations such as Missionary Church that ally with (but are not formal members of) the movement, agree that the church's role should be to welcome people, not to judge them.

Although the United Methodist Church is not evangelical in any "official" capacity, many members adhere to the principles of the evangelical movement. Evangelical Christians constituted a sizable proportion of the membership of City Church, even though its leadership was entirely liberal, and Missionary Church's clergy and laity were almost entirely evangelical. In evangelical belief, Christian love and sin must both be understood in light of a central truth of Christianity, expressed in John 3:16.[12] To these members, this passage meant that believing in Jesus, the Son of God, would lead to eternal life, which they locate in Heaven, while not believing in Jesus leads to condemnation, to an eternity in Hell. Accepting Jesus as your savior means that you "ask him into your heart" and that you have an ongoing relationship with him through prayer. As you walk with Jesus, inspired and illuminated by the Holy Spirit, you increasingly understand God's way, his plan for you. Given their belief in the central importance of Christ for each individual's salvation, evangelical Christians uphold the Great Commission (Matthew 28:19–20), which they read as Jesus' charge to "go . . . and make disciples of all nations," teaching others about what Jesus has told them and the good news of Jesus' birth, death, and resurrection to save the world from sin. [13] In this theology, if people reject the opportunity to accept Jesus as their savior, then they reject their only means of salvation. In this view, Christian love demands that believers do whatever they can and are called to do to help others find the path to salvation.

These basic beliefs act as an anchor for their adherents as they struggle to be "in the world but not of it," to be "Christlike" as they respond to and try to uplift the fallen world around them. These beliefs guide people as they try to answer the questions and resolve the complications of contemporary daily life, including homosexuality. These Christian ideals resonate with and are often articulated in terms that echo the American ideal of tolerance— Christian love, compassion, acceptance, and welcome. To many of those who spoke with me, to show Christian love is to show others unconditional acceptance and compassion, realizing that all human beings fall short of the glory of God. It is to realize that while people all live in different situations, the many differences between them are minute in the eyes of God, and people should not allow these differences to get in the way of showing each other compassion. One reason to practice this love is to show people how God loves them, to help them to accept Jesus as their savior, and to attain eternal salvation. With a belief in original sin, the evangelicals in each congregation with whom I spoke took as given that God forbids some behaviors and condemns some dispositions (such as a disposition to selfishness); they believed that in walking with God, people can gradually come to leave behind their sinful ways, whatever form their predisposition to sin takes.

Unlike Fred Phelps, whose "God hates fags" approach places him in the extreme fundamentalist camp, members of City Church and Missionary Church who believed that homosexuality is sinful repeatedly invoked the phrase "love the sinner, hate the sin" when talking about how Christians should deal with homosexuality. The phrase responds to a problem these members confronted not only with regard to homosexuals but with regard to non-Christians as well: Which is more loving, to accept people as they are, even if it may mean their eternal damnation, or to show people what it will take for them to go to Heaven, even if it means seeming to be intolerant from a secular perspective? Are there ways to tell others about the means to salva-

tion without appearing to judge them? How to reach out to non-Christians
without driving them away or seeming judgmental—this is a problem that
many of the evangelical Christians I met took seriously and grappled with.
This struggle takes place around homosexuality as well.[14]

At City Church, those who strongly believed homosexuality to be sinful
appeared to be a minority; the clergy tended to support joining the RCP, and
most members of the congregation, many of whom might have objected, ab-
sented themselves from the debate. Thus, the vocally "traditional" members
of City Church had to articulate their views on the matter more often and
more clearly than their counterparts at Missionary Church. Although those
at Missionary with this view did not have to make their case, because it was
taken for granted, members at City Church had to both articulate this view
and to challenge the pro-gay assertion that they lacked compassion.

City Church members Rosario and Bill Burkhart, for instance, expressed
both their belief in the sinfulness of homosexual behavior and their desire
to show Christian love. They considered it "blasphemous" to state that God
would endorse homosexuality; however, they were quick to invoke their
Christian duty to love everyone and to try to help uplift their fellow sinners.
I posed a scenario to them, asking:

> What about a man who'd say, "It wasn't until I was able to understand
> my homosexuality as a gift from God that I understood how being able to
> love one other person brings me into the love of God." Have you heard
> people say that?
>   Rosario: Of course. What do you say to that? I think we should love
> everybody. I mean, I don't, if you're including sex in that, that is indeed
> to me blasphemous.
>   Dawne: It's blasphemous to say that God would . . .
>   Rosario: . . . that homosexuality is a gift of God. That is clearly listed
> under sin throughout the Bible.

Here, we see Rosario articulating both Christian love, "I think we should
love everybody," and a rejection of homosexuality, which she saw as "clearly
listed under sin throughout the Bible."

Her husband Bill responded with a similar distinction to the question of
whether homosexuality is a gift from God. He said:

> Well, it's basically apples and oranges. Sex being a gift from God,
> that's quite true. It's how you use it. If you happen to be a homosex-
> ual, if you're really born homosexual and not made so—like many are

converted, so to speak, to it later on, [that is] they weren't born that way. Being born like that would make it a preexisting condition, like if someone is born with their genes in a certain order that make them more susceptible to drinking, for example, something like that, then he's got all the earmarks of somebody that would be, he's born with that tendency. We're all born with tendencies, and they're all downward directed to start with, thanks to Adam and Eve, but it seems this is a condition that needs to be dealt with, understood, it would seem to be part of the cynical force at work in the world. You hear people won't believe in the devil, they believe in a negative force that certainly isn't doing us any good; it can't have our welfare at heart.

I think a homosexual finds himself, or herself, with this condition, and they have spiritual experiences and want to get deeper into the church and into their life with Christ and so on, but they don't know, I think some of 'em don't understand that that's what it is, that it needs to be dealt with. In other words, you don't lock the drunkard out of the church because he drinks, you try to help him. Not that a drunk should be encouraged to drink just because that's his chosen lifestyle. We're not gonna back you up in it.

I think the worst part of it for me is to hear people say, "Well, they're just as good as we are," which is true, but missing the point, but if they don't know, if they're not honestly and completely exposed to the scriptural interpretation that some of us give it, then that's a problem for a Christian. We should be open on the Godward side, the side of righteousness, so that any new light that comes out will find a place to shine.

For Bill, to compare homosexuality to God-given sexuality was like comparing apples and oranges; these are simply two different kinds of things. In Bill's analysis, not all homosexuals are born with that tendency, but even if they are, they, like all human beings, have inherited some downward tendency thanks to the fall of Adam and Eve, and a negative force that "can't have our welfare at heart."[15] In Bill's view, the church must welcome the homosexual, just as it must welcome the drunkard. And just as the drunkard should not be encouraged to drink even if that is his "lifestyle" choice, neither should the homosexual be encouraged to practice what places him or her in that category.

Bill continued, and we hear him struggle with the problem of the political discourse of equality. He said the "worst part" was hearing people say, "Well, they're just as good as we are." He acknowledged that homosexuals are fundamentally as good as anyone else, but to maintain that homosexuals are just as good as "we are," in Bill's view, missed the point that all people "should be open on the Godward side," so God's new light may shine in. This is not to say that Bill objected to the idea of equality; rather, he did not see equality as overriding the truth of Scripture, that homosexuality is one sin among many.

Bill and Rosario saw homosexuality as sinful according to Scripture, but they were also quick to point out that no human being is free from sin, regardless of sexual orientation. We see this in Bill's comment that "we're all born with downward tendencies," for instance.

Another member of City Church, Mark Montero, also believed homosexuality to be sinful, while recognizing that sin is not the sole province of homosexuals. Mark attended one of City Church's four reconciliation meetings where a number of people attacked him for his insistence on homosexuality's sinful nature, implying that his beliefs were uncompassionate. In a one-on-one conversation with me later, however, he wrestled with the implication that his views betrayed a lack of compassion, saying:

> I honestly do believe homosexuality is more a matter of choice. I'm
> not saying that it's easy to unmake choices. You've made a choice and
> you've lived that way for a long time. . . . I think the thing that I said
> about alcoholism is a good example. Everyone says that it's genetic. But
> it doesn't mean if you're genetically predisposed to be an alcoholic that
> you'll end up ruining your life drinking. There's more of an overt sense
> of self-destruction with somebody who's really strung out on alcohol
> in a bad way. The analogy there is to say that just because something is
> genetic doesn't make it right. That's all. Okay.
>
> Just because you're genetically predisposed to be one way or the other
> doesn't mean that you don't have [volition] . . . you have your work,
> you're a person . . . you can decide to do what you want to do, right?
> I think there's something really losing if you don't believe that about
> people, otherwise we're all just sort of robots.

When I asked him about people I had spoken to who believed that they had no choice about being *heterosexual*, he responded by saying, "I think that's a lie. I mean, everybody is attracted to one degree or another to men and women." When I asked how he knew that, he said that the mice his college roommate had owned would have same-sex sexual activity when given the opportunity.

In this discussion, Mark critiqued the argument he had heard repeated at City Church, that if gay people are all born gay, then they cannot and should not change. First, his analogy to alcoholism made the point that people are all born predisposed to inappropriate behavior, and that they can exercise moral volition and discipline and live in a godly way. Second, he universalized the moral burden to exercise sexual restraint, placing himself and all of humanity in the category of potential "homosexuals."

Mark observed from his own life, and those of his old roommate's mice, that everyone potentially wrestles with the temptation of homosexuality, that everyone has an inclination toward polymorphous sexuality, that everyone is naturally attracted to both men and women. For Mark, the choice to abstain from same-sex sexual relations is a choice any moral person can make, and many do. A popular pro-gay argument is that homosexuality is genetically inherited and therefore cannot be changed or controlled. Although this view implies that gay people are a fixed set of people (which, in Mark's view, denies them volition), Mark emphasized that sexual morality, including that regarding same-sex sexual desire, is a universal concern that all people have to wrestle with to some extent or other. Mark thus placed himself in the category of persons whose volition requires moral strength; seeing himself as no different from gay men and lesbians, he demonstrated the very essence of compassion, literally "feeling with" those who struggle with nonmarital sexual drives. In this way, Mark transcended not only the earthly sexual drives but also the earthly drive to distance oneself from others.

Other members who saw homosexuality as sinful believed that Christians, united in the church as the body of Christ, could collectively serve as a parent or shepherd, helping members to find and stay on God's path. While Mark Montero confronted people about what he saw as their erroneous belief that homosexuality was acceptable, thereby opening himself to the critique that his own Christianity was uncompassionate and therefore flawed, his fellow City Church member, retired librarian Ron Wilson, had learned to avoid such scrutiny by not speaking out and by showing love and compassion. Ron shared his own struggle to reconcile Jesus' command to love one another with the command to strive toward sinlessness. At the time of our interview, he had just come to a two-part resolution to these struggles, with one method for dealing with homosexuals who are quiet about their sexuality, and another for those who "reach out." First, however, he expressed his starting point, saying:

> As I read the Bible, it says very clearly that we are to love one another.
> Jesus said it in the story of the Good Samaritan: "You will be known as
> my disciples by the way you love one another." So the question is, how

do you put all of this together? I have no problem with that, in fact, I
think it's part of our job, that we reach out to everyone. If you come here
seeking God's grace and help for your life, then, "Welcome!" because
that's what we're all here for. If you were to come, saying, "I'm not doing
anything wrong, I'm just fine," and continue to live in a manner that
God says is not appropriate, that's a problem, and how do *I* deal with the
problem?

  And for a long time I have thought that part of my loving other people
was to not let them go running off willy-nilly. Take my children as an
example. Certainly, if my children were engaged in harmful, potentially
harmful actions, I would be the world's worst parent if I did not try to
bring this to their attention and help them not to do it.

  Now, to what degree and how does my view of homosexual activity
work into the church community? Well, that's something I've been
struggling with for a long time. And, frankly, I was sort of frustrated and
didn't know what to do about it. The idea of "just anything goes," the
extreme of that view, now, I just don't see how we can deal with that.
Being here, trying to be part of a loving, supportive community, trying
to help one another, I think is ideal. It doesn't always happen. Maybe it
doesn't ever happen. But, that's the goal certainly.

Here, Ron expressed his worry that those who advocated changing the
church's stance on homosexuality supported a view whose extreme version would mean "just anything goes." He could not support "just anything
goes," in part, these comments suggest, because he saw the church as a place
where people should love and support one another by helping one another
to transcend harmful tendencies. To let members run off and do "just anything" would be for the church to help them to condemn themselves to
Hell, just as letting errant children engage in harmful actions would be to
fail at parenting. His experience as a parent taught him how to deal with
people who fail to know what's good for them and helped him understand
his obligations in such a situation.

  Ron continued, explaining how he had decided, as a member of City
Church, that he should address homosexuality at the practical level:

The more I think about it, the more I think I have to be affirmative in
what I believe. I don't think that I would be correct in never saying
anything. But what I say, and how I say it, and to whom I say it—it has
to be done very carefully, and in a sense, in my view, only after I have
earned the right to say it. If somebody walks in off the street and I start

lecturing them, well nobody's going to get anywhere that way, and all it's going to do is frustrate everybody, or else send me on an ego trip, which is not the purpose of all this.

Well, certainly, if anybody asks, I feel it's important to simply say what I believe in a kindly and supportive manner.

Ron developed a careful strategy, balancing a response of love and kindness with his duty to share his beliefs when the time is right. Ron knew that lecturing would shut people off to his message and might put him on "an ego trip," which would be inappropriate. If the congregation follows a "don't ask, don't tell" policy like that governing homosexuals in the U.S. military, then Ron's reading of Ezekiel helped him to see other people's sin as between themselves and God. He elaborated:

If they don't ask me, well then what do I do? If they are living a quiet, "don't ask, don't tell" life, then basically I have come to the conclusion that, from this eighteenth chapter of Ezekiel that I was talking about the other day, it's only a matter of their personal life. I think that I have just recently come to the conclusion that what the Bible is telling me is it's *their* business. What I do with my life is *my* business. And it's my responsibility to deal with it. And if I don't, there will be a price to pay. Similarly, I have come to the conclusion that's true with them.

Their sin was between them and God, and Ron's was between him and God. If he did not deal with his own sin, he would have "a price to pay," implying that homosexuals would have a price to pay if they did not "deal with" their own sin. Ron had determined that he would not be punished for knowing of their sin and saying nothing, if "it's only a matter of their personal life."

On the other hand, he continued, if the "don't ask, don't tell" policy were not followed and "this lifestyle started reaching out to other people," then Ron would have to speak up. I asked him what he meant by "reaching out," and his explanation turned toward opposition to the genetic argument:

Well, some people believe that homosexuality is purely genetic, that is has no social content. I'm not sure that's true, I just don't know. At this point I'm going to assume that it's not necessarily true. Therefore, if some person was reaching out to other people, and encouraging them to be involved in a homosexual lifestyle, I just would not feel right in not doing anything. What I would do or what I would say, I just haven't the foggiest idea. I don't know that the situation will ever occur. But if it did,

I just don't think that I would ever feel right, be able to live with myself,
if I didn't say something. But I think that would be a condition in which I
would not just be able to say, "It's somebody else's business," because at
that point, I don't think it's just one other person's business.

If a homosexual encouraged others to be homosexual, in Ron's view, then a
line would have been crossed. His live-and-let-live strategy would then be
inappropriate; he would have to speak out.

Like Ron, fellow City Church member Rosario Burkhart also raised the
concern about what to do when someone made their homosexuality known.
Having made clear that her business as a Christian is to accept people as God
accepts her, she added:

But while I accept them, it does not mean that I will not go to people who
openly behave like that, and *make* me aware of that, and say you are
indeed sinning, according to the Scriptures. Be aware of it, because I am
not going to come to Judgment Day, and have God say, "I am holding
you responsible, because you had an opportunity to do something about
this, and you did not."

Rosario, like Ron Wilson, attempted to balance the church's ideals of love
and acceptance with the belief that God holds his people accountable for their
actions. Like Ron, she also conveyed that other people's public and unapologetic avowals of homosexuality tested *her*. They put her in a position where
she risked falling out of God's favor if she did not articulate the sinfulness
of homosexuality.

In these comments, we see members struggling. They struggled with
their own experiences and beliefs, and they struggled with the gay movement in the church and its accusations that church tradition is intolerant,
petty, unloving, and heterosexist. These members did not distance themselves from homosexuals; they saw homosexuality as sinful, but because
they did not believe it to be any more (or less) innate than their own dispositions toward sin, they held no special place for homosexuals in the range
of sin. They disagreed strongly with Fred Phelps's "God hates fags" message, and found it unchristian. They believed that God forbids some things
that human beings are inclined to do. For them, transcendence meant rising
above all of the temptations that dog humanity, and, in that way, growing closer to God. A certain kind of subtlety and nuance in this theological
perspective developed in the context of City Church, a congregation on the
road to affirming homosexuality—there was hardly a simply parroting of

Scripture or church doctrine. In fact, these beliefs were developed and articulated in resistance to what City Church's leaders taught and preached. Yet even Fred Phelps had to employ some form of everyday theology, for certainly nowhere does the Bible say "God hates fags."

Transcendence and the Godly Ideal

Clearly, members have built a wide range of beliefs on the proposition that homosexuality is sinful, beliefs shaped by the understandings of God and Scripture that make sense to them in their own lives.[16] Within that range, the theological and social environment at City Church influenced many church members; it made them focus on defining sin and determining how to deal with unrepentant sinners compassionately. In a place such as Missionary Church, where no one publicly challenged the notion that homosexuality was sinful, members could develop their theologies by focusing on the positive things that God desires for people. In this trend, believers saw people transcending their human "fallenness" by growing toward God's ideal, much the way children mature with the love and guidance of their parents. People could grow toward God's ideal, especially by growing toward the ideal, heterosexual family model God created as told in the story of Adam and Eve.

Maureen McConnelly, with whom we opened this chapter, exemplifies the kind of thinking taking place among the under-sixty generations at Missionary Church. She understood God and the church as taking the same parental or shepherding role articulated by City Church's Ron Wilson. Maureen used the extreme case of gay cannibal serial killer Jeffrey Dahmer to show what Christians' duty to love meant to her, saying:

> My basic premise is, God tells us to love everyone as ourselves. That doesn't mean you condone everything somebody does.
>
> It was interesting when that whole Jeffrey Dahmer thing came, you know, people's emotions were so high. And I said, "You know, I'm sure that some of you would have difficulty with this, but you know what? His mother still loves him, and God still loves him, no matter what he's done, and how awful it is. Do I condone any of it? Oh, heavens no! I think it was all just so bizarre and sick! And sad, but that doesn't mean that we shouldn't love and care about him." And that really is true. And, therefore, if there are things that people do that are wrong, you don't love and respect the wrong things, but you do have a responsibility to love and respect them.

For Maureen, the church should show everyone the same love God has for them; the church is on earth to show people God's love, not human judgment. At the same time, Maureen believed that God saw some actions as sinful, across the board. Turning her attention to less spectacular examples, she continued:

> With the kids, I mean, I'm very clear. You know, most of the gay couples here happen to be men. But there are a couple that are women. I think they are fascinating people, they're wonderful neighbors, I enjoy them totally. But I'm not going to tell my children that I condone their lifestyle. And I can say, I don't know why they are gay, practicing that way, or doing that, and it's not really my business, and I don't know how to judge them. You know? There are lots of issues now, about the whole gay issue, the genetic qualities, and things like that.
>
> But on the other hand there's also things written biblically that address it. It's like, we're all driven, hormonally, but God says, "For the best *quality* of life, I don't want you doing that prior to marriage. This is something that I hold for the married." So God set rules, and did he do it to make us all unhappy? No. He did it because he knows that makes life *the best*. And we have choices on whether we choose the best or less than the best, and we all make mistakes. And that's kind of how I tell my kids.

The more quotidian examples of Maureen's gay neighbors led her to a subtler approach to understanding sin and God's intentions. God made certain ways better, she said, and for "the best quality of life," people must follow God's rules. God knows that his way is the best, and his way includes loving and accepting people, and having sex only within heterosexual marriage.

As we saw at the beginning of this chapter, praying for people allowed Maureen to intervene in their lives without creating conflict or acting out of apparently worldly concerns. Furthermore, she saw sharing that feeling of transcendence in the world as itself the way to practice Christian love. In her understanding, people who continued to practice homosexuality and refused to confess that it is sinful could not have that feeling of combined security and release. If they accept Jesus as their savior, she implied, they will eventually come to renounce all sin, including nonmarital (and thus homosexual) sex. For her, freedom was not about rights but about a better life in knowing the Lord.

Maureen, like the members of City Church we have heard from, saw homosexuality as sinful, but she focused even less on biblical prohibitions than people at City Church, where the relevance of prohibiting passages was questioned and needed thus to be affirmed. As a result, Maureen's theology of sin took on a slightly different valence. Her understanding of sin had to do with a distance from God and the perfection of God's transcendent ideal. For her, sin came about when people relied on an earthly understanding of freedom rather than a godly understanding. She tacitly made clear the difference between these two understandings of freedom with reference to the gender division of labor:

> In the household, in the family, there's gotta be a head of the household.
> You know, the Scriptures of submitting can get so twisted, but if you
> really look at that and read them, it's really saying, "Yeah, submit to him
> as the head, as the leader, 'cause every group needs one leader." But what
> does a good leader do? He pulls on the benefits and talents of his group,
> and that's what the head of the household is to do.

In her understanding, God intends all families to have a husband, a wife, and children, and for the rest of the family to submit to the husband's headship. This leadership should not be "twisted," however, for, in Maureen's interpretation of the Scriptures, the husband should draw on the benefits and talents of the family, just as a skilled leader would with any group. Here, Maureen explained how God's transcendent way supersedes conventional, secular understandings of equality, while reconciling the traditional patriarchal family model with contemporary ideals. For instance, while affirming that every group needs a head, she pointed out that proper headship required a leadership style akin to the collegial management approach advocated for contemporary workplaces, drawing from the strengths of the group. In her view, when families organize themselves on these principles, life works out better; God alone might know why, but ultimately God's way is the best.

She then made an analogy to being gay, comparing it to the other imperfections that characterize humanity. She remarked that she knew some people for whom being gay was a choice conditioned by circumstances such as abuse, but then added:

> But I also know some personally that, from the day they were born, they
> just didn't feel comfortable being the male or female that they were. I
> look at that and I think the reality is that there are mistakes. There are
> handicapped people too. There are people that are retarded. We are not
> perfect. God does not make us all perfect. Does God make allowances
> for that? Yes. How does he make those allowances? Does he say, "Well,
> for you it's okay to do that"? I don't believe so. I believe that he sends

options. And if you are in a close relationship with him, he tells you
how to cope with it. I also know of homosexuals who have been in both
situations and have become very close to the Lord and felt that [gay sex]
is not something he wanted them doing. And he's helped them alter
that. . . . And are their lives more of a struggle? To me, it's just like an
alcoholic; it's just like a handicapped person.

It's like this: Can I get sexually aroused even though I'm not married to someone? Yeah. But does that make it okay for me to go have
[extramarital] sex with him? No. I think the same principles apply to
everything.

Maureen's experience affirmed for her that going against God's plan, ma-
nipulating the system, is never right, no matter how tempting it may be.
Maureen knew people for whom homosexuality had been a choice, for instance, because of their histories of abuse, as well as those who had been
gay or lesbian their whole lives, born that way by "mistake," like a "handi-
cap." She implied that being handicapped distanced someone from God, and
I doubt she meant that.[17] Rather, she seemed to see homosexual desire as
a human imperfection, one which may be worked with and overcome, one
that is neither sinful in itself nor an excuse for sinful behavior.

In Maureen's view, no cause of homosexuality would excuse people
from having to live in accordance with God's way, which she saw laid out
in Paul's letters.[18] Maureen could understand why someone might want to
live as gay or lesbian; nevertheless, she saw such a life as sinful. In her view,
God sends options, and people are free to choose God's way or their own
way. But it is simply never right to go against God's way. God has the ideal
plan, and those who defy it are framed not as dissidents rebelling against a
perceived oppressor, not as criminals flouting social standards for their own
gain, but as children who don't know any better or as handicapped people
who cannot do better.[19]

Maureen's account of God's ideal family pattern resonates with the popular understanding that Adam and Eve are not only the first people God
created but God's model for how human beings should interact, within and
between the genders. Maureen framed prohibitions on homosexuality and
same-sex marriage as part of the essence of God's transcendent and overriding truth. This approach was echoed by others, at City Church as well as at
Missionary Church, who did not need to justify their belief that homosexuality was sinful.

Andy Gilmartin is such a person, a Christian psychotherapist (with a
Ph.D. in theology) who I met when he worked for an ex-gay Transforming

para-church ministry. As a counselor who worked with people who struggled against their homosexuality, Andy believed that God intends for people to find fulfillment in heterosexual marriage, but he was less dismissive than many people of the good that comes of homosexuality. He saw gay, lesbian, and bisexual identities as meaningful and important to people who have them; he believed that God could intend for people to take on such an identity for a time, and that the love in gay and lesbian relationships is real. He believed that homosexuality is a step some must take on the road to wholeness, though it is not a viable finishing point in and of itself.

Distinguishing himself from the more "doctrinaire" proponents of ex-gay transformation, he stated:

> A lot of our people in this movement are pretty doctrinaire, but I'm not. There's not really much in the Old Testament I take literally—well, except Genesis 1:2, that first creation story. God created Adam and Eve; I'm pretty doctrinaire about that. I believe that's how God intends for us to interact in the world, within the genders and between genders. I take the rest of my understanding of Scripture from that starting point. (Reconstructed from notes)

In Andy's analysis, when God says the first man should not be alone, it is of critical significance for each of us today that God gave that man (Adam) a woman (Eve). Just as Maureen saw Scripture as an overall message about God's plan for families, Andy understood Scripture as a story about the relationship between and within the genders; it may be that this starting point framed his subsequent interpretations, or it may be that his experience shaped his view of the Bible—most likely, as his beliefs grew and matured he experienced both. Andy saw something timeless in contemporary church norms regarding sexuality, linking them to God in a way that even some liberals found compelling.

For instance, some members of the relatively liberal City Church did not wish to claim that homosexuality is sinful across the board, yet they had reservations about fully equating homosexuality with God's ideal sexuality. These members did not agree with those who took the "traditional" view, denouncing the congregation's move to affirm homosexuality. By distancing their theology from scriptural prohibitions on homosexuality, they could find ways to show compassion. When we look at the comments of City Church member Carol Johnson, a high school principal, we can see how people's experiences with intolerance as well as Scripture can combine to form an everyday theology.

Carol believed that calling homosexuality sinful was intolerant, judgmental, and, in that way, unchristian. She stated that homosexuality was
"fine" with her because "we're all people," thus affirming the Christian ideals of universal love and compassion. However, on the subjects of same-sex
marriage and the ordination of gay men and lesbians as clergy, she had reservations about changing the denomination's standing policies against opening
these institutions to gay men and lesbians:

> I was talking to this one couple that, well, they just wish we could just
> leave things alone, because they're afraid that we'll be having gay mar-
> riages in the church, you know, and everything, so there's some fear
> there.
>   Dawne: So do you think that could happen?
>   Carol: Not a marriage per se. I could see—and this would be for
> heterosexuals as well as homosexuals—commitment-type ceremonies.
> Not ceremonies, but a blessing of commitment or something.
>   Dawne: So you think that could happen *here?*
>   Carol: I could see that happening here. But it wouldn't be like a
> marriage-type thing, it wouldn't be perceived as that. I think it would be
> much more low-key. I think that would really upset people.
>   Dawne: How do you feel about it personally? I mean, in general, do
> you think that the denomination should change, or do you think that it's
> right the way it is?
>   Carol: I think that for the ordination, I pretty much prefer that it's
> the way it is.
>   Dawne: Okay, so you don't like the idea of having "practicing homo-
> sexuals" as ministers?
>   Carol: Well, I think, in a sense it's the same conflict that a lot of
> people brought up, including myself, that you have Adam and Eve. So,
> it's not that you condemn other people that aren't the same way you are,
> it's just that . . . it's not necessarily what was originally in the Bible.

While Carol could state that she supported the church's ban on ordaining
gays and lesbians, she hesitated to express her own thoughts on same-sex
marriage; she was uncomfortable with the idea but struggled to stay out of
the debate. In a congregation where many prominent members of the congregation and pastoral staff thought that any position that did not advocate
full acceptance of homosexuality in the church was politically motivated and
religiously backward, it was difficult for people with ambivalent views to
articulate them. She shared with me her understanding that God originally

intended for people to be heterosexual, but she articulated it differently in response to her daily experience. She did not, however, simply believe what she was told. Her views reflect a struggle to make sense of what she knew to be true, even as some truths competed with others.

Carol found herself in a difficult position. She had said earlier that she thought it unchristian to leave her church over the reconciling congregation issue. The "ugly" response to gay men and lesbians she witnessed from her fellow congregants was unchristian too. By claiming that gay men and lesbians were "fine" and that she was fine with them, she seemed to position herself as someone who did not see homosexuality as inherently sinful. She did not cite and apparently did not find relevant the scriptural passages frequently cited by those who claim the opposite.

Her desire to not "condemn other people that aren't the same way that you are" conflicted with her belief that ordination (and possibly marriage) should be denied to "practicing" homosexuals. Carol traced the contemporary Christian ideal back to Adam and Eve, the Bible's first couple.[20] Carol thus rendered today's family ideal of one-man-one-woman marriage as the timeless universal God created when he made humanity, and thus, posited marriage (and its affirmation) as a mechanism that can help people transcend the everyday world and become closer to God.

Transcending Human Rules

Christians like Maureen McConnelly, Andy Gilmartin, and Carol Johnson depart from seeing sin as a list of forbidden acts, and move toward a focus on sin as distance from God's ideal. I suspect that they make this move because they realize that Scripture forbids many things not commonly understood among mainline Protestants to be sinful today: men shaving their beards; women speaking in church, exposing their heads, or teaching men; eating pork or shellfish—even divorce and remarriage, which Jesus himself decried (according to Matthew 19:3–9), are allowed in UMC doctrine.[21] Many people we have heard from, nevertheless, take as God's timeless ideal those passages that appear to denounce homosexuality.

Not all mainline Protestants accept that those particular passages are timeless or even reflect a timeless ideal. Rather than seeing prohibitions on men lying with men or women lying with each other as akin to the commandments not to steal and murder, some members see those passages as akin to Paul's remarks about women and Old Testament purity codes.[22] These members cite historical uses of Scripture to keep women from church and secular equality and to legitimate slavery as examples of earthly, politically motivated, and even cynical misuses of Scripture. God's truth does appear in Scripture, these members insist, but not in context-specific laws or misread allegories. Rather, God's truth is itself found in the overall message of Scripture: to love God and others first, foremost, and always.

Although it is possible to rely relatively directly on Scripture and believe that homosexuality is not sinful,[23] supporters of the pro-gay Reconciling Congregations Program at City Church tended to have a view of Scripture and sin that was harder to pin down. Many City Church members believed human language to be too small to encompass the vast depth of God's command to love. Overall, many pro-gay members took a liberal theological perspective and saw Scripture as something that states many contradictory things and that thus requires not only study but patience to use properly. At one level, these theological liberals were suspicious of humanly acquirable knowledge, hesitant to see everyday knowledge as being from God. Liberals' views might seem at first to resist the notion of everyday theologies. However, something in these people's everyday lives makes their approach to theology make sense to them.

For many people I spoke with whose pro-gay stance derives directly from their theology, the question of specific scriptural passages is nearly irrelevant. For them, the key to being Christian is to follow the teachings and example of Jesus over other Scriptures. The overarching message of Jesus was one of love and spiritual transformation, not of rule-abidingness. Their account of Scripture seems to imply that if God's truth transcends time and social context, it transcends the social context of the times in which the Bible was written; so for Christians to hear God's truth, they must not limit it to what was written. In their view, appeals to specific passages in the Bible, whether there are one or eight or a thousand, miss the central point of Jesus' message, that the center of righteous living is not the rule of law but the rule of unbounded and unconditional love. They agree with the tenet that sin is not an item on a list of bad acts but rather a state of being separate from God. In their perspective, no one can determine what sin is for another person, and, thus, denouncements of others' homosexuality are not really in keeping with Christian faith.

When I asked City Church member Linda Renaldi, a human resources specialist in her mid thirties, whether homosexuality were sinful, she replied:

> No. I don't think premarital sex is a sin either. I *do* think promiscuity is
> a sin; I think it's sinful if you use people just for sheer physical pleasure,
> or lie to them, or become obsessed with one aspect of your nature. I
> mean, God made sex pleasurable. And is the argument that it's just

for reproduction? Well then, why is sex still pleasurable after menses
has stopped? It's not logical to me! That before and after, you know.
Little children from the age of infancy masturbate because it feels good.
So before you can have children and after you can have children the
sensations are pleasurable. It's one of the joyful things God gave us. It's
like all kinds of things are gonna happen, but meanwhile there's this
really cool thing you can do with your body that makes you feel better.

I don't think sex is as wrong as some of these people [other members]
might. I think you can abuse it like you can abuse everything, you know,
eat too much, drink too much, lots of other things you can do too much,
so, no.

Linda based her definition of sin on hurting, using, or lying to others, or
becoming obsessed "with one aspect of your nature." Thus, in spite of Jesus'
own words on sex outside of marriage (and some of her clergy's), Linda saw
contemporary premarital sex as not necessarily sinful either, if it does not involve mistreating others or becoming obsessed. Furthermore, for something
to be categorized as a sin, it must be "logical" to her.

She did not see any reason to believe that the morality of sex was any
different from that of eating—in her experience, things that are pleasurable
are *good*, when not abused or abusive. Linda distanced herself from those
who would argue that sex is only for reproduction and saw its pleasurable
qualities as gifts God gives people of all ages. In her view, the pleasure of sex
is a gift in itself, not a reward for or enticement to reproduction. People can
abuse it, putting it as a goal before the love of God and others, but it is, as
the *Discipline* says, "a good gift of God."

Linda did not always have such a strong view on homosexuality. In an
interview, she explained how she came to be a part of the reconciling congregations task force early on in the process. She had been brought to it in
part by Patrick Nelson, her good friend in the congregation, a gay man and
the task force's first chairperson. Linda recalled:

I didn't have any grand plan of being an active part of the Reconciling
Congregations movement until I got to be pretty good friends with
Patrick, and that's really how the whole thing started with me. And to tell
you the truth, I didn't know how I stood on the issue when it all started.
I mean, I'm a fairly political person, but you certainly do get brainwashed
when there are parts of the Bible that tell you that this is wrong. And
now that I've done a lot more study, my opinion has definitely changed,
but when I started, I didn't know how I felt about that at all. [. . .] But

Patrick just felt like he ought to round it out a bit more with people, and I sat in on a meeting where a member of this congregation literally came across the table at him and told him that he was going to burn in Hell and that he should repent and that she no more wanted his kind in the congregation than she would a murderer or a child molester or whatever.

Well! That pretty much solidified things for me! It became very clear how I felt about this issue and what I thought. It's like what [Reverend] Nicki [Parnell] says at the end of each service, "Do justice, love mercy, walk humbly with God." I'm like, which one of these people are doing that, where do I align myself? It was just a no-brainer for me from that point on.

Linda demonstrates clearly how her understanding of Scripture, God, and morality was shaped by her experience. For Linda, this scriptural passage from Micah 6:8,[24] recited by a City Church pastor as a benediction, came to exemplify what God's central message was in light of the physical aggression and dire pronouncements against homosexuality that were used almost weaponlike against her friend.

I asked her about the scriptural prohibitions on homosexuality:

Okay, if someone came up to you, personally, one on one, and said, "I've always been told that homosexuality is a sin, I read the Bible and it says right there [pointing figuratively] that this is totally unacceptable," what would you say?

Linda: Well, I would ask them who told them it was wrong, and try to get to the basis of it, and I would also talk about lots of places in the Bible that are written contextually. You know, like, if I'm married, and my husband dies and he has a brother, I'm supposed to have sex with him to continue having children. Well, guess what? I'm not gonna do that! It's not gonna happen! You know, there was a covenant with God in the desert that we have to circumcise our male children. Well, you know, Christ's covenant was to have eliminated all that. If I have a son, I'm not going to cut off the tip of his penis. I think that's really barbaric. Okay? I'm not gonna do it. And you know, I'm supposed to have my head covered in church—well, I do today because I'm having a bad hair day—but you know, I'm not going to do that all the time. I mean, Paul said women can't even speak in church. Nicki [Parnell] delivered the sermon today. She's gonna burn in Hell?

There are all kinds of things in the Bible that were contextual, from the historical and sociological perspective, and I think some of those passages [that people interpret as antigay] are some of them. And I think some of those passages are also misunderstood. What about Sodom and Gomorrah, whether that's a hospitality issue or a homosexual issue? So I would just talk to them about it and try to understand and try to, you know, maybe give them some different ways of approaching it. Everyone has to make their own mistakes.

As Linda talked about how to deal with people who believe that homosexuality is sinful, she implied that they do not have an understanding of the context in which the Bible was written. For Linda, the Bible is a guide, and many of the stories and rules in it need to be understood as historically specific to the time in which they were written. In her view, Christ made some of the rules unnecessary to his followers, such as the circumcision law and other Levitical codes, while other passages, such as Paul's instructions about women covering their heads and not speaking in church, came from a particular social context and do not apply today. Biblical denunciations of homosexuality also come from these two kinds of writings, she implied. Linda referred to the interpretation that the sin for which God rained fire on Sodom was the sin of inhospitality, a common interpretation among pro-gay clergy and laity.[25]

For Linda, the central mandate of Christianity is to act in a Christlike way, to love others. In her view, this message is simple and easy to understand, in spite of the Bible's many specific passages that require study:

I can't pull it out of the Bible. I don't know Hebrew and Greek and Aramaic, I can't translate the original texts of the Bible, so I don't really know what's written down, 'cause I can't translate it myself. And every time you translate another language, you imbibe it with your own—the things that have happened to you, your educational background, your socioeconomic background—you change it. Words are code, and you have to know the code. So, all I can go by is what Christlike behavior is. And it's very easy to tell. That's a really easy barometer.

Dawne: It's very easy to tell . . .

Linda: What's Christlike and what's not. Gee, what's Christlike behavior? Worshipping with people who you might think are sinners, or are different from you, or you don't understand? Or, dumping them? Gee. What's Christlike behavior here?

The simple truth for Linda was that, to be Christlike, when the opportunity arises, you must worship with people who are different from you, not "dump them." She set up this opposition between "worshipping with" and "dumping"; in doing so, she closed off the possibility of loving others while believing that their behavior is sinful. Here, Linda used simplicity to silence debate. For her, the bottom line was that to be Christlike is to love others, just as for those who believed homosexuality to be sinful, the bottom line was that God intends for sex to take place between a man and a woman who are married to each other.

Linda implied that sin was not something to be known by looking for biblical rules, but something to be transcended by being Christlike and loving. City Church members Nancy Cook and Ruthie Shafer expressed an understanding of sin similar to Linda's, both articulating the abstract notion of sin that was implicit in Linda's comments. They also maintained another key aspect of liberal theology—that God constantly reveals truth to people.[26]

Nancy Cook, whose social justice work brought her into contact with many different cultures, based her beliefs on the idea that there is a truth that supersedes much of what people can perceive in the world by reading or looking or by debating intellectual ideas. Truth, she insisted, is not simple—a view that seems related to her efforts to create cross-cultural understanding. When I asked her how she would respond to a hypothetical church member who believed homosexuality was sinful, she replied by using a language of semiotics to analyze sin, saying:

> Well, I would ask, "What do you mean by the word 'sin'? What reality are you pointing to?" And that's what this twentieth-century theological revolution was trying to get people to look at. What reality in mind is sin? It's not just a list of things that are no-no's. What is sin? Sin is something that everyone participates in. Every human being. Yes, the church is for sinners. It's for every single one of us, and that's much more profound than just dos and don'ts. You could say that's a moral code of ethics, but I don't think that's as profound as sin. And the reason I think this theological revolution is important is that it forces people to think ontologically, to think existentially about life, their lives, to try to translate things into things that are true, rather than something they read, something that itemizes, or debates this intellectual idea over that intellectual idea.
>
> We have no clarity with that word [sin]. And I don't think that in the Bible they are dividing people up into this group and that group. The

Christian message is about every human being struggling with their own life. And in so doing you form your opinion about other people's lives too. In the Old Testament, the Ten Commandments was a social structure, it was law, that helped people structure themselves.

In Nancy Cook's understanding, sin is not a list of bad acts. Rather, it is something personal, between the individual and God, and, thus, others cannot know the nature of a person's sin. She saw the definition of "sin" as unclear. The ultimate message of Christianity is about the individual's relationship with God, a view that helped her see judgment as inappropriate. Rules about improper behaviors, in her view, help people to structure themselves into a society. She saw these ideals coming from a merging of the opinions people develop in their individual relationships with God. However, she seemed to state that human rules should not be confounded with God's ultimate rules.

I pushed Nancy further on the question of the sinfulness of homosexuality. People who leaned toward conservative evangelical Christianity tended to see sin as something a person would do less of as he grew and matured in his faith. Thus, being selfish, being unloving, hurting others—these might be signs of where someone still had some distance to go in his walk with God. I pointed out that even if someone looked at sin as a state of separation from God, she could still see homosexuality as one of numerous kinds of behavior one would not do if one were truly listening to and drawing closer to God, maturing in faith. I posed to her this view:

> A guy I know would say, "Yeah, we all have sin, and before I was mature in my faith, I was tempted by porno[graphy] shops." He would be tempted to go in there and now that he's mature in his faith he knows that it brings him further from God. He says the same thing holds true for homosexuality, that you can be tempted to have sex with someone who's the same sex as you, but when you're mature in your faith, you realize that it is bringing you further from God's intent.
>
> Nancy: Well, I'd ask, what do you mean, first of all, by "God," and what is God's intent. This guy's got a list of dos and don'ts that he's interpreting as God's intent. Being mature in faith means— I'd want him to define all that. I might agree that you should discipline yourself and your sex life, and what helps you discipline your sex life is getting maturity, maybe, on whatever your values are. He's making a presupposition again about what it means.

Nancy's first response to this argument was to ask what my acquaintance meant by concepts such as "mature in faith," challenging what she perceived as his definition of sin as a list of "don'ts." She next turned the conversation to the social construction of morality, to distinguish social mores from sin by relating prohibitions of homosexuality to eighteenth- and nineteenth-century support for slavery:

> But just like, for example, slavery. I guess some people were always clear that it was a brutal thing, but it was associated with society and necessary. But then some people were brave enough to say, "God's will is that we don't have slavery." And then other people were saying, "God's will is that slaves are necessary, because our society is supreme, white society is supreme." They said, "No, it's not." So, they decided not only that they would get rid of their slaves but that they would try to lead other people. That was, you could say, sociologically a new aspect of God's will becoming apparent. So, for me this dialogue that's happening now, this opportunity to affirm a new part of God's will, is a new dialogue.

Before addressing the question of pornography, she compared the current debates over homosexuality to the nineteenth-century debates over slavery. Just as God's will was made apparent in the social process of debates over abolition, she implied, so too can God's will be revealed through today's debates. By comparing the traditional church stance supporting slavery with the traditional church stance opposing homosexuality, she likened the two sets of traditionalists to each other, cutting off the possibility that the current traditionalists are right while those who supported slavery were wrong. She espoused the liberal theological view that God's truth becomes ever more apparent, suggesting that the older, more "traditional" view of homosexuality would eventually die out, and people would understand homosexuality to be as much a part of God's Creation as slavery is not. She thus avoided making an overt judgment by making an implicit one, equating a traditional church stance that is now almost universally understood as having been wrong with the current "traditional" argument about homosexuality. I brought her back to the question of pornography:

> So where would going to porno shops fit in? Is that an okay thing? If someone could say "anything goes," you know?
>
> Nancy: Well, and that's where social structures do come in. I'm really not as liberal as the ACLU. I don't think anything goes if it's

hurting someone. For me personally, this kind of information feeds people damaging ideas, it reinforces images of mistreating other human beings.

Dawne: So you draw the line at hurting other people.

Nancy: Yeah. It's something that manipulates people. For me person-ally, it's a waste of time and money, it's destructive, for *me*, to do that. Not that pornography isn't a part of life, whatever form it comes in. But should there be laws against porno shops? Is that what you're asking? If there's a study that can definitely link porno shops to child abuse, rape, multiple killings, then we should definitely close them down. And I definitely wouldn't want one in my neighborhood.

For Nancy, sin is not about dos and don'ts. But did her distaste for pornog-raphy presuppose a list of dos and don'ts? Nancy quickly made it clear that she, unlike the American Civil Liberties Union (ACLU) in her mind, did not believe "anything goes," as she drew the line at hurting other people. As it was for Linda Renaldi, hurting people seems to have been a "don't" for Nancy, because it violated the commandment to love others.

On the other hand, Nancy distinguished the various judgments one could make about pornography from its being sinful. She also distinguished between her personal tastes—she did not want a porn shop in her neighbor-hood—and a more rational basis for determining whether porn shops are harmful and should be legally banned. For her, a standard of harm deter-mined whether something should be illegal. A standard of harm could also determine whether something was demeaning and encouraged violence. She verged on saying that hurting others is sinful, but hesitated to pin sin down to a question of harm. The reason for this reticence seems to be Nancy's anxiety that human language and human concepts cannot convey the truth about what is godly and what is sinful, as she was eager to ask what others mean by such terms.

Nancy did not account for the possibility that homosexuality is sinful, nor did she explain how she could know that it is not. Rather, she simply refused to accept that anyone can know sin for another person. By refusing to define sin, Nancy, like the others, might risk taking a stand that "anything goes," regardless of her own claim to the contrary. How, many would ask, is the church, Christianity, supposed to know how to guide people, how are individuals supposed to know how to live, if the church cannot discern God's guidelines? For that matter, if religion is wholly individual, why should any-one go to church at all? Why not stay home and worship in a religion of one?

These blanks begin to be filled in by Ruthie Shafer, a forty-two-year-old human resources director and member of City Church. She spoke of her view of Christianity and the Bible as demanding a life of wholeness and connection to other people, rather than a list of dos and don'ts. She explained her overarching theology as follows:

> First of all, through my own experiences, my own pursuit of spirituality and some study of the Scriptures, I think in order for any person or group of people to call themselves Christians, they are in some way espousing a set of values within the context of the New Testament. And within that context, the messages which I believe are most important are those that we have in some way documented to be as close as possible to the message of Christ himself. And if you go back and take a look at those Scriptures, you find that not only is there very little discussion about an issue as discrete as this, but in general there's very little in terms of topical dos and don'ts. There's a very broad message, a very commanding message, and for most of us, one that's difficult to implement, which is a wholeness of connection with other people. So my frustration [with the debates at City Church] was that any contemporary community of faith would actually need to come together and consider excluding anyone, in any way.
>
> Particularly, if you go piece by piece in terms of parable and Scripture, you find in some contexts how shocking it would be that people who consider themselves Christian would set aside others. And what would be the basis for that set-aside? And even within a context in which you would say, "I believe that person to be in sin," then of course if you follow the New Testament then that is in fact the mission of Christ.

Here, Ruthie began by explaining what Christianity meant to her. In her view, a godly experience could only be had in connection with other people; transcendence could not be solitary. For Ruthie, the argument about homosexuality was *not* that God never placed homosexuality on the "don't" list, so therefore it is on the "do" list. Rather, she saw the story of Jesus as a story about inclusion and wholeness, one that excludes no one. In fact, even if one considers someone to be in sin, one must still follow "the mission of Christ" and welcome that person into the congregation. This is a point with which many of those who believe homosexuality is sinful would agree. Thus, Ruthie articulated a Christian basis for the "tolerance" argument accepted overwhelmingly by those who spoke to me from all sides.

Ruthie built on that view, expressing a classically liberal Christian view of God's revelation as ongoing and part of God's vast creation, the "boundless variety" of which serves "to keep us alive and healthy and exciting." She continued:

> Sexuality within that context is only one variable, and it's one in which we should glory and understand the joy. It's not one in which we should narrow our vision to some limited way in which people should or should not exist under certain circumstances.
>
> I think that people get confused about identity and behavior. For me, there is a moral context within all human behavior, but it has very little to do with your identity. It has to do with the choices you make and how you choose to live out your loving capabilities. So I think we have issues to deal with in that arena as well. Who I am is not a moral choice in terms of my sexual identity. I did not choose that. I came fully equipped with that. I did not wake up one morning and say, "I believe I'm going to be a heterosexual." It didn't happen that way.

In Ruthie's experience, transcendence comes from seeing oneself as part of God's amazing creation, connected to other people, to God, and to the entire universe. Morality is about the choices people make, and sexual identity is not among those choices, which she knew in part because she knew she did not choose her own sexual identity. Ruthie saw identity as given to a person by God.

For these pro-gay City Church members, people can transcend the earthly realm by reading Scripture in the context in which it was written and by learning to love in a Christlike way, not by judging others as sinful. By making this argument, these members moved the church's spotlight off of gay people and onto those who believed homosexuality to be sinful. However, they did not challenge head-on the argument that homosexuality was sinful. They left that question unanswered and wondered why the "other side" was so recalcitrant. When confronted with the claim that homosexuality was sinful, which seems clearly spelled out in the Bible, these members might seem to some to dodge the question by responding, "What is sin, anyway?"[27]

Scripture and Everyday Theologies

Members of both congregations looked to what they knew about God, through Scripture and tradition, for guidance as to how God wanted people to live. They sought comfort, guidance, and transcendence in what they saw as the eternal word of God. However, some parts of Scripture can be harder to discern than others, and some can seem more dated or irrelevant than others, depending on people's own lived experience. Because people disagreed on how to interpret it, Scripture could fail to bring a feeling of transcendence. Scripture is an important key to transcendence, but if a sense of unbounded connection is a feeling of transcending human divides, of oneness, then conflict over Scripture is the very opposite of transcendence. Members looked to Scripture to naturalize their understandings of God's will, and they looked to what they knew about God to help interpret Scripture. Were this reciprocal relationship to come to light in the wrong way, it could threaten to denaturalize both.

Were members to come together and say to each other what they have said in this chapter, they would confront just how different their visions are, not only of Scripture and sin but of God. Indeed, some members saw God as a parent who laid down particular rules to show people the best way, or even to simply mark his followers from outsiders. Others saw God as a creative force of love and compassion, which lacks the agency to say "yes" or "no" but which inspires people toward interpersonal connection and mutual care. These ways of viewing God tend to be mutually exclusive, although some people alternate between the two, or personify God as a way to grasp the infinite.

For Robert Wuthnow (1998), these differences reflect an age-old difference between the spiritualities of home and quest, tabernacle and pilgrimage. These differences in turn draw from the different historical periods in which people are raised or with which they identify. To those from times and places of stability, the idea of an unchanging and unmoving God makes sense, a God found in a place of worship like a tabernacle. To those experiencing life as a constant or repeated upheaval, a God that transcends time and place, that draws people together and provides answers in a tumultuous and uncertain social climate, makes more sense. With this God, people must search for answers and find fleeting views of the sacred. Wuthnow sees these two different kinds of spirituality characterizing different believers. I found that some people gravitate toward one ideal or the other, but many more seemed to combine the two, seeking out some kind of stability in God *because* they experienced the world as so unstable. Regardless of whether members gravitated toward the ideal of the tabernacle or the quest, no one involved in these debates seemed to accept one view of God as handed to them in stone. They all synthesized everyday theologies that helped them to hear God's voice in and through their widely varying and often unpredictable experiences.

Church members agreed in many ways on what ideals God embodies—love, communion, transcendence, truth, righteousness; their shared ideals allowed them to worship together and at times experience unfettered bonds of communion. Yet within each congregation, members differed with respect to what those ideals mean for human beings. Most members believed that God's word is timeless; some believed that word to be reflected in traditional church doctrine that must be reaffirmed. Most members believed that God's love and wisdom are infinite; some believed this to mean that this love and wisdom are ever unfolding and that they become apparent to human beings through the processes of history, and that the church must adapt to keep up with God's ongoing revelation.[28]

Members' very different beliefs about sexuality stemmed, in part, not only from different experiences but also from very different beliefs about the nature of God and creation—who or what God is and what God intends for people, what human life is about. Debates about homosexuality can be so explosive because they threaten to bring out the fact that the one timeless and true God in which members believe can appear to say widely opposing things to different members. Members' views can range so widely because each, as a member of numerous overlapping communities and with widely different experiences, does not simply absorb what is taught as church doctrine but engages with those teachings in terms of her or his own social experiences.

For all its transcendent qualities, Scripture can fail at times to bring people together in transcendent communion if they disagree over what it means. Both congregations dealt with this potential for conflict, but given their different understandings of God's revelation, they approached the problem of intracongregational conflict quite differently.

chapter FOUR

Community and Dissent

Let us therefore no longer pass judgment on one another, but resolve instead never to put a stumbling block or hindrance in the way of another. . . . Let us then pursue what makes for peace and for mutual upbuilding.

—Romans 14:13, 19

Church members develop everyday theologies in response to the wide range of experiences and ideas to which everyday life exposes them. Their congregations play a large role in the development of these everyday theologies, of course, but not the only role; members do not generally believe everything they are told. Church leaders do, however, seek to guide people on the paths they see as righteous, and to maintain their congregations with integrity. On occasion, people's everyday theologies can conflict with each other or with church doctrine, and such conflicts may threaten to denaturalize the transcendent connection between religious communities and God. Thus, congregations need to deal with conflict in ways that cohere with church teachings.

Church members tend to assume that those who disagree with their morality disagree because they are either ignorant of God's truth or because they do not prioritize what is right. But none of the people I spoke with were essentially ignorant or evil. Regardless of their disagreements, the members I heard from were articulate about their beliefs and theologies; all could explain their understandings of God, and all demonstrated a desire to be loving and caring, even to those they believed to be wrong.

People in both categories sought to transcend the earthly and to grow, and help others grow, closer to God. And yet they were in conflict, sometimes painfully, over homosexuality.

This chapter explores how each congregation accounted for and handled dissent. Because of the different understandings of God that predominated at Missionary and City Churches, these congregations responded differently to conflicts over homosexuality. Most Missionary members believed that God gave one truth, so dissent could be excluded from the congregation's everyday functions—in effect, it could be dismissed as rooted in either ignorance or deceit. In contrast, many members and leaders of City Church believed that God's truth could be revealed in many different ways. Thus, dissent could not be excluded outright but had to be processed, discussed in such a way as to enlighten all involved about God's message. In spite of believing that God could reveal truth in many ways, though, the leadership in the congregation (both lay and clergy) tended to believe that there was one godly way to deal with homosexuality, and that was to welcome and affirm gay men and lesbians. Rather than simply exclude dissent, the pro-gay leadership at City Church enacted what Michel Foucault (1977) termed "discipline." That is to say, rather than silencing dissent, they sought to have dissenting views stated and discussed in such a way as to enforce certain norms of membership.

The Meaning of the Word at Missionary Church

At Missionary Church, members believed that God gave humanity his word in Scripture, and that although people may have difficulty understanding it, his message is unchanging and eternal. In this view, God's word is laid out for all time in the Scriptures, and these indicate that Jesus is the way to salvation. As a man I met at a regional Confessing Movement conference told me over lunch, "[The debates over homosexuality in the church] all come down to a basic question: We [conservative evangelicals] think God's revelation was laid down in the Scriptures for all time, while they [members of the RCP] think he makes new revelations all the time." Given their belief that God revealed one eternal and unchanging truth, which is represented in Scripture, Missionary Church members needed to account for how people could think something different, and the answer could be either ignorance or deceit.

While believing that God's word appears in Scripture, members of Missionary Church also realized that it could be hard for human beings to understand. Different passages are intended to be read in different ways, and some parts might seem, from the inherently limited human perspective, to conflict with others. At Missionary Church, how clearly a member understood God's message was an indicator of one's "maturity in faith." It was perfectly acceptable to ask questions about God and faith, to seek to learn more about God's plan, but it was understood that such questions indicated ignorance of God's answers. God understood that humans were fallen and that it was the human lot to struggle to understand his love, but clearly one would have fewer questions as one studied, prayed, listened to and read Scripture, and heard the messages of clergy. Having fewer questions did not mean that one could think one had all the answers, however. The members who were recognized as most mature in faith were those who recognized that God could always teach them something new, and who tried to speak humbly about their knowledge and experiences in faith. Arrogance itself would indicate a failure to understand God's way.

Missionary Church member Betsy Meisensahl and I had a conversation about how to understand the Bible. Betsy affirmed that the Bible is all true but believed it could take some historical and contextual analysis to understand. For her, this need could pose problems for faith; it could raise questions about how people are to know which parts to take literally and which need to be understood in context. Betsy described how different parts must be read in different ways, as histories, as poetry, as illustrative metaphors, and as potentially conflicting eyewitness accounts that must be understood as particular individuals' perspectives. Any difficulty people have in interpreting the Bible, she made clear to me, would be due to human limitations, not to any incoherence on the part of the Bible or God.

Given this large range of reasons not to read various scriptural passages as literal truth directly applicable to contemporary life, I asked her about the pro-gay arguments that make the case that the prohibitions on homosexuality are not literal truth directly applicable to life today (for example, that injunctions against "homosexuality" referred to idolatrous temple prostitution as opposed to the egalitarian, loving relationships of today). She responded, "First of all, the Bible was not written only for the day in which it was written. I think it was written, and those words hold true, for all time." In her view, temple prostitution may not be the form homosexuality takes today in the United States, but some things in Scripture transcend the time and place in which they were written. Homosexuality is one of those things, in her view; it was an abomination when it happened in the form of temple prostitution, and it is an abomination now.

Betsy continued, describing the rules in the Old Testament that were deemed unnecessary after the coming of Jesus and those that persist:

To have the most understanding out of the Bible, it also helps to know
what the cultural background was and why something was such an
abomination. There are also rules in there about not wearing clothing
that's made with two different fibers mixed together. And there are
all kinds of things in there about what you should eat and what you
shouldn't eat and all that. For the most part, it's a tough distinction,
because I believe that all of that falls under the Old Law, and that we're
not held to the Old Law. You don't gain eternal life by following all
the rules. It's telling you you gotta get away from all the rules. But at
the same time, we have the Ten Commandments. Do you keep everything that was said there? Do you pick out certain parts? It's a tough
debate.

Betsy wrestled with ways that context could help believers understand the
Scriptures. She found that it helped to know why, in the culture of the time,
something was considered an abomination. Such cultural understanding can
help make sense of why God forbade blended fabrics and certain foods when
the book of Leviticus was written, but does not forbid them to Christians
now. She implied that part of that had to do with Jesus' coming, and his
replacing the Old Law with the New Law. "You don't gain eternal life by
following the rules" was something she derived from Jesus' life and teaching,
but, on the other hand, she hesitated to see that remark as Jesus' negation of
the Ten Commandments. It is hard, Betsy said, for human beings to know
which rules God thinks are true today and which are not. But, for her, that
potentially denaturalizing confusion comes out of human beings' own imperfection, not because Scripture is inherently ambiguous. She later cited
2 Timothy 3:16, "All Scripture is God-breathed," to affirm that Scripture
had its own coherence.

Although Betsy affirmed that Scripture itself was coherent, she nonetheless wrestled with her personal understanding of what God intends. She
said:

Boy, when it comes down issue by issue. . . . What do we still believe is
true, versus what we don't. It is awfully hard to defend: yes, I believe
God still holds us to this one, but no, he doesn't hold us to that one. I
don't know. You almost have to go, "I believe our individual convictions
are based on what God reveals to us." And I'm not saying that he speaks
to me in a voice I can recognize, or even that I open the Bible and I read
something and, yes, I know that's what God is telling me right now. But I
guess I think he begins to form our convictions to be in line with his.

For Betsy, confusion about Scripture could be sorted out as God revealed his wisdom to an individual. In Betsy's view, then, this confusion results from immaturity in faith—God hasn't *yet* spoken to someone on a certain point because that person is at an early stage of transformation. The answers are clear to God, and become clearer to people as God speaks to his followers, as he gradually forms their convictions to be in line with his. Ultimately, maturity in faith seemed to be a measure of the extent to which a member could reconcile seeming contradictions in Scripture without violating the congregation's foundational assumptions about God and Scripture, including that Scripture itself is God's timeless, coherent, and explicit truth.

Just as failing to know God's plan could indicate immaturity in faith, so could failing to love others. Tina Harrison addressed a question about whether gay people were welcome at Missionary Church, saying:

> We knew Thad for a long time, but we never knew he was gay. And [my sister Phoebe] actually liked him. We thought they would get married. And then we come to find out Thad is gay! And so I told my sister, "If you really love him, you know, as long as he's totally faithful to *you*, and *denies* that . . ." I remember when she kind of struggled with that. Of course, now she says he was never her boyfriend.
>
> But when my family found out, see, my dad never liked him anyway. Because my dad, my dad is a Christian, but I don't think he gets it sometimes, it's not right to judge people.
>
> So, in other words, if you came [to church] and you never told anybody [you were gay], nobody would ever know. But if you came out openly, I hope that we would be friends and love this person, and speak the truth, *in love*. And, you know, that's what Jesus is all about: speaking the truth in love. So, befriend the person. Even when we have people of a different color come to our church, it's so funny to watch, because you can see people aren't comfortable with it. Somehow we all want everybody to be the same all the time. [. . .]
>
> The whole point of church is to help people accept Christ as their savior. When I became a Christian, I didn't change overnight, and I wouldn't expect that a gay person would either. I would expect that if they accepted Christ as their savior, then they would slowly begin to see the selfishness [of practicing homosexuality].

As Tina tried to explain how she believed the church should respond lovingly to gay people, she made an analogy to church members who were uncomfortable with nonwhites in church. She described those who were uncomfortable with nonwhites as "funny," but she moved not to place herself above them by using the first-person plural, saying "sometimes we all want . . ." She dismissed their discomfort, seeing it not as socially ingrained racism but as immaturity in faith. She thus denaturalized the racism rooted deep in others' worldviews, but she did it without attacking them.

If ignorance is one side of the problem of people believing the wrong things about God, the other side is deceit. As we saw in the last chapter, members were mindful of Paul's warning to the Ephesians not to be childlike and follow the deceitful scheming of pretenders. Tina saw racist Christians as childlike and ignorant enough to believe deceivers who abused Scripture to gain support for their own godless agendas. Tina saw biblical endorsements of racism, such as those used by the Ku Klux Klan or supporters of slavery before the Civil War, as the result of deceitful scheming and remarked:

> Because there's just too many ignorant people. Not ignorant, I shouldn't say that. Well, ignorant just means lack of knowledge. So, Bible-ignorant. It's easy to sway people. If you're a Christian you should be feeding on the Word, because that's what gives you your life, and daily confessing your sin, because that's what cleanses you. We daily feed our bodies, and most Americans take a shower every day or a bath, but many Christians don't read the Bible. They just go to church and hear what Pastor Richard says. It's very easy for Christians to get swayed when they're like that, because they're not reading what the Word says.

For Tina, ignorance or deceit alone could explain readings of the Bible that differed from the understanding she saw as eternally true. Tina implicitly likened homosexuals and RCP supporters to the ignorant and childlike members who did not know God's way. She thus rendered them incapable of critiquing her worldview in a way she would have to engage.

Although Tina did not go so far as to pinpoint certain homosexuals as deceivers, other members did. When I asked Jan Erikson, a longtime Missionary Church member in his early sixties, for an interview, he expressed his frustration with the pro-gay RCP, saying:

> That Reconciling Congregations movement is a bunch of yahoos. [. . .] All they care about is money and bringing up the numbers [attracting more people into congregations]. They don't care about saving souls, because souls are of no use to them. Money is. And they destroy churches.

The Gospel is the final word, and it doesn't change. I don't want to talk about homosexuality. If a homosexual wants to come to the church, let 'em in the church, they're a sinner like me. We're all sinners. Homosexuality isn't my problem to deal with, but I've got my own, different sin to deal with. If you want to bring your sin to God, welcome. Come on in, but don't talk about it, and don't preach to my children.

You know, they snuck a homosexual assistant pastor into a congregation [in a nearby town] without telling the senior pastor. That's the kind of thing they do. They want to say it's like race or gender, but it's not; it's a choice. I've had it with those yahoos. They're tearing apart the church. (Reconstructed from notes)

Jan based his understanding of the sinfulness of homosexuality on Scripture, more specifically, the Gospels, whose meaning he said never changes.[1] His understanding of the Reconciling movement's sin went beyond their support for homosexuality, however. In his view, the Reconciling movement cared only about money and nothing for souls. They "destroy churches"; they want people to believe homosexuality is not a chosen and sinful status. Jan was careful to note that he, too, like all human beings, was a sinner, and sinners are welcome in the church. Homosexuals might have their sin to deal with, but what the Reconciling Congregations movement did went beyond that level of everyday sin, into the realm of deceitful scheming. He thus naturalized any threat they may have posed to his understanding of God's truth by categorizing them as greedy deceivers.

Dissent within the Flock

Given that Missionary Church believed that God revealed one coherent truth in writing and/or inspiring the Bible, and that those who did not understand it were either ignorant or intentionally deceitful, dissent did not have a central place in the experience of faith. God's message was laid out in Scripture and accessible to all who opened their hearts to him. To argue with what the whole congregation apparently knew to be true would put one in a position of being seen as either ignorant or arrogant. Ignorance was part of the human condition, but to give oneself to the Lord meant humbling oneself and admitting that one's human inclinations had resulted from sin.

There were some disagreements in the congregation, to be sure. Members disagreed about the nature of God, they disagreed about church policy, and they disagreed about homosexuality. But none of these disagreements was central to the life of the congregation, and each was handled in a way that reinforced the belief that God's one central truth, as they understood it, was supreme.

During my time at Missionary Church, I heard what sounded like very different understandings about God's relationship to social stability and change. Pastor Richard often preached on the theme that God shakes up people's habituated life patterns, for instance, by demanding that various prophets and disciples abandon their families and livelihoods and do God's work.[2] A number of members repeated this theme to me, explaining God's demand for people not to separate religion from secular life, getting out of the habits of selfishness and greed that characterized work and consumer life. On the other hand, in an adult Sunday School class one day, Mary Ann Burgess, a new member in her mid fifties, expressed her belief that God loves order and hates chaos. She thus saw family patterns and lifestyles since the 1960s—including homosexuality—as unacceptable to God, who created the earth and heavens to bring order out of chaos.[3]

These views might seem contradictory: a God who shakes up society versus a God who loves order and stability. But these views did not overtly conflict at all during my time there, because they did not need to. For instance, with reference to homosexuality, the former could mean that God called people to abandon the habituated selfishness of modern life—including homosexuality—while the latter could be cited with the assumption that homosexuality was a symptom of social decay. The knowledge of God's timelessness, and the timelessness of his prohibitions on homosexuality, allowed potentially conflicting views to work together as evidence of God's vast and coherent plan.

There were of course conflicts about how the congregation should deal with the denomination's gradual acceptance of homosexuality. Early in my time there, the congregation held a meeting to brief members on the Reconciling Congregations Program and the Confessing Movement in the denomination. Before an audience of forty members seated in rows in the gathering hall, Pete Vogel, a member who was active in the Confessing Movement, gave a presentation on the Reconciling movement, including details about the Reverend Jimmy Creech's (his real name) ecclesiastical trial for blessing a same-sex covenant ceremony in October 1997. He also talked about the Reconciling movement's "worship of the goddess Sophia" as a feminist intervention on behalf of women who had bad childhood experiences with their fathers and thus did not like to think of God as a father.[4]

Among those at the meeting was Herb Grayson, a long-time member of the congregation from the era before the Evangelical United Brethren (EUB) denomination merged with the Methodist Church to form the United

Methodist Church, which it did in 1968. At the end of the meeting, Herb stood up and said something potentially controversial. Becoming increasingly animated, he said:

> This church [the UMC] is going crazy and they don't care about God or Jesus or anything. We [the EUB] joined the Methodists thinking that they were about upholding the teachings of Jesus Christ, but now they've gone too far with this Sophia nonsense and all this. The only thing they care about is money! We have to hit them where it hurts and withhold our apportionment! Nice guys finish last! We have to hit 'em in the pocket book, 'cause that's the only place they'll feel it and that's the only thing they'll listen to. We have to withhold our apportionment, and if that doesn't work, I don't see why we shouldn't just leave the Methodist Church. We have to play hardball with these people because that's what they're doing. Nice guys finish last!

Members became animated, in a jocular way, as the group muttered about Herb's comments and shared jokes about Sophia. Sitting behind Pastor Richard, I jokingly asked him if Jesus had said somewhere that "nice guys finish last." (He did not reply.) No one directly confronted Herb's assertions about the denomination and how to deal with the proponents of change. As Herb went on, though, Pastor Richard rose from his chair in the audience and quietly said something like "Now, Herb," but not loud enough for Herb to hear him right away.

Participants in the meeting did express their disagreement with Herb, but not directly. Pete Vogel and another member pointed out that not all of the historically Methodist congregations supported the Reconciling program but just a certain small group within the church. A little later, as the volume in the room decreased, Pastor Richard exercised his leadership by standing up and saying that he believed the way to influence the church was to stay in it, pay the apportionment (each congregation's annual dues to the denomination), and keep their right to vote and witness to the truth.[5] Here, as we might expect of a forum of this sort, jokes, distracted mutterings, and delayed comments all helped to defuse what could have become a conflictual situation. Members either chuckled at Herb's animation or joked about liberal Methodists' supposed goddess worship; they thus paid little mind to his particular demands. They did not seem, at the meeting, to see Herb's passion as an indicator of his faith, nor did they appear to see him as righteously inspired.

Although someone with Herb's dissenting beliefs could voice them in the congregation with little fear of reprisal, Missionary Church members who had gay relatives or who did not think that homosexuality was inherently sinful avoided mentioning this kind of dissent. One older member told me he believed homosexuality was a gift from God, but he stipulated that I not tell the rest of the congregation he believed that. Likewise, in interviews with other members of Missionary Church I was surprised by their live-and-let-live views on homosexuality, as I had never heard them suggest any acceptance (or rejection) of homosexuality in church forums. These members avoided stirring up controversy and disrupting their congregation.

For instance, member Jackie Richards, a social worker in her mid thirties, told me about her disagreement with the rest of the congregation's dominant stance on homosexuality, confessing that she did not have "the guts" to challenge her congregation. She remarked:

> I don't have proof, there's just comments here and there. But if you took a poll, I feel pretty certain that I'm in a real minority here, in accepting homosexuality. [. . .] This whole [antigay] movement is starting to be in our church. I think they're smooth, they're starting in the meetings, and [printing antihomosexual pieces in the newsletter] [. . .] To be honest, I don't have quite the guts to stand up in front of the whole church and say that I don't agree. Hopefully there'll come a time when I could do that, when we could do that. But I'm not gonna be the first one. I hate that. But I'm not the one that's ready to go out on a limb and say, "Blah! Let's accept this person for what they are, and just help them to get a relationship with Jesus Christ." [. . .] I don't think it's my position to change anyone. Or convert anyone into a heterosexual lifestyle because that's what's right. I don't believe that.

Jackie believed that she did not "have quite the guts" to oppose what she saw as an antihomosexual movement in her congregation, but it was not simply lack of guts that kept Jackie from challenging her congregation. At Missionary Church members could easily dismiss those who expressed disagreement with beliefs widely accepted to be the timeless truth. If Jackie were to express her disagreement to the congregation she would risk them seeing her as either ignorant or deceitful. Jackie's brother was gay, and though he lived in another city, she feared that telling her fellow church members about him would subject her to their belief that he should forsake his partner and change his sexual orientation. Jackie herself would risk losing something, were her friends in faith to know of her disagreement with them. Jackie taught a Sunday School class and was a respected leader within the congregation. Judging from what was said about others who appeared to lack maturity in faith, and given the apparent belief in the congregation that she was relatively mature in faith, she might well have risked losing some social status and some of her credibility as a church member.

Without intending to exclude any particular persons, Missionary Church managed to exclude certain kinds of conflict. The members' sure knowledge that God's truth was laid out once and for all time did not allow for meaningful debate about essential matters. After all, to do so would seem to put God himself up for debate, a perverse notion if ever there was one! The notion that God never changes allowed members to suture together very different beliefs about God, knowing that the limits of the human brain could make God's word seem confusing, but that ultimately everything made sense to God. That notion also excluded certain beliefs from consideration. Members believed that scriptural prohibitions on homosexuality were timeless and that doubt about such timeless principles indicated either a lack of spiritual maturity or godlessness and deceit. Thus, no one who disagreed about homosexuality spoke up about that belief. Their silence then perpetuated the belief that prohibitions on homosexuality were timeless.

The Meaning of the Word at City Church

At City Church the congregation was dominated by a liberal understanding of God, which posits (a) that God is vast and powerful enough to speak to many people in many different ways, and (b) that God did not become inactive after the official codification of the Bible, but can reveal the truth to people in new ways all the time. This view comes out of the crisis that evolutionary theory posed for American Protestantism in the nineteenth century (Marsden 1980). In this view, the story of Jesus' life, which some liberals believe to be empirical fact and which others see as wholly or partly allegorical, serves as an allegory for how God shakes up (denaturalizes) oppressive human belief structures and social systems with radical, revolutionary love. Martin Luther King Jr. and Mahatma Gandhi, regardless of their different religions, both delivered God's message of love, thus changing people's hearts and, in the liberal Christian view, bringing about the kingdom of God.

To theological liberals, Scripture is central as a message of love. People may read all or parts of it as allegory, but regardless of how much is allegorical, in this view, the central and recurrent message throughout the Old and New Testaments is that people should treat one another with love. They believe that the Ten Commandments, Levitical law, the lives and teachings of the prophets and Jesus, and Paul's letters to the early church all point repeatedly to the centrality of loving God and neighbor. The details of the stories must be understood in context; for instance, Paul's exhortations in the Epistles to women to not speak in church were written in a particular time and place and by a particular man. Similarly, injunctions against homosexuality, whether written by Paul or appearing in the Old Testament, are particular to the times in which they were written and do not refer to the kinds of same-sex relationships existing today.

The members of Missionary Church also saw love as central to Christian life, but they tended to speak of Scripture as coming first, as God's message telling people how to go about the business of loving God and neighbor. In the liberal theologies of many City Church members, Scripture's main idea is one of love, and once one understands that message one can go back and interpret specific verses. Scripture was seen as central because of this timeless message of love, so God could reveal the meaning of that lesson, as well as the nature of creation, in different ways throughout time. Love and Scripture are both important in both theological perspectives, but they relate to each other in different ways, with very different implications.

When I asked liberal City Church member Ruthie Shafer about homosexuality, she remarked:

> I believe that it [sexual orientation] is a biological design; I do not believe that it is a social condition or that it is a lifestyle choice. As many of my friends say, it is not a lifestyle, it is a life. I believe we are, to use a contemporary image, but I truly believe it, that we are a rainbow of God's Creation. [. . .] And I think that when we deny that we are denying God's genius of creation. I think we're about to learn more. As our own technology moves forward, we'll be able to describe the foundation of how we are who we are, because some of our gifts really do come with us, and may have been there for generations back. And as we explore it, much like exploring the cosmos, we'll begin to see how incredibly simple and yet complex and extraordinary the whole thing is. So I have a great and deep appreciation for the design of mankind and all living things.

For Ruthie, the idea that God inscribed homosexuality in people through biology gave her the certainty that homosexuality was part of God's genius

of a diverse and complicated creation. People do not always understand the
genius of God's Creation, in her account, but just as we have learned more
about the planet and the universe, we can learn more about humanity's variation with the help of science. Not only did she not see homosexuality as
sinful, she saw any such judgment as closing people off from God.

Such a view might seem to lack any moral compass at all, and indeed
there were members of both congregations who saw such liberal theologies
as "sentimental" and leading to an "anything goes" philosophy in life. Liberals such as Ruthie were aware that they could seem to think "anything
goes," but clearly they did not think this at all. Ruthie, for instance, made
clear that sin meant denying God's love to people—and such sinners would
receive the wages of their sin. She continued:

> But, see, I believe that all of us who exclude others from the faith are
> messing with "the Man," as they say. That is a big no-no. That is a big,
> big, big no-no. Scripture says be very, very-very concerned if you are
> a person who helps to move one of these little ones away from God.
> I mean, there is some very strong imagery in that. So anyone who is
> involved, I think, in making people feel uncomfortable, even if it's as
> simple as someone whom you know to be gay walks into the church with
> their partner and you turn your head and you don't welcome them; I
> believe that you will be accountable for that. Yes, I do. And if you have
> formed [antigay] collectives, where that's your mission, and you are part
> of that set of politics, oh, I don't want to be around; it's not going to be
> any fun. I don't know what all the penalties are, but I know that there's
> a current life penalty for that kind of mindset; it's a kind of living death
> that people can experience when they are in that politics.

For Ruthie, God is love, God is the life force, God is expressed in the vast
diversity of creation. To know God is to open your heart to that vastness,
to choose to practice love in everything you do. God's power is with those
who choose to live in that kind of love, and others know when people have
it. To deny the value of diversity is to close oneself off to God, to experience
a living death. Although the experience of this love is hard to express, for
Ruthie the consequences of being in a different mindset are readily apparent
as a living death, as well as in whatever other consequences God might have
in store.

As she elaborated, she expressed pity for those whose view of God differed from hers, because she saw them as closing themselves off to parts of
God's Creation:

The first thing that comes to mind is all the wonderfully diverse people in my life, and I think, *why would you not want this?* Why would you not want this? What kind of a world are you living in, in your little box, when there are so many wonderful people and ways of approaching things and experiences to have? Why would you want people to be so small? It must be pretty bad at your house. And so there's a part of me that always pities what they're losing, because I know you can't be involved in that without paying a price today. Who knows what the ultimate price is. But I don't know how you can be connected to God. I mean, aren't you moving away from the life force, if, in fact, your goal is destruction, segmentation?

For members such as Ruthie, a theology could be called "liberal" because it meant that God's love is given liberally, that there is plenty for everyone.[6] At the same time, this view can cast those who disagree as unloving. In a theology where love is central, to characterize someone as "unloving" does not necessarily mean that they are "filled with hate," however.[7] Although apparent contradictions in Scripture posed a problem for theological conservatives such as Missionary Church's Betsy Meisensahl, those contradictions were embraced by liberals as different contextualized instances of God's overall message of inclusive love. However, just as those who disagreed with conservatives' foundational assumptions could seem immature in their faith, the same dynamic appeared for the liberals—in spite of their claim to embrace diversity, they could pity but not embrace those who disagreed with and threatened to denaturalize their key assumptions.[8]

The Conflict at City Church

Although Missionary Church members rarely aired their dissenting beliefs, at City Church dissenting beliefs were invited. City Church's dominant view of God meant that disagreements had to be respected and discussed, but this invitation to dissent made it harder than it was at Missionary Church for members to feel connected to one another and to God. It is in its absence that we can most clearly see that church members seek communitas—Turner's term for a sense of unbounded community and connection.

Unlike at Missionary Church, the clergy and many of the more active lay members at City Church believed that God's revelation continued throughout human history and that God spoke to different people in different ways. The gift of prophesy did not die out in biblical times; such leaders as King and Gandhi used their prophetic gifts to teach humanity about love and justice. If God could speak to many different people in many different ways, even through different religions, then it was not people's role to silence others about their walk with God.

Thus, at City Church, issues surrounding homosexuality had been debated. The result was what members described as "pain," "anger," and "wounds." Four years before I attended the church, the congregation had begun to study homosexuality and the Bible and to consider joining the RCP. For two years, members of the pastoral staff conducted classes based on both sides of the debate.[9] A committee of members called the reconciling congregations task force had arranged educational and outreach activities, such as bringing in speakers and arranging movie outings, but the task force felt that the church was not getting any closer to joining the national Reconciling Congregations Program. With a few exceptions, members of the task force felt that their efforts were largely ignored.

When they were not ignored, the attention was by no means entirely positive. When the Reverend Fred Hershey, the liberal senior pastor, taught a course called "What the Bible Says about Homosexuality," a participant in the congregation taught his own class in a church meeting room called "What the Bible *Really* Says about Homosexuality." This person, John Brown, reportedly taught participants that homosexuals were very likely to molest children and openly accused Fred Hershey of not being Christian. Throughout the process, a few other members similarly attacked and besmirched Reverend Hershey and his wife Rebecca. John Brown saw the unspoken politics of pro-gay education and responded with his own political organizing, including contributing to phone and mail campaigns urging members not to support the task force.

Sensing that the educational process they had initiated was unproductive and that the personal attacks were becoming too hostile and frequent, the task force's activities culminated in a congregational meeting intended to form a consensus on the question of whether to join the RCP. The date of that meeting, October 20, 1994, was recalled in infamy long after the meeting was over. Many members who attended the meeting would, when I was with them two and three years later, describe it as "painful" and "raw." Linda Renaldi, for instance, described that meeting as a nearly unbelievable event in the history of her congregation:

> It's like something you'd read about: "A riot erupted in a church base-
> ment, when they were like . . ." And it's like, whoa, stop! This is [the
> big city]. It's 1995, or 4, whenever it was. So, it's disheartening. It just
> set everyone back. It's like, God, is this where we are? You shaking your

finger at me and me shaking my finger at you and you getting so upset
and crying and *you* crying? And people just breaking down. I mean,
grown men sobbing. On both sides. Very raw. And look, we're all so
desensitized. You see all this stuff on TV, and it's like this doesn't happen
in real life. All these people are sobbing and yelling in a room, and you're
like "Whoa! This is better than *COPS*."[10]

Dawne: But if you saw it on TV, you wouldn't believe it: "Yeah, like
that's gonna happen!"

Linda: You'd be like, yeah, that's a script. That's not real. Then all of a
sudden you're like, this is a little more real than I've bargained for. How
vociferous everyone was going to be, how big this was going to be.

At that meeting, many members gave impassioned, angry, or tearful comments. John Brown had loosely organized opponents to the process, whom
he was reported to have directed from the balcony overlooking the meeting
room. Some people stood up and announced that family members, including
some who had been members of the congregation for years, were gay or
lesbian.

The effects of that meeting were still felt late in 1996 when I began attending. The meeting had resulted in the writing of a compromise statement,
declaring City Church a "reconciling congregation," with lowercase letters
to indicate that gay men, lesbians, and bisexual persons were indeed welcome in the congregation but that City Church was not allied with the national RCP movement or officially a Reconciling Congregation.[11] The four-
paragraph statement, written by members with a range of views, began with
a history of the congregation from its nineteenth-century beginnings in a
settlers' fort. The third paragraph read:

> We welcome all people to the life of this congregation. We believe that
> we are all sinners in need of God's love and grace and that God, through
> Jesus Christ, intends the church to be a community which incarnates
> love, grace and justice for all people. Holding true to that belief, we
> welcome and encourage all persons, including gay men, lesbian women
> and bisexual persons, in all aspects of our Christian life together.

This statement appeared in the church bulletin each week, but little else was
said about homosexuality, in part for fear of sparking another controversy
or reopening old wounds. An unchallenged (to my knowledge) history of
that period, read to various groups of members two years after the infamous meeting, summarized the intervening years: "Unfortunately, progress

ceased as offended parties licked their wounds, resentments festered, some members left for other pastures, and the [reconciling congregations] Task Force activity was minimal."

During the first exploratory period, members on both sides found themselves often frustrated, angry, and hurt. The sides were clearly delineated. Even people who advocated "moderation" risked being labeled as either supporters or detractors. Those who didn't fit on one or the other side tended to stay out of the conversation, despite others' efforts to bring them in. With this polarization came frustration. For instance, Ron Wilson and his wife Rhonda were long-time members of the congregation, who had chosen City Church because they wanted their children to be exposed to the diversity and vibrancy of a large downtown congregation. Both Ron and Rhonda took very seriously what they saw as the mandate to show Christian love, and Ron especially felt that to simply proclaim that homosexuality was not sinful dismissed God's word as revealed in the Scriptures.

About the congregation's process of discussing and learning about homosexuality and the RCP, Ron remarked:

> We could have done it in a better way, but that's beside the point. I can't go back and change history.
>
> Dawne: What would have been a better way?
>
> Ron: Well, it was pushed too fast, in my view. I know the people in the reconciling congregations committee had felt that they were ignored, that this was getting nowhere, and I guess they finally decided that they just had to push. And when they pushed, things began to break off. I think we just needed a lot more time, and I'm talking in terms of months if not a year or two. More time to try to find small groups to talk about this; other discussions; have outside speakers who were not so highly partisan. We had some outside speakers—well, unfortunately some outside speakers we had were highly partisan pro. And they caused me more trouble, in my view. I would have been far better off if I had not gone to that meeting. Because I came out of there just so mad, I could have chewed nails and spit tacks. One guy, as far as I am concerned, my reaction to what he said was that he was trivializing the Bible. And saying it just doesn't make any difference. When I asked a question, "What does the Bible say on this," and he took, in my view, the most ridiculous and trivial point he could find and quoted that, and it just irked the living daylights out of me.
>
> I went home and steam was rolling out of my ears. My poor wife was really alarmed. I was really upset. And I don't know how many [meet-

ings] I missed. I stopped going to some things at this point. There were some other things, but I just said I can't deal with that. I'm not going to put myself through that again. I think we needed to find reasoned, quiet, more balanced approaches.

Ron felt "irked" not only because he thought that the RCP supporters dismissed him and his beliefs but because, in his view, they dismissed the Bible and would not take his questions seriously enough to account for how their views might be based on God's word. The debate was dominated by people who wanted to avoid conflict, and to do that they could not reveal the ways they disagreed fundamentally with Ron's theology. Instead, they dismissed his concerns as trivial.

RCP supporters, too, felt frustrated with the process. Linda Renaldi, speaking out at a congregational meeting to discuss homosexuality and City Church's recent history, recalled the incident mentioned in chapter 3 in which a fellow church member leaned into her gay friend's space and threatened him with Hell. In the meeting, Linda related the experience as one that affected her understanding of the whole church, saying:

> Well, I feel very strongly on this issue, and I feel like I'm always going to be butting heads against the people who feel very strongly the other way. It's hard; I lost faith in this church when I saw someone practically come across the table at a close friend of mine. And I think it's really hard when someone comes at your friend, or your daughter, or father.
>   Jeffrey Parker [a lawyer in his early thirties]: Or yourself.
>   Linda: Sure.

On the occasions when theological differences over homosexuality put people in a position to air their differing beliefs, the result was that people like Linda lost faith in the church. Throughout the congregation, members observed the ill effects that the "polarization" of City Church had on the Christian life of the church.

When I asked Reverend Curtis Oakes, an assistant pastor at City Church, what had happened at the meeting of October 20, two years prior, he responded:

> There's something we did wrong there. It shouldn't have been as painful as it was. People were saying things about each other, and about some of the clergy, that were really hurtful.
>   That debate, it was painful. It was hurtful. The problem is that there

always has to be a third option. When two sides are so divided, and everyone starts to get such a personal stake in being on either one predefined side or its opposite, they end up saying things they can't possibly support or maybe even believe. The positions get solidified, and the third option, not the middle, but outside that debate, is where the answer and resolution lie.

The thing that was missing two years ago was love. In Corinthians, as you know, the Corinthians were all fighting with each other and Paul says to the Corinthian church that without love, you have nothing. Wisdom fades with age, and he goes through all the things people thought they had, and pointed out what's wrong with them. And the one thing that matters is love, but people were saying some really hateful things here. I think love is the most important thing.

For Reverend Oakes, Christians are called to love, but the polarization made people lose sight of that, acting hatefully, causing each other pain.

Keith Appleton made similar observations, remarking:

I dropped out of the RC debate early on. People were being too mean, on both sides. I didn't want to end up disliking people I liked. On the one side, people were saying gays were going to Hell, et cetera. On the other side, people were saying things like "You're the same people who were opposed to letting blacks in the church and letting women be ministers. If you're antigay, you're also racist and sexist." They'd say that, but I mean they have no idea where people stood on that or where they would have been back then. (Reconstructed from notes)

Later, when I asked Keith about whether he thought City Church should hold same-sex covenant ceremonies, he replied:

Yeah, they should, but they can't right now. It would tear the church apart. [. . .] To get into that debate would put me in the place of people being mean, and I don't like that. I don't want to be there.

People on each side try to punish each other; each side sees it as *we* have to win and *they* have to lose. They can't just sit down over dinner and argue about it. It's too important to each side to win or destroy the other side. And they *should* be discussing it. Christians should be discussing it, because it gets to the very heart about what they believe about relationships and society. (Reconstructed from notes)

Overall, Keith's comments point to the ill effects of polarizing debate.

Ruthie Shafer was not a member of City Church at the time of the October 20 meeting, but her understanding of polarization echoes what Curtis and Keith said about that meeting:

> To the extent that we come together, and spend time together, and we learn from each other, in formal and informal ways, then we will evolve as a community. And so you and I have differing opinions, and our opinions will be modified and our approach will be different. That's the healthy way to do it. The polarized way of doing things, in *human* methodology, at the other end of the line, is you and I have a disagreement and it escalates and escalates and we become polarized not just because of our ideas but now because you're pushing me. So now I must become positioned with my ideal because it's my weapon, and the ultimate of that is war. So as Christians we've been given, if you will, tools for working with each other and caring for each other, but we fall short in using them.

For Ruthie, polarization was "human" and fallen, rather than God's way of love. Like Linda, these members all saw how the congregation's polarization led them away from what church should be for. Linda "lost faith" in her church when she saw someone "come across the table at" someone she loved, just as others felt that conflict went against the purpose of coming together as Christians. Overall, Keith Appleton's observation seems quite apt. For disagreeing parties in the church to have a discussion "over dinner" would reveal their very different beliefs about relationships and society. It would also reveal their very different understandings of who or what God is and what God intends for people. And as all of these members suggest, conflict gets in the way of what church is for: using my earlier language, we might say conflict disrupts communitas, the transcendent feeling of boundless connection among people all engaged in the same pursuit. Conflict denaturalizes people's deeply held beliefs, by showing that what seems obvious to one might seem misguided, ludicrous, or blasphemous to another. Instead of helping people to forget their earthly bonds, these conflicts "wounded" members, forcing them to remember their embodied, worldly selves.[12]

Restoring Communitas, Suppressing Conflict

The discussion between Linda Renaldi and Jeffrey Parker took place in a series of reconciliation meetings held two years after the congregation's meeting of October 20, which I attended at the beginning of my time there.

Because of the unsettled outcome of that earlier meeting, the reconciliation meetings were designed to "move forward" while managing the church's underlying conflict. By attempting to "heal wounds" in the church, the organizers were trying to restore a level of consensus and community that had been missing within the congregation.

The organizers of the reconciliation meetings intended for these meetings to generate a new consensus. These organizers, clergy and members of the newly reconvened reconciling congregations task force, sought input from members of the congregation's administrative council and an individual whom they asked to represent the "traditional view." Their goals for these meetings reflected the two conflicting ideals City Church maintained for itself—diversity and community. To foster a sense of community rather than divisiveness, organizers agreed that the meetings should not be called "debates." They would be open for people from all backgrounds and opinions to express their feelings in order to try to help heal the congregation's two-year-old wounds. As a community that valued diversity, City Church would allow its members to share their feelings with one another so they could come to understand one another better.

On the other hand, the organizers also wanted to move the church forward, and forward, to most of them, meant toward becoming a Reconciling Congregation. To this end, each meeting would be attended by a pastor from a nearby Reconciling Congregation to answer questions and allay fears about homosexuality or the RCP. Task force members believed that education was the key to overcoming conflict. This meant that they assumed that those who disagreed with them were, to some extent, ignorant. To be a place that truly welcomed diversity and showed God's love to the world, RCP proponents believed that the church had to affirm the sacred worth of gay people and advertise to the world that gay people were welcome there, by joining the RCP.

In this way, members of the task force sought not to exclude conflict but to bring it to light so it could be neutralized. Rather than silence disagreement, they invited opponents to articulate their beliefs so the reconciling congregations task force could address their concerns through education. Like most members of psychotherapeutic, social work, and related professions throughout the late-nineteenth and twentieth centuries, the RCP supporters believed that those things they defined as problems would be solved if people could simply talk about them. (See Foucault [1965] 1988, 1977, 1978.) Part of the conception of these reconciliation meetings was the assumption that resistance to the RCP was deeply rooted in the psyche of individuals.

In planning these meetings, members tried to create a group therapy kind of environment, structuring them so that members sat in a ring of chairs, with a facilitator rather than a lecturer. Facilitators of each meeting were instructed to read a prepared statement about how people should speak in turn and not attack one another. Participants were told explicitly that these meetings were not debates but a time for each person to allow others to express their feelings and concerns. Although the organizers may have hoped, in the backs of their minds, for psychotherapeutic breakthroughs to be made at the meetings, the reality was that these groups were instrumental in furthering the reconciling task force's agenda of affirming homosexuality and welcoming gay men and lesbians.

At these meetings, RCP proponents tacitly recognized that the congregation associated the issue of homosexuality with painful contention. Proponents thus used the meetings to try to reframe it as an issue about which the whole congregation could agree, an issue of welcome rather than sin. Linda Renaldi was, for a time, a vocal proponent of City Church joining the RCP, and she had been on the reconciling congregations task force. At the meeting that she and Mike Tennison (a forty-three-year-old lawyer and one of City Church's few openly gay members) attended, Linda and Mike tried to disengage the question of "welcoming gays and lesbians" from any source of disagreement. Thus, they had to attempt to divert conversation from the central question at hand: whether or not the church professed homosexuality to be sinful.

At one point the Reverend Bob Welsch, visiting the meeting from a Reconciling Congregation, attempted to direct the meeting to the politics inherent in any decision regarding homosexuality in the church.[13] In the following segment of the conversation, Reverend Welsch stated that the RCP does not consider homosexuality sinful, pointing out that if it is to truly welcome gay people, a congregation must state unequivocally that homosexuality is *not* inherently sinful. In explaining the national terrain of the homosexuality debate in the denomination, he remarked:

> So along with the Reconciling Congregations movement nationwide, there are also these grassroots movements going on. Now, there are others [such as the Transforming Congregations] who say self-avowed gay people can't be welcome as gay, because they are *unrepentant* sinners. That's another disagreement that exists there.
>
> Linda: But the Reconciling Congregations is very clear about being a welcoming group and not being political.
>
> Reverend Welsch: Well, the RCP says gays and lesbians are no less persons, no less whole or sinful than heterosexuals, and don't need to

repent of their being gay. That if you have a wholesome, loving relationship you are living as God intends. The Transforming Congregations say
you have to repent of your identity, be celibate or whatever it takes.

Throughout the conversation, Reverend Welsch, himself a prominent RCP
activist, stressed that being a Reconciling Congregation meant taking a stand
and publicly stating that homosexuality is not sinful. Linda attempted to
steer the group around the question of politics by positioning the pro-gay
position as one of compassion and welcome.

Meanwhile, members attending the meeting expressed concerns that the
RCP would take on "advocacy" and "split the church." A long-time member,
seventy-two-year-old Ethel Patti, interjected:

> My fear is that this issue is going to split the church again.
>
> Jeffrey Parker: Well, a difference, I think between just being a rec-
> onciling congregation with lowercase letters and joining the national
> program, in a lot of people's minds, is that the way it is now, we're in
> control, but if we join that movement, then we're not in control. What's
> the danger of the Reconciling Congregations Program changing to do
> more political or advocacy work? We have carefully avoided the theologi-
> cal issue of sinfulness here, but what if *they* don't?
>
> Glenn MacArdle [an attorney in his late forties]: I think that's where
> education would come in.

Here members struggled to dissociate homosexuality from politics, advocacy, or conflict, and, thus, from the question of whether or not homosexuality was sinful. Glenn MacArdle offered "education" as the solution, thus
positing that disagreement was rooted in ignorance, while suggesting that
"education" would help to *dispel* the notion that the RCP was political.

Reverend Welsch subtly suggested that splitting the church might not
be such a bad thing, given that the alternative would be injustice, but, once
again, his attempt to embrace the political nature of this divide met with
resistance from City Church's pro-gay members. He remarked:

> It has a lot to do with people's feelings on the issue, and the identity they
> want for the church. I know that many years ago, when City Church
> decided to become racially diverse, they lost people. [Ethel interjects,
> "Oh, yes."] I know this historically to be true, and when the Methodist
> Church decided to side with the abolitionists that led to a split that went
> three ways.

Jeffrey: But I'm skeptical that the RCP won't only be welcoming.

Linda: But then we could leave it if we decided not to be a part of it any more.

Mike: With any small organization, to think about joining a larger organization, you have to weigh what you get out of that, and decide when being a part of a larger organization will be mutually beneficial, and terminate the relationship when it stops being so.

Here, again seeking to dispel the notion Reverend Welsch reasserted, Linda and Mike both employed an argument based on administrative procedure to evade the question of whether the RCP would become political. Although they privately agreed with Reverend Welsch's stance—that the church must identify itself as reconciling and declare that homosexuality is not sinful in the eyes of God—they took the public position that the congregation could withdraw from the organization at any time.

The glare of the silence about sin, mentioned above by Jeffrey Parker, became even more obvious to some participants toward the end of the meeting, when another participant, Barbara Jennings, interjected:

But do you accept that homosexuality is sinful?

Linda Renaldi: But, you know, Barbara, that's what we're tap-dancing our little hearts out to avoid discussing.

Barbara: But no, I have heard people say that they accept that. I think this should have started with twenty minutes of conflict management.

Glenn MacArdle: But this isn't supposed to be a debate.

Barbara: I just mean because that training helps people to really hear what each other is saying. I mean, to really listen, to drop your stereotypes, and really hear what people are saying.

Barbara, the director of a nonprofit organization, expressed frustration with the way participants had avoided discussing whether homosexuality was sinful and the way people avoided "really listen[ing]" to one another. This avoidance of debating the political issue, the divisive issue, in fact, the *real* issue—whether or not homosexuality is sinful—characterized the discussions at City Church as well as at Missionary Church. To discuss whether homosexuality must be considered sinful or not would clearly show that the question of God's intent, the nature of God and God's definition of sin, could be a subject of disagreement. Such a discussion would show that people understood God and sin in terms that made sense to them in their own lives. The paradox of this congregation was that its central premise that God can speak to people in different ways would, if demonstrated too overtly, rock the community's foundation. For liberals in the congregation, God could speak to people in different ways, but there were limits to what God could say.

A discussion of sin would serve as an observable example of how people could worship together with very different beliefs about God. The question of homosexuality's sinfulness divided both the City and Missionary congregations, but the divides remained invisible as long as no one engaged in debate. Members could proceed with their worship *as if* God relayed one clear truth. They could sit, pray, sing, and worship together in their sanctuaries confident that they worshipped the same God, whose eternal truth existed on a plane beyond any human squabbles or concerns. They proceeded with that worship unhindered to the extent that they avoided invoking their underlying conflict.

Conflicts within the church hindered these members' experience of God, and led them to feel that they had been distracted from Christianity, as we saw above. When City Church reopened the question of joining the RCP, Linda expressed to me her own frustration with some of the members of her congregation, adding that frustration was not the best response to the conflict:

> I guess what we're all hoping is that [the congregation's administrative council] will vote "yes" [on joining the RCP] and then we'll just deal with it; I mean, that's what I'm hoping. That's kind of where we are. Just trying to get it done and move into the positive phase of it. [I've made] my contribution to it, but I'm *over* it. I'm like, I have a major chip on my shoulder with people who don't get it by now. I get to be more emotional about it than anyone else does. I'm like, "Okay, remember when we didn't let black people in? Remember when we didn't let women in[to the ministry]? When will we stop ignoring the lessons of history?" You know, in fifty more years it'll be aliens [from another planet]. We're gonna let them in too. It's just, "Hello! Wake up! It's not your job to judge who gets in and who doesn't. So just shut up, or get out." That's kind of where I am right now. Which is not the best attitude to have, obviously.
>
> Dawne: What do you think would be a better attitude?
> Linda: For me to *love* them, love them for not loving, and try to focus on this whole healing process. I just have trouble getting past the audacity. And you know, [one opponent] is trying to learn, and evolve, and I think it's really *cool*. And I think they really care about City

Church, and I know everybody does. Everyone cares about their walk
with their God, and they care about the church, and I know everyone
is as passionate in their beliefs and as sincere about it as I am. Usually
I can get to a common ground with people. That's what I do at work, I
coach people, I communicate—people skills are my strength. And I get
such a hard-on about it that I just get pissed off. It's kind of like, you
know, "Enough. Pray about it. Think about what Christ would do, what
is the Christlike thing to do?" It just shouldn't be this hard. So I lose
patience.

For Linda, the debate should not have been as hard as it was; she had become
impatient to the point that she felt she was not obeying her Christian duty
to show love.

Later, Linda explained why she hesitated to agree fully with Reverend
Welsch at the Reconciliation meeting. In her view, to go beyond simply welcoming gay people through the church doors, to acknowledge that homosexuality is not sinful, opened doors to other discussions she wished not to have
with people who could not even bring themselves to publicly state that they
would "welcome" gay people into the church. She referred, for example,
to the potential controversy that could erupt over the *Discipline*'s rule forbidding the ordination of "self-avowed practicing homosexuals" (¶304.3).
Linda said:

We have to go on record as saying, "It isn't wrong. It's okay." And then
that leads us down the whole path of, okay, ministers, what's "self-
avowed practicing"—I mean, that phrase just cracks me up, like they
were teasing, "Okay, you're a self-avowed nonpracticing woman." I
mean, how do you say that you are not practicing something that you
innately are? You know, I might be celibate, but I'm still heterosexual. So
this just doesn't make any sense to me just from a logical standpoint.

Then the whole issue of how do we feel about same-sex marriages.
How do we feel about adoption? How do we feel about raising children?
I don't think we're ready to go down that path. I do not want to go down
that path with these people. I can barely make it down the path that I'm
on, to be a Reconciling Congregation. So I think that's the dichotomy, if
that's what you were referring to.

When I asked why she did not want to entertain these central issues in her
congregation, she replied:

Because we can't even get them to agree that the church should be open to all people. How can we get to any kind of agreement about whether homosexuals should be ministers, about whether homosexuals should be married in the church, about [gays adopting or raising] children—you know, there's no way. I mean, something so fundamental as the basic question, should the church be open and welcoming to everyone, and do we need to make sure that we're clear and even overstate that if possible, is that okay? Yes or no? To me, that's a no-brainer. We shouldn't be having all this trouble, and if we're having all this trouble about this, which to me is a no-brainer, these other issues, where I can understand why people might be more upset—marriages, children—you open a whole 'nother Pandora's box with these people. I prefer to keep that locked, within this group. I'm happy to pursue it with myself. But I don't think I can go down there with everyone.

Linda did not want to open up to debate what she saw as harder questions—those about same-sex marriage, gay people raising children, and the ordination of "self-avowed practicing homosexuals"—when the congregation had trouble with what struck her as a "no-brainer," "the basic question, should the church be open and welcoming to everyone?" To address these questions would risk opening the door to deeper conflict, to more frustration, and cause her to lose more faith in the congregation than she had already.

These harder questions of marriage, child rearing, and ordination were avoided in the reconciliation meetings and elsewhere at City Church. In fact, Reverend Hershey, who supported the ordination of gay candidates, had early on taken the question of same-sex marriage off the table for debate at City Church, drawing criticism from RCP members elsewhere in the city. For Linda, though, and other members of City Church (like Keith Appleton quoted above), the big questions were not something they wanted to discuss.

Given the problems these debates had caused at City Church, we might wonder why the leadership insisted on asking people to articulate their disagreement. They might have been more like Missionary Church, where people could feel love and community because major differences were more effectively silenced. Instead, they invited discussion not to vote democratically on the proper Christian response to the RCP but in an effort to create the changes they believed fulfilled God's mandate. This was observed by Mark Montero, who believed homosexuality to be sinful and opposed City Church joining the RCP. Mark had been vocal in his belief in the sinfulness of homosexuality at one of the reconciliation meetings. Citing both that meeting and a luncheon talk by an outside pastor who was an RCP proponent, he told me:

> This Reconciling Congregation thing, if you observe the way they're carrying it out, it really is a very targeted, sort of one-sided thing. They're pushing this thing through. It's not "Well, let's go and really find out how people feel," it's "Put 'em in a room, make them feel uncomfortable, have this minister say that if you think that homosexuality is a sin then you're probably likely to get out a gun and shoot a homosexual if you meet one." And then say, "How do you feel about the issue?"
>
> The guy sitting next to me, the minister from [a neighboring Reconciling Congregation]. [. . .] His discussion was very similar, "If you are opposed to this, then you're a homophobe, you're sick, you're like, an apartheid"—whatever, you know—*fan*, that sort of thing. So I just think it's hopeless, that they would actually find out how people feel by doing that. I don't think they want to know how people feel.

From Mark's perspective, the activities surrounding the RCP question were advertised as times for open discussion but were actually heavily biased against the view that homosexuality is sinful. Convinced that RCP supporters had their minds made up and were closed to discussion with their detractors, Mark saw those who held the traditional view being painted as supporters of apartheid or pathological killers, just as Ron Wilson saw that view being dismissed as ridiculous and Keith Appleton saw it lumped together with sexism and racism.

The pro-gay liberals at City Church did not wish to set people up in this way; they wanted to be loving and open. They believed that this conflict came at this moment in history as a revolutionary moment, that God was breaking the church open as had happened in the Civil Rights and women's movements, as they believed had happened when Jesus confronted the rule- and tradition-bound Pharisees with his radical teachings of universal love. Believing that God was leading them, they saw it as their Christian duty to enlighten others and to open the church to all. In effect, however, they seemed arrogant and dismissive. Although they may have hoped to achieve the dramatic breakthroughs of psychotherapy in some members, they settled for a more modest approach, offering their knowledge and experience, while avoiding the question at the heart of the struggle—the question of whether homosexuality was sinful or not. To allow that discussion to take place would be to reveal that sane, mature, loving, and intelligent Christians could disagree about what sin is, who or what God is, and what God demands of people. Revealing this divide could easily have split the church, pitting members with different theologies against one another, each side believing itself to be led by God.

Dissent and Discipline

At Missionary Church, people did not express conflicting views, but at City Church leaders periodically invited people to express their disagreements. At City Church, these invitations allowed painful and divisive debates to explode throughout the congregation. The congregation then sought to manage conflict not by excluding certain views, which would go against their dominant liberal theology, but by managing it: "education" was intended to teach opponents of the RCP that their fears were unfounded and their beliefs in tradition misplaced and pharisaic, regardless of what they actually believed.

In spite of the congregations' very different theologies and their very different implications for Christian action, however, members of both congregations tried to suppress dissent and conflict. Both congregations saw certain conflicts, including those over homosexuality, as something their church should avoid. Congregations might engage in conflict over how to renovate their building or whether or not to have a program for homeless people.[14] But when a conflict gets to the heart not just of what it means to be a member of a congregation but of who or what God is and what God intends for people, that is a conflict best avoided, as even to have such a debate would seem to reduce God from the timelessness they see God as defining and inhabiting. "Putting God up for a debate" was a phrase often used by members to establish the impropriety of such theological discussions within a congregation.

In these two congregations, the different theologies shaped the institutional possibilities for debate, which in turn shaped the outcomes. Throughout his studies on topics ranging from insanity ([1965] 1988) to criminality (1977) and sexuality (1978) Foucault explored and illustrated two major types of power and social cohesion, exclusion and discipline.[15] In the earlier model, power works by silencing and excluding dissent. Exclusion or punishment corresponds to a classical understanding of power. Under this model, lunatics spent their lives outside of society, riding on ships of fools; people found guilty of crimes against the king were tortured and executed or imprisoned for life. In short, those who disrupted society were simply excluded—banished, locked away, or killed. In the other model of social control, people were not punished but disciplined—rather than excluding a few extreme or unlucky cases, societies began to police everyone, not just at the level of behavior but at the level of thought and feelings. Psychoanalysis, a method of curing ailments by encouraging people to talk about everything in their minds, figures prominently in Foucault's model of modern social control. Clearly both forms of power coexist.

For Foucault, one method is no better than the other; there is a trade-off. He paints bucolic pictures of lunatics roaming freely across the countryside without a care in the world, of people experiencing a vast range of sexual pleasures with no lasting consequences—as long as they did not get caught and tortured to serve as examples. Although we might question his bucolic portrayal of this mode of power, his image of modern, disciplinary power rings dismally true. In Foucault's understanding, modern discipline has no happy-go-lucky side; people police themselves and each other's thoughts, languages, and identities constantly in formal educational and corrective institutions, as well as in everyday interactions. No one is excluded; the ideal of "inclusion" is thus ambivalent—inclusion in the community is at the same time inclusion in this form of policing.

We can see these ideal types played out in the differences between these congregations. It would be false to say that Missionary Church is less modern than City Church. But City Church's dominant liberalism and its trust in the therapeutic model are reflected in its members' approach to conflict. At Missionary Church, the meetings about homosexuality were configured as lectures: the audience faced forward to receive information from the expert. At City Church, the meetings tended to be held in a circle whenever possible. Leaders sought to position themselves as facilitators, and everyone was encouraged to share her or his feelings and beliefs. These differences stemmed from the congregations' different views of God—whether as an authority figure who had delivered one truth or as a figure that could take many forms and speak to people in many different ways. City Church was liberal and trapped in a contradiction; God could speak to people in many different ways, which meant that God spoke to those whose views conflicted with the leadership of the congregation. Yet if someone believed a more "traditional" view, City Church members had no way of knowing whether it was the voice of God or whether God's message had simply failed to come through to that person. All views were equal in principle but not in practice, as Mark Montero observed.

On the surface these congregations had very different ways of dealing with dissent. But, in fact, people's resistance to City Church's attempts to exercise discipline suggests that discipline is itself another form of exclusion. City Church's approach also posits that dissenters must be ignorant or deceitful, or perhaps just allowing free rein to their anxieties and prejudices.

Both congregations idealize radical inclusiveness, but both must draw the line where they see the opposite of God's intent.[16] These foundational assumptions are ultimately not open to negotiation, regardless of what model a congregation employs to deal with disagreements about God. In fact, rather than accusing dissenters of ignorance or deceit, when members perceived a threat to their foundational assumptions, they often turned to a language of "politics."

chapter FIVE

The Problem of Politics in Church

If members experienced conflict as a distraction from God and church, most defined politics as the very antithesis of religion. This chapter explores those definitions of politics. Missionary Church member Al Delacroix, a computer programmer in his forties, criticized the Methodists' focus on "social issues" rather than the Bible. One day over lunch he remarked:

> I've had a problem with the Methodist Church for a long time. It has involved itself with social issues on way too many occasions. One of the things that I like about the Baptist church when I was going there was that as children were growing up they were being taught the Bible, not social issues. [When] we got out of the Baptist Church we began to get into social issues. Well, I got out of the Baptist Church right around 1960. Well, you can imagine what kind of turmoil we went through in the next decade, because we went through Vietnam, we went through the Civil Rights [movement], we came through so many different things that our church was just constantly in turmoil over, you know, "What should we be doing? What should we be doing?"
>
> Basically, my feeling is if you're a church, you should concern yourself with Christian doctrine and the Bible, period. That's it. Why get all tied up in all that other crap. Okay, that's a nonmissionary attitude, but it's the way I feel. I think we've got a lot of religion in theology, but we don't

have much Jesus Christ, is what I'm trying to say. That's where you find
God. But that's just the way I feel.

And so it's been my effort to try to put some Jesus Christ back into
it. And it ain't been too unsuccessful. But if it tears up the church, it just
does. There's just no guarantee that anything's gonna stay together.
Families don't stay together. Churches don't stay together.

Al took a stand, disagreeing with many Christians, both liberal and evangelical, who believe that the church's role is to uplift fallen society. The social gospel movement in Protestantism, which was involved in the period Al
talked about with issues such as the Vietnam War, civil rights, and feminism,
was based on the belief that it was the church's sacred calling to make the
world a more loving place that affirmed the human dignity of all people.[1]
Likewise, the evangelical movement includes smaller movements that see
social issues as one arena in which to carry out what they see as a sacred
duty to "evangelize," to uplift the world by telling the good news of the
gospel, that fallen humanity can be redeemed through Jesus Christ. These
are very different belief systems, without a doubt. However, in his desire to
avoid "get[ting] tied up in all that other crap," Al disagreed with both. Furthermore, even in disagreeing with his church about its place in the world,
Al still attempted to avoid direct conflict by repeating that his views were
personal, not political; he described them as "just the way I feel."

Al was hardly alone. Many members of both Missionary and City congregations thought that politics was the opposite of church, God, and the
spiritual. When they thought of transcending the fallen world, they thought
of transcending politics. For these members, the church could best be a place
to encounter God when it allowed people to forget or suppress the divisions
and hierarchies that characterize daily life, when it minimized conflict. Especially surprising, even some *activists* defined "politics" as the opposite of
"good" motivations. This chapter explores how, given the controversies over
homosexuality in their congregations, denomination, and society, members
defined the category of "politics" and, in turn, defined its opposite.

In this chapter, I look at how members of Missionary and City Churches,
and their larger denomination, used the terms "politics" and "political," by
examining what categories they defined "politics" against. In exploring what
different people meant by the term "politics," my own definition should be
clear from the outset. There was a great deal going on in these congregational debates that I would term political, but that need not be a bad thing. I
define "politics" as pertaining to the reproduction or negotiation of relations
of power and privilege. This is a very broad definition, drawn to a large extent

from Foucault, under which nearly anything can be said to be "political." These two congregations sought to become less imperfect and worldly by seeking to transcend the worldly realm, by trying to create the sense of timeless and boundless, radical equality of communitas. When members sought to distance themselves from what members considered politics, however, they often had the effect of simply defining themselves as apolitical without disrupting the very political social divisions and hierarchies that structured their congregations.

In looking at the processes through which people define religion as the opposite of politics, I draw from the broad schools of thought known as structuralism and post-structuralism. Structuralist linguists and anthropologists call our attention to the way that language works relationally—we name things to delimit them from what they are not. The linguist Ferdinand de Saussure ([1915] 1983) pointed out that the terms we give things are not inherent in those things but are arbitrary.[2] Even a word such as *apple* does not naturally spring forth from the fruit but is an arbitrary sign that developed through human interaction to distinguish an apple from other fruits, from other parts of the apple tree, from things that are not food, and so forth.

Post-structuralism agrees that human beings order the world through language, but it sees social power working organically through those systems of categories. People inherit language to a large extent, and the power that inheres in it, but language still has a capacity to change and develop. Post-structuralists, such as Jacques Derrida, Michel Foucault, Eve Kosofsky Sedgwick, and Judith Butler, point to the ways that categories can work hierarchically, and even nonhierarchically, to reproduce power.[3] The gendered categories of male and female, for instance, imply certain things about what it means to be male and female, including hierarchies of strength, intelligence, valor, and the like. These hierarchies come to seem "natural" because of how we understand gender as physical difference and, therefore, as indisputable (Butler 1993). Similarly, by establishing a division and hierarchy of sacredness between the categories of religion and politics, members can assign different people to those different categories, thus creating hierarchies among people as well.

Sociologists, too, have examined how people categorize themselves and one another, thus defining in-groups and out-groups, who belongs and who does not, who is on the outside that defines the boundaries of the inside. Sociologist Kai Erikson (1966) analyzed the witch trials of the Massachusetts Bay Colony, examining how witches were defined as outcasts in order to reaffirm the group identity of the insiders. More recently, sociologist Arlene Stein (2001) saw similar things happening in municipal debates about homosexuality in a small town in Oregon. In the debates I observed, however, this process of defining in-groups and out-groups was not a one-way street. Even if only on their own, participants in the debate all engaged in the process of defining what religion was about and, therefore, whose beliefs and behavior were or were not consonant with the church's purposes.

In spite of the existence of conflicts, most members belonged to a congregation because they wished to feel ever closer to God; they wished to connect with that which is "greater out there," to be part of something beyond the stress, selfishness, disconnection, and politics of everyday life. In this chapter we look at the fluid concept of "politics" and see how congregation members used the concept to stand for a large part of human interaction that they repudiated. This concept served as an outside to another concept: church. Members often referred to church in a way that was ambiguous, meaning at least two different things: their own particular congregation (as in "let's go to church"), and the "body of Christ" (Christianity in general, as in "do not tear the Church asunder"). The flexible category of politics served as the opposite to this flexible ideal of "church," but this flexibility worked in different ways. The fluidity of the word *church* helped, in effect, to craft the local congregation as part of the transcendent body of Christ; this fluidity helped to remind members to keep their eyes on the bigger picture. The fluidity of the concept "politics," however, was more complicated.

Dehumanizing Politics

In the last chapter we saw how pro-gay members of City Church tried to discipline other members, in part because they desired to keep the church whole and in part because conflict itself disrupted their religious experience as members of a congregation. Debates over homosexuality made many members of City Church feel personally wounded and disrupted their faith in their congregation. Meanwhile, members at Missionary Church did not have such debates and thus had faith in their congregation as a loving and welcoming place. In both congregations, however, members set up an opposition between church and conflict, and between church and politics. Members opposed church to politics in a variety of ways; this is the case not only because politics seemed to bring with it conflict but also because politics highlighted the sometimes opposing interests people brought with them to church, and because politics grounded people in the very world they sought in church to transcend.

Congregations deal with many different kinds of conflict all the time, ranging from what color a carpet should be all the way to questions of deep theological significance, such as these debates over homosexuality. Any conflict has the potential to be both highly heated and political, depending on its context and the actors involved. Different members might see a conflict as political in different ways. I define a conflict as political when people experience it not as a matter of simple differences of opinion that might change with simple conversation but as something that has to do with people's entrenched interests, including their understandings of the proper relations between themselves and others. The category of the political is very slippery, however, and different people can define certain things as political in one situation but not another. Furthermore, people can use the term to delegitimate those things they do not want to discuss.

Sociologists have argued that the ideal of the separation of church and state gives "the church" moral cachet and apparent objectivity in those "political" disputes that take place in government and public administration. In their research on religious ideals in American political culture, sociologists N. J. Demerath and Rhys Williams (1992; also Williams and Demerath 1991) find that Americans value the ideal that religion is separate from the cynicism and interests of "political life," and that this notion of separation gives religious groups moral authority in public debates. The Constitution's separation of church and state contributes to an American ideal that the church is outside of the cynical and calculating interests of the political sphere, that it has no "interests" in the electoral sphere and thus has a legitimate voice to articulate the objectively "moral" viewpoint in political disputes.

I would add that this separation also works to build and maintain the ideal of the religious sphere as a space free of the dehumanizing powers of politics. I advocate a broader definition of politics than Demerath and Williams, however, one that sees political disputes as not simply debates among legislators and the like. When people (sociologists or otherwise) equate politics with the state, they neglect the broader negotiations and workings of power and privilege, the politics inhering in everyday life. Everyone has a stake in power and privilege, even if they do not wish to be better than other people or to wield control over others. In secular life and in church, the privileges and power people do have can be a lot harder to see than the privileges and power others have over them.

Many members believed that the church could and should guide society at large; even though liberals and evangelicals could have some different ideas about what people and government should be doing (for example, increased funding for social welfare programs versus ending legalized abortion), both thought the world would be better if everyone followed their ideas. Despite this, most of the members I encountered in these two congregations valued the belief that the church is free from politics so that they could find *refuge* from the political world. For one member to accuse another of being "political" was to accuse that person of bringing secular, petty concerns into the sacred realm, of putting the interests of power before the demands of morality, tainting something pure and diminishing something wondrous.

Church members' resistance to mixing worldly concerns with church was highlighted in a casual lunch conversation about sexual morality that I had one day with some of City Church's Young Adult group members. Someone asked Keith Appleton and me what we thought about the case of a young man, Ralph, who dressed provocatively and went out to pick-up bars. Keith called the young man's behavior "promiscuous" and thus immoral.

Curious about the bases of churchgoers' truth claims, I asked how he knew it was immoral. The discussion became predictably uncomfortable and we continued it later over electronic mail (E-mail), where Keith told me it would be impossible for him to explain to someone who did not share his moral language (namely, me) why anything would be immoral. In this e-mailed comment, he wrote:

> When we discuss families, you and I have already found we have completely different frames of reference, so that when I say something you hear it through a filter that I simply can't get around. I've tried. Doesn't work. Same with sexual morality. Yup, I believe there is a right and wrong. I don't think we CAN discuss HOW I "know" right or wrong, because I don't get the sense of a shared language with which to express it. [. . .]
>
> With that avenue shut off, I'm tempted to use the "public language" of saying how I believe sexual promiscuity is harmful to the young man's development of an appreciation for healthy sexual and emotional and intellectual relationships, but that's not a satisfying answer. It is an answer for a world in which everything needs to filter through political screens, and I think political screens are humanity killers. I just can't play that game.

Keith based his morality on something that he could not explain to someone who did not already share his moral vision. He followed a major strain in Christian history, seeing morality as the ultimate, indefinable good for its own sake. To define morality in terms of "health" would be to diminish it by turning it into something focused on mortal goals rather than God. Keith did not wish to explain whether or not promiscuity is immoral in the secular language of what constitutes "healthy sexual and emotional and intellectual relationships." In fact, he equated answers based on healthy emotional development with answers based on "politics." What links these two concerns? In distinguishing morality from both the language of healthy development and the language of politics, it appears that Keith distinguished moral concerns from any goal-based or secular concerns.

Furthermore, in Keith's explanation, "humanity" included both an earthly, or public, aspect and the transcendent ability to know God and God's will. Something must be free from the requirement of "filter[ing] through political screens," in his view, since these screens are "humanity killers." Given the opportunity of using a secular rationale to answer questions about morality, Keith did not or could not answer. To explain his decision, he then invoked Stephen Spender's 1988 novel *The Temple*, identifying with a Weimar-era German character who "lives for things that have nothing to do with politics," who lives to be free from having to be "for or against" people and policies. By refusing to define the basis for his morality, Keith elevated that higher aspect of "humanity" that is not phrased in the language of for-and-against, the killing language of politics.

Keith Appleton dichotomized "humanity" and "politics," where outside the political language of for-and-against lies a space of unadulterated, living humanity. Other members of both congregations volunteered distinctions between politics and religion, in a variety of different contexts. Maureen McConnelly, a high school teacher who attends Missionary Church, distinguished the functions she sought in church from politics, even while allowing that politics may be an important area for Christian intervention. For instance, she remarked on the political debates happening in the church at the denomination's statewide Annual Conference, whose divisive and pro-gay tenor had upset Missionary Church's representatives to that conference:

> I look at church as a time to be with the body of Christ, other people,
> and that's mandated biblically. God wants us to do that, support each
> other. And I do that. I try *not* to get involved in the political aspect of it.
> Sunday, when I went in, I think it was in the Sunday School class, what
> was being said [about heated conflicts over homosexuality at the Annual
> Conference], I don't get real involved in that, because I feel at this point
> in my life what I'm looking for is a place that we can attend as a family.
> [. . .] Maybe there'll come a time that I can be politically involved in
> issues like that, but I tend to be able to separate that.

While allowing that she might become involved in political debates later, Maureen opposed the political work of the church from the part of the church she herself sought, the part that she saw mandated by God. Politics, she seemed to say, is not about being with the body of Christ, not about supporting each other, and not about being together as a family. She was not alone; these were the aspects of church attendance church members tended to value, no matter how extensive their involvement in controversial debates.

Missionary Church member Al Delacroix believed that political or social action by the church distracted members from the Bible and Jesus Christ, as we have seen. In spite of his desire that the church not debate controversial social issues, including homosexuality, Al did believe that Christians might improve the secular world. He said:

> I can honestly tell you this, if the worst thing [two gay people] ever did was getting married, they've got it *made* in heaven.
>
> I know that people who are perfectly straight murder people, cut off little kids' fingers and send them out running, and screaming, "Next time I'll send you his head. Guido." I mean, people who have totally no respect for other people, they could care less—I know perfectly "good" people who could care less if people are starving to death in the streets, sleeping outside. You know, where's the Christianity in that? Why don't they focus on that?
>
> Why don't we go to some nation like Rwanda. Or what's the other place, Zaire? Places where people not only can't get along but actually have mass murders. We send troops to Bosnia and Herzegovina, and all those places over there, so that people won't kill people. We send guns to a country that's using guns. What's wrong with this? Why aren't we sending missionaries? Why aren't they going? Teaching Muslims to get along with Christians and vice versa? Why aren't we in Northern Ireland? No idea. They're Christians and they can't even keep from killing each other. So the fact that there are some hostilities here about homosexual marriages, I'm not surprised, not at all surprised. But I won't be out marching. I didn't march against Vietnam. I haven't said a whole lot about [President] Clinton. I make a joke every now and then.

In these remarks, Al implied a distinction between homosexuality and problems such as violence and people going hungry, which he thought should be Christians' focus. In areas where everyone could presumably agree that atrocities are being committed, Al believed it would be more appropriate for the church to engage the world. But even such a widely shared value, and one about which he spoke passionately, wouldn't move him to take it up as a cause. He remarked, "But I won't be out marching. I didn't march against Vietnam," again seeming to indicate that "being out marching," whether to support same-sex marriage or to protest violence, would not be essential Christian action. Returning to his earlier point about social issues, we see how marching, in his view, would contribute to the "turmoil" that detracts from what should be the real foci of the church—the Bible and Jesus Christ.

Al could imagine the church doing good in the world, but he did not advocate doing anything to create turmoil, even if it would mean moving the church to do that very good. Other members did engage in political or social projects in the name of the church, but many of them also expressed ambivalence about "politics." Twenty-eight-year-old seminary administrator Pete Vogel participated in church politics a great deal, helping to organize the activities of the Confessing Movement for the Annual Conference of which Missionary Church was a member. Even so (or because of that), he was even more explicit than the others in his critique of the debates between the Reconciling and Transforming/Confessing movements:

> I almost see the Methodist Church as too quick just to celebrate an identity. So, for me, I would have a hard time, I mean, there are some folks [living a homosexual lifestyle] that have [histories of] abuse and things like that. If we're in ministry together, then let's bring those people to a point where they can deal with the pain and experience the healing and experience the redemption, rather than using them as a political toy. And I think that's what we're doing. Both sides are using homosexuals as tokens for their own agendas. I think the loser is not going to be the Reconciling or the Transforming [movements], it'll be the person who's in need of healing.

Pete defined politics as using people for agendas, using them as "a political toy"; and elsewhere he made the analogy that it was like kings and queens using pawns to fight their battles. Like Keith, Pete saw this sort of instrumental thinking as contrary to the work of God in the world, even though Pete seemed to see mental health and healing as within the proper realm of the church.

City Church's Ruthie Shafer appeared to identify with political organizing at the other end of the spectrum, associating the struggle for the acceptance of homosexuality with the nonviolent struggles for civil rights for African Americans and with Gandhi and his followers' struggle for independence in India. She also distinguished politics from the proper function of the church, as we saw in the last chapter, describing as "political" any organized collective attempt to make gay people feel unwelcome in the church. She saw that kind of politics as directly in conflict with God and thus creating penalties both eternal and in this life, in the form of a "living death."

On the other hand, Ruthie accepted as proper and godly work that others saw as political. Drawing from her understanding of civil rights activism, she remarked: "Yes, I do have great faith that there's a way to follow the path of Gandhi and Martin Luther King and all the others before us that have shown that you can make huge social change, that you can warm the hearts of mankind, and you can do it in peace. Yes, I do." For Ruthie Shafer, as we saw in chapter 4, the human way of doing things was to be divided, to polarize people, to escalate conflict. Leaders like King and Gandhi had power to "make huge social change," she pointed out, but that force came from individual factors: their spirituality and their ability to "warm the hearts of humankind." In Ruthie's analysis, their power and ability to transform the world came from their "healthy" way of doing things, rather than the "*human* methodology" of polarization and war. While Keith focused on the aspects of humanity that allow people to transcend political divisions, Ruthie focused on the earthly flip side of humanity, the divisions human beings create. In spite of this different focus, both defined politics as destructive of one's own or others' humanity, while they believed that the church had the tools to build humanity up.

Dick Featherstone also went to City Church but disagreed with Ruthie Shafer on the church and on the political role of Martin Luther King Jr. In Dick's view, politics and church should be strictly separated, because pastors, for all their strengths, have no experience in "the real world." Talking about what he saw as the traditional basis of Christian doctrine, he stated:

> Those are what we should put our emphasis on, what the Apostles' Creed says, as opposed to some way-out left-wing social cause; like I say, the Methodist Church is the first one to hop on anything that comes down the pike. And again, we create a lot of ill will, and have historically, for those reasons. And again, the minute it's gone, something else comes along, and so forth.

I asked for examples of things Dick saw causing ill will, and he replied:

> I like Nicki Parnell okay; I personally think she's one of the best if not *the* best bedside ministers we've ever had. But again, her theology is one

of liberation theology! Okay, I mean it's quite obvious, when she starts talking, where she's coming from, you know, standing [. . .] with the Indians and all that type of business, which again to me has absolutely nothing to do with Christianity! Okay?

Dawne: So, does that create ill will? What are you saying?

Dick: I don't know if it creates ill will, but it doesn't do anything to foster the church, okay. It's just something you have to live with, forget about, and so forth.

Dawne: So, what kinds of things foster the church?

Dick: Well, I think one, there's really only one commandment, Matthew: Go into the world and Christianize the world. Which we do hardly any of, as opposed to, like I say, getting involved with every political issue that comes down the pike. And again, just my personal opinion, I don't think the church, or the clergy, have any more ability to deal with political causes; in fact, I think they're less equipped, because they have not had any practical experience in dealing with the real world, okay?

Here, Dick clearly demarcated the roles of religious and political leadership, seeing social justice theology as unchristian. For him, Christianity should be about Christianizing the world and tending to the sick.[4] It had no business dealing with political causes. Dick's directness made me laugh, and he then laughed and elaborated that the clergy's lack of "practical experience in dealing with the real world" made the church distinctly unqualified to address politics and make the necessary compromises.

Recalling the number of Dick's fellow City Church members who had cited the Reverend Martin Luther King Jr. as an inspiration, I asked, "So what about Martin Luther King?" He replied:

I guess, if I were black, I guess I would think a lot of Dr. Martin Luther King, okay. Being white, I don't think he did that much. I don't think he's a priest. I don't think he's a prophet. I don't think he's any of that bullshit. [I laugh.] I mean, really. I think he was a political leader. He fought for people. Like I say, if I were black, and so forth, I could possibly identify more with what he did. He surely didn't do anything for my race, or my people, that I see.

Dawne: So, he was clergy, but do you think he was an effective political leader?

Dick: Yeah. He was. Okay, but again, I don't know that you can go and say—he got out of the clergy realm and into the political realm.

Arguing with those who have claimed King's civil rights leadership to have been prophetic, Dick dismissed that claim as "bullshit." In his view, King was not a spiritual leader such as a prophet or a priest; he was a "political leader" who "fought for people."

Dick established an interesting equation. He asserted vehemently that King stepped out of his role as a spiritual leader when he became a political leader and fought for people. If Dick were black instead of white, however, he said he might identify with what King did. (Likewise, he might have found that "standing . . . with the Indians" was in keeping with God's will and the Christian mission, were he to identify with those goals.) However, in Dick's view, King "surely didn't do anything for my race, or my people." Dick did not identify with him. Dick implied that he would have experienced King's leadership as spiritual leadership if he were black or, in other words, if he had identified with it. Instead, he experienced it as political, since King was "fighting for people," but not Dick's people. When King pointed out that a difference of power and privilege already existed, he appeared to Dick to have created the divisions that Dick had not needed to notice before.

In his personal honesty, Dick Featherstone revealed a striking truth about politics and spirituality in church. Calling a movement "political" can be a surface-level strategy to delegitimate that movement in the church. However, Dick's comments reveal a much deeper experience. On the one hand, he equated "identifying with" a movement, seeing it as fighting for yourself, and categorizing it as prophetic spiritual leadership. On the other hand, he also equated disidentifying with a movement, seeing it as fighting against yourself, and categorizing it as purely political. For Dick, as for many others, the language of for-and-against is clearly the language of politics. On the other hand, the language of spirituality unites a certain group of people with similar goals into a boundless whole; it does not split people up; it is not a vocabulary for talking about inequalities and injustices; it is the unspoken language of simply "for."

Prophets and Politicos

When the church operates with tacit power and privilege, it fails to live up to its own ideal of being a place for all people to commune with God and the body of Christ. It is in part because King brought to light this very tension that many Christians look at him as a prophetic leader. Yet as Dick Featherstone shows, different interests contribute to deciding whose leadership constitutes prophesy and whose constitutes politics. As members found themselves confronted with intense conflict in their church lives, they struggled to define prophetic versus political leadership.

One moment in which people sought to distinguish between political and spiritual leadership occurred in the autumn of 1997 in regard to the Promise Keepers' rally in Washington, D.C. The Promise Keepers characterized themselves as a men's spirituality organization, sponsoring arena-filling rallies whose goal was to better society by encouraging and helping men to take responsibility for their families.[5] Many feminists, including the National Organization for Women (NOW), saw the organization as antifeminist; they saw the Promise Keepers urging men to "take responsibility" for their families as a thinly veiled attempt to roll back women's equality in families. For instance, they quoted Promise Keeper Tony Evans urging men to take back their role as leader in the family:

> Sit down with your wife and say something like this, "Honey, I've made
> a terrible mistake. . . . I gave up leading this family, and I forced you to
> take my place. Now I must reclaim that role." I'm not suggesting you
> ask for your role back, I am urging you to take it back . . . there can be no
> compromise here. If you're going to lead, you must lead. . . . Treat the
> lady gently and lovingly. But lead! (National Organization for Women,
> Promise Keepers Mobilization Project, n.d.)

When the Promise Keepers held their rally, NOW denounced it in the national press as an attack on the women's and gay movements, citing the organization's ties to Religious Right leaders and its organizers' remarks on gay men and lesbians, women, and abortion rights, and warning of a future of gender-based slavery akin to that depicted in Margaret Atwood's *The Handmaid's Tale* (see Ireland 1997). The Promise Keepers maintained that they were a spiritual organization whose goal was to help men take back their biblically mandated roles, re-creating a society with Bible-based gender roles, racial reconciliation, and Christian unity.

In an adult Sunday School discussion at City Church, thirty-six-year-old Mindy Reynolds explained that she saw the Promise Keepers' goal as holding men accountable to God. She expressed her exasperation with NOW and other feminist groups' protesting the Promise Keepers rallies and took issue with their charge of antifeminism:

> The Promise Keepers are wanting to get men together in Washington
> [D.C.], and I don't see why those women are protesting them. I think it's
> really exciting. Not everything has to be political. Why do they have to

call it political? If women can get together and no one complains, why shouldn't the men? If they're going to go back to their families, and help with the kids instead of working so much, then that's good. If you're just doing something, and I attribute something bad to your actions, that's just my bad thinking. If the Promise Keepers are getting together, and the women want to say that they're being political, that's because the *women* are the ones being political.

We can see how Dick Featherstone's equations help us to think about this debate. From the perspective of the National Organization for Women (NOW) feminists, the Promise Keepers fought against the gains made by the women's movement, thus the movement was political rather than spiritual.[6]

Mindy Reynolds did not identify with NOW but with the Promise Keepers' goal, seeing it as encouraging men to be accountable to their families and to help out with their kids. From Mindy's perspective, the Promise Keepers were not fighting against her, but *for* her, regardless of her own family status. She identified with their goal. Thus, she saw their "get[ting] men together in Washington" not as political but as spiritual leadership.

Mindy characterized political analysis as "bad thinking." She concluded that the women of NOW must have been guilty of bad thinking; if they could see what the Promise Keepers do as political, the women of NOW were themselves guilty of that charge. In the discussion, the matter at hand was NOW's warning that the Promise Keepers wanted to take away women's equality in the home. In Mindy's view, opening a public debate with this allegation made NOW guilty of being political. Furthermore, Mindy equated women's "getting together" with the Promise Keepers' gathering, asserting that "women can get together and no one complains." Here, Mindy erased from consideration the countless individuals and organizations who *do* complain about feminist organizing and protesting, including many supporters of the Promise Keepers.[7] She thus enacted what it would be like to think guiltlessly in the context of patriarchal domination, to think in terms other than "politics."

Finally, Mindy echoed Keith's desire for a haven. The Promise Keepers could help create a haven from the effects of contemporary economic instability and long work hours if they would move men to reorganize their time so they didn't "work so much" and could "help out with their kids." "Not everything has to be political," she said, expressing a desire that the Promise Keepers march be an innocent and "exciting" space, a place where they could get men together to move toward the goal of getting families together. In asserting that "not everything has to be political," she seemed to express political exhaustion, a feeling that "everything" has been made political and negotiable, and to no good end.

Dick Featherstone's suggestion, that one sees as spiritual only those movements with which one identifies, and that one sees as political those movements from which one perceives an attack, can also help us to understand the debate about homosexuality as it took place nationally among the leadership of the United Methodist Church. In 1996, a group of pro-gay clergy circulated a statement of conscience, "In All Things Charity" (IATC), urging "prayerfully and with humility" that the UMC change its antigay doctrine.[8] It stated that "Scripture, tradition, reason and experience convince us that 'the practice of homosexuality' is not in itself 'incompatible with Christian teaching'" and that the church's refusal to recognize and bless same-sex unions and ordain gay clergy is unconscionable. It also said:

> Standards of sexual morality and wholeness in relationship are not differentiated by gender or sexual orientation. Fidelity, mutuality, and the rejection of "all sexual expressions which damage or destroy the humanity God has given us as a birthright" ([*Discipline*] ¶65G) are to be expected equally of all persons regardless of sexual orientation.

A number of clergy and laity soon circulated a rebuttal, "The More Excellent Way: God's Plan Re-Affirmed." The statement distanced the pro-gay position from spiritual leadership by equating it with politics. It began:

> Although the authoritative witness of Scripture and Christian tradition teaches that the practice of homosexuality is a sin and that persons who practice such will not inherit the kingdom of God (cf. I Corinthians 6:9–10), this witness has been diminished, ignored, and demeaned by individuals, groups and organizations within United Methodism who are committed to *a political agenda that is destructive to the nature and mission of the Church* and the moral fabric of society in general.

And it concluded:

> We pray that the Church will move beyond this needless debate over an issue settled centuries ago and upheld throughout history by the unanimous witness of Scripture and Christian tradition. God's plan for humankind is not subject to modification according to the whims of personal experience or opinion. The Church will not abandon its biblical

teachings on sin, repentance, forgiveness, salvation and sanctification in order to accommodate a culture at odds with the Gospel of Jesus Christ. Neither will the Church diminish its commitment to the sanctity of the marriage covenant and the integrity of the office of the ordained ministry in order to salve the consciences of a *politically motivated* constituency which knows not the radical demands of the life of holiness and discipleship.

We call upon the Church to recognize again its unique nature as the Body of Christ, "a chosen generation, a royal priesthood, a holy nation, [God's] own special people" called out of the darkness into the marvelous light of God's mercy and grace (cf. 1 Peter 2:9–10). As a people called of God, let us leave behind this distraction and move forward, shining forth the light of the Gospel of Jesus Christ into the dawning of a new millennium.

We stand as servants of Jesus Christ, our Risen Lord and Savior. (Emphasis added)

These passages posit that people who see homosexuality as compatible with Christian teaching neglect God's teachings and are informed not by Christian duty but by secular culture and politics. The beginning statement draws from Scripture to point to the virtual timelessness of prohibitions on homosexual behavior and casts people who disagree with that interpretation as dismissive of the Bible. The concluding section of the statement fixes homosexuality as outside "God's plan for humankind" according to the Church's "biblical teachings on sin, repentance, forgiveness, salvation and sanctification." Likewise, it characterizes the demand for same-sex covenant blessings and the ordination of "self-avowed practicing homosexuals" as "whims of personal experience or opinion" and as "accommodat[ing] a culture at odds with the Gospel of Jesus Christ." These clearly unholy preoccupations are equated with "politics."

The statement repeatedly characterizes the pro-gay movement in the United Methodist Church as political, as "committed to a political agenda that is destructive to the nature and mission of the Church and the moral fabric of society in general" and "a politically motivated constituency which knows not the radical demands of the life of holiness and discipleship." By using the term *political* in this way, the authors and signers of "The More Excellent Way" define the IATC statement and signers as the opposite of the church way, as political. The church way, by extension, is the opposite of their secular motivations. The church will *not* accommodate a culture at odds with the Gospel; the church does *not* abandon the Bible; the church *knows* that the radical demands of the life of holiness and discipleship include commitment to the sanctity of the marriage covenant and the integrity of the office of the ordained ministry. In calling their opposition political, they invoke nature (God's order) as its opposite, thus defining politics and a pro-gay stance as unnatural and their own position as what simply *is*, the truth that should go without saying.

Both statements engage in a struggle for the power to define the church's proper stance. At one level, one can simply call something "political" in the church to delegitimate it. More important, this delegitimation takes place at a deeper level; as the speakers in this chapter so far have shown, when a church member identifies a statement or action as against oneself, as something to disidentify with, she or he is far more likely to see that statement or action as political, and not of the church.

Clearly, no matter how members define politics and the church, they see these things as antithetical. This is not to say that these members are apolitical. They are very concerned with politics, about opposing themselves to politics. Generally, members define politics as divisive, polarizing, sepa-rating the body of Christ, creating ill will—in short, as the opposite of com-munitas. The apostle Paul warned early Christians not to tear the church asunder. But very profound differences of opinion and faith existed in both congregations, creating the potential for conflicts on matters as deep as who and what God is, what God expects of Christians, and what life on earth is about. Furthermore, when members distanced themselves, the church, and righteousness from "politics," they left themselves few avenues for dealing with the inequalities that structured their social worlds—few avenues for actually creating the unbounded equality they idealized.

Disavowing Politics

Missionary Church members Al Delacroix and his wife Lucy have gay friends and, as they put it, they "don't care." Lucy, like Al, saw debates over the sinfulness of homosexuality as distracting from the real goals of Christianity. At one point in our conversation, Al and Lucy rejected the rigid family patterns idealized by many evangelical Christians, which led Al to reflect on his understanding of love as something that goes beyond models of the nuclear family. Both agreed that families have never all mirrored the nuclear family model of two parents with kids, and Al remarked:

> It's never been that. We had a lady who passed away in Florida. She and one other lady had been living together all their lives. When this first

one died, all of us [from work] attended the funeral. It was like, it was a relationship. [. . .]

You know, it's somebody, if you love somebody you just love them. It doesn't matter if it's the same or opposite sex or whatever. Go back to [the scriptural story of] Ruth following her mother-in-law around. I mean, that was tremendous. And today somebody like that would be considered kinky, strange. The family unit can be so many things that it's not fair to pigeonhole and say, like Ward and June [Cleaver, 1950s TV series parents]—is that their name? It's not fair to do that to people. I know a lot of times when we moved into a community we'd suddenly become part of somebody else's family.

Lucy agreed, adding:

But it's weird to say, "Okay, *this* is a family and nobody else can be a family," to be exclusive. Just like [saying someone can't be Methodist or can't be Christian for some reason]. Come on. Some of these people are gonna be so shocked when they get to Heaven and see who else is there. They may not even want to stay!

Al and Lucy rejected the historical idealization of the nuclear family that many evangelicals hold as sacred. They saw the love of same-sex couples and the pain of the death of a partner as the same for heterosexuals and gay people, rejecting any idea that heterosexual love was better than homosexual love.

However, they both insisted that actually *challenging* the implicit hierarchy of hetero over homo would be disruptive. When it came to marriage, or any public statement of being a homosexual, a language of invasion and harm emerged. I asked Lucy about same-sex marriage, and she replied:

Well, I'm wishy-washy on marriage. I think it's their business. But the thing is, I don't want it thrown in my face. I don't want to know what you do in your personal life. I don't see how that enters in—I know it enters into what you are as a person, but it doesn't enter into what you do at work, how you interact with your friends. I guess it's that in-your-face attitude that I don't like. Well, my best friend Rick is a homosexual and somebody had to tell me this two years after I moved away. And they were like, "Everybody in the world knows this," but it just never . . . you know, *I* didn't know. We didn't talk about it. I just knew he was fun to be with and we had a good time together. That's all I really cared about.

> If they want to get married, that's fine. But if they want to get married in the Methodist Church, the Methodist Church doesn't allow it. That's what they say. So, my opinion would be, instead of trying to force it down somebody's throat, okay, go start your own congregation.

On the one hand, Lucy supported marriage and sexuality as private matters, so private that even her friend kept the fact of his being gay from her. Lucy contrasted Rick's silence to a more violent image, where same-sex marriage would be thrown in the faces or forced down the throats of the UMC.[9] Leaving the United Methodist Church to start a new one would be preferable to confronting it, as confrontation was, in her imagery, akin to violence.

Likewise, Al preferred that a new congregation be formed rather than to see continued conflict within the UMC. He underscored their feeling that causing conflict is anathema to the purpose of the church. When I asked him what he thought about the UMC's ban on ordaining "self-avowed practicing homosexuals," he responded:

> I got no problem with that. If somebody wants to be a minister, and they want to be a homosexual, okay, go somewhere else. Every day I get up and I drive to work and there's a speed limit. I might want to run eighty miles an hour, but there's a speed limit. If I choose to go eighty miles an hour, I'm gonna get a ticket. I'm gonna have to obey the law one way or another. I'm gonna obey it or I'm gonna pay the price. And if you decide that you want to be a homosexual, and you know that the Methodist Church has got these rules that say we absolutely will not, then go somewhere else. The word of God is not just Methodist, it's a lot of other things. If you just really are dying to be a homosexual minister, go to the Baptist Church, they love 'em! [Pause. We all laugh.] Just try to get in that door! Try to get in that door! Ooh!
>
> Lucy: Especially Southern Baptist!
>
> Dawne: Okay, well, we've established that's not going to happen, where are they going to go?
>
> Al: Well, they may even have to start their own church. The homosexual movement would not be the first group to start one; Methodism was an offshoot. If you can't work within the group, get out of the group and start your own group. Even with a job, sometimes the organization will go in one direction and you either move in that direction or you go and start your own or you find somewhere else to go. It's just common sense. But why go in and just try to make it a battle all the time? What's the point of that? All that does is make you draw lines in the sand and

choose sides. That's not what the Christian faith is supposed to be about. That's just my opinion, for what it's worth.

Like Lucy, Al affirmed that church policy was not something to be negotiated, but something to either be supported or abandoned with the starting of a new church. Here, the American spirit of enterprise promises to solve the problem. Likewise, a joke about a denomination known to be less accepting of homosexuals than the UMC deflected attention from Al's portrayal of the UMC as an intolerant place that gays called to ordination should leave rather than engage. Clearly, Al and Lucy had wrestled with problems of sin, tolerance, exclusion, and belonging, and they had concluded, contrary to the majority in their congregation, that homosexuality may seem strange to many people, but it is simply a different way to love. Regardless of that, for them avoiding conflict was the key to spiritual transcendence.

By shunning conflict, Al, Lucy, and other members of Missionary Church obscured any hierarchy that may already exist in the church. Lucy's comments on same-sex marriage and her friend Rick illustrate a dynamic where gay people are seen as technically equal but where a double standard operates. He was her friend, they enjoyed each other's company, and he never told her he was gay.

Lucy and Rick were good friends, but one wonders how egalitarian their friendship would be if Lucy ever mentioned to Rick that she was married and had children, or any feelings, hopes, fears, or weekend activities that might have hinted at her sexual identity. Lucy had a privileged position in her relationship, because Rick did the work to manage information about his homosexuality. This does not preclude their relationship being close and meaningful. Rather, it points to the power and privilege inhering at all levels of life, including those we often think of as private and intimate.[10]

There were members of both congregations who believed that the church had a duty to uplift the world. However, while Missionary Church was fairly uniform in its avoidance of *internal* politics, City Church had its share of social gospel Christians who believed that the church's duty to God and the world is to shake the complacency that allows injustices to continue, even within the church. In the Young Adult Ministry's Sunday School class, for instance, a new facilitator used a curriculum that linked scriptural passages to such worldly conditions as overseas sweatshops and union activities. Many members of the class supported the facilitator in using this curriculum and thought it was important to understand how the world worked. At the same time, other members fell away from the class, longing for the days when a different discussion leader had focused more on personal feelings and personal spiritual growth and seeing the new leader's politics as "depressing."

This chapter has shown how people struggled continually to maintain the church as a space free from politics, a space filled with transcendent beings who could leave behind the political world that exhausted them. In doing so, they struggled to maintain a naturalized sense of morality, in spite of the many potentially competing languages of morality available for doing so. In effect, to retain a sense of themselves and their moral viewpoints as timeless, they distanced themselves and their viewpoints from the repudiated category of politics. To retain church as a transcendent space free from politics, they took care not to invoke the structural exclusions and hierarchies associated with the fallen, secular world. Al and Lucy Delacroix, for example, equivocated about allowing marriage to same-sex couples and ordination to "self-avowed, practicing homosexuals." Their struggle to reconcile their own conflicting beliefs was, in a sense, a struggle to remain unmarked. Denying same-sex marriage rights would mark them as constrained by human rules and prejudices; allowing same-sex marriage would disrupt churches and mark their members as participants in politics.

Many members of both congregations strove to maintain an unmarked position of transcendent humanity.[11] This unmarked humanity was a goal and reward of church attendance. However, not everyone in these congregations could maintain a perpetual state of being unmarked. Indeed, many of the self-identified bisexual, gay, transgendered, or lesbian members in these settings experienced a double bind. If they allowed the church to persist in its exclusions, they would be perpetually denied access to the feeling of transcendence and communitas.[12] On the other hand, if they pointed out the discrepancies of power and privilege—the politics, by my broad definition—already existing in the church, they risked being marked by those politics, marked as distant from God and guilty of "bad thinking."

In the women's movement of the early 1970s, the phrase "the personal is political" reflected an emerging understanding of politics as having two sides: oppression and liberation, isolation and community. As women came together in small, politically motivated communities to talk about problems such as rape, discriminatory healthcare, domestic violence, and depression, they confronted these problems as political and oppressive, not just "personal." The feminist consciousness-raising movement was hardly a utopia, even by its own standards, but it saw politics in both oppressive isolation and community resistance.

In the quarter century since that movement's heyday, a more one-sided understanding of politics has taken over. In striving for good, members of these congregations defined politics as dangerous and impure, selfish and heartless. In doing so, they could tacitly create a category of what "politics" was not, and affirm their own membership in that antipolitical category. In spite of its ambiguity, however, it would not do us much good to dispense with the word "political." It is much more useful to scrutinize it, to see how it is used, what it means, and what its effects are. If politics is rooted in current events and concerns, the opposite is timeless. If politics is self-interested, the opposite is selfless. If politics is base, the opposite is lofty. If politics is isolating and combative, the opposite is about togetherness and caring. If politics is about negotiation and compromise, the opposite is about timeless truths.

To call something "political" also implies that it is somehow artificial, as opposed to what is natural. Politics is about negotiations, subject to the compromises and current demands of human beings, struggling with one another to come to an agreement. Its opposite is timeless and not subject to human whims and struggles for dominance; it transcends those human processes. Even in the Enlightenment language of politics, rights are natural to human beings; they are not subject to political debate, but inalienable. Of course, who exactly counts as a human being is subject to change, a historical fact that reveals the power and privilege that underlie this system of categories. Regardless, this opposition between "politics" and the "natural" serves to naturalize members' claims; when their moral language confronted the danger of being exposed as socially contingent, members could invoke politics as the antitheses of whatever they held as ideal.

Politics is a slippery category. Even as these members use the term and define it as the opposite of the church, it is not simply a synonym for "evil." To effectively naturalize its opposite, it needs one set of referents to which few seriously object. There are some things that no one disputes are political—elections and some mass demonstrations, for instance. To tell the participants in such events that they are political actors with political motivations can often be a quite uncontroversial statement. It is that element of objectivity that distinguishes the slippery category of "politics" from a category such as "evil," which not a lot of people consider themselves, outside of the movies. To call something political sounds far more objective than to call something evil.

When members call something "political," however, they often do so to distance themselves from other elements of the political—its smallness, its cynicism, its roots in a specific time and place, its controversy, its self-interest. The speaker need not identify which elements of the "political" she means, and the referent takes on the scarlet letter of politics, the fallen side of human interaction. Members thus effectively cast themselves as beyond politics by disparaging other things as political. But these members are not apolitical. Many are deeply concerned with the category of politics, and all are engaged in relations of power and privilege. By distancing themselves, and righteousness, from politics, they leave themselves few avenues for addressing the social problems that make daily life, and sometimes church life, seem disenchanted and fallen.

I said at the beginning of this chapter that I see much in these congregations that I would call political, but that this is not necessarily a bad thing. From the feminist consciousness-raising movement, other left movements, and Foucault, I borrow a definition of politics as both ubiquitous and ambivalent. The "political," by my definition, includes both the reproduction of power and challenges to it. Like members of these two congregations, I believe that politics is about negotiation. Those members who spoke of negotiation, however, saw it by and large as negative. This is where I differ from them, for indeed the only thing my definition of politics naturalizes is the pervasiveness of power in human interaction and the demand for negotiation rather than silence about that power. When we broaden our sense of what is political, we open ourselves to denaturalizing the world around us, our relationships, our sets of categories.[13]

As these debates make clear, homosexuality has come to be associated with politics, a development that poses a major stumbling block for gay people in the church. Due in part to church and secular debates about homosexuality and gay rights, many members equate homosexuality with politics, fallenness, and secularity—in short, things most churchgoers consider to be the opposite of their church ideal. The problem for gay church members is to disengage from politics and the fallen world, to find ways to achieve or retain the unmarkedness essential to experiencing church communitas. From the perspective of those who both struggle and worship within such equations, the idea that church is a space free from power and privilege is an ideal that can seem far from reality.

For people whose belonging in the community and whose full humanity and fundamental equality to all others was problematic, the politics present in the church could be quite visible in everyday life. Yet they too wished to belong in that space of unproblematic personhood previously retained for the white, the heterosexual, the male, and so forth; they too wished to inhabit that space of innocence and transcendence, but their mere entry into it would problematize that space. Maintaining silence about church members' conflicting interests did not make those conflicting interests disappear. By refusing to allow conflict to emerge, members allowed discrepancies of power and privilege to continue, contrary to the church's need to spark in all a feeling of the radical equality of communitas.

chapter SIX

Body, Spirit, and Sexuality

Being involved in a political debate could disrupt members' lives and experiences of church; being the subject of such a debate is a whole different story. This chapter explores the subjects of these debates: sexuality, gay men, and lesbians. Brian Dodge was a quietly gay man in his thirties and a member of City Church. When I asked him whether he thought homosexuality was sinful, he replied:

> This is my perception of other people: When they hear the word "homosexual," many of their thoughts go right to the sex acts. And, from my standpoint, the fact that I am homosexual or gay has much more to do with support and bonding with an individual. [. . .] More so in past experiences [than] with women that I have dated . . . sharing, the intimacy and the sharing. It is part of that, but that's not my premise of what comes to mind. It's when I form that bond or attachment with another individual.
>
> Dawne: There are people who are antigay who would say, "Sure, that emotional bonding is great, and we should all be nurturing each other, and if two people who are of the same sex love each other, or have an emotional bond, that's fine; they just can't have sex."
>
> Brian: And in my mind I don't have sex in a committed relationship. Maybe it goes back to people's definitions. And in my definition, five or ten minutes is sex. But when I share my emotions and everything that goes along with me [he

laughs] it's a four to five hour experience [I laugh and nod]. It's making
love. And that's part of that bonding, it's not just a quickie or whatever
you wanna call it. There's something that's shared that I don't think
is there unless two people are very close, and that's straight or gay or
whatever.

Brian distinguished love and intimacy from the physical sex acts that may
have accompanied them. By making this distinction in response to a question
about sin, Brian explained how it was that he felt he could be gay, be physically and emotionally intimate with someone with whom he shared a bond,
and be in a "right relationship" with God. In effect, he claimed that although
"sex" might be sinful, "making love" and sharing intimacy are spiritual.

As a member of a congregation where homosexuality captured seemingly everyone's mind and threatened the congregation's peace, Brian had
to negotiate the dichotomy between spirit and body that sometimes invisibly
structured the way many members thought about life (at Missionary Church
as well as City Church). In this opposition, spirit is equated with godliness
and transcendence while the body is its absolute negative: equated with an-
imality, earthliness, and fallenness. The spirit is sacred, the body is profane.
By no means am I saying that members all hated their bodies or hated sex.
The spirit/body opposition has a life of its own, structuring the way many
Americans think so that it is hard to imagine that something, or someone,
could be both spiritual and physical at once. In these congregations, where
most members saw heterosexual marriage as the only thing that converts
bodily sex into something spiritual, anyone seen as being sexual outside of
marriage became marked in opposition to the spiritual, as sinful or carnal.

This opposition between godly spirit and sinful body grounds much
American Protestantism, as well as much of Western thought. This distinction is commonly linked to particular views of God and sin that have roots
in the writings of the apostle Paul and later Augustine.[1] However, we must
recognize that the dichotomy between spirit and body is a social creation. In
fact, it is a political distinction, whose meanings have changed as people have
used it for a variety of purposes. For instance, in European and North American thought, white Christian women, and nonwhites and non-Christians of
whatever gender, have been seen as particularly grounded in their bodies.
This view has been used to cast these groups as less spiritual or even less human than white men (or white Christians in general), and therefore needing
to be tamed, managed, or suppressed.[2]

The distinction we have already seen between the transcendent and spiritual church and earthly, physical politics is but one version of the theme

of the opposition of spirit and body, a theme that members must negotiate constantly. Other parallel oppositions include those between morals and science, between marital and nonmarital sex, and between right-relationship and sin.[3] In each case, members struggle to attain spiritual feelings by transcending the bodily, fallen, or physical. This happens through the feelings generated in church activities, feelings of connection, of warmth, of release, of being filled or overwhelmed or accepted or loved in a sublime, ineffable way. However, attaining a feeling of transcendence—whether in church services, pastoral counseling, committees, Bible studies or prayer or fellowship groups—is never complete. Church members have bodies, and they see each other as bodies—in fact, they see some as more rooted in bodies than others.

Church: A Haven from Sex?

Before examining in depth the more overtly social negotiations of the body/spirit distinction, it is important to get a taste of what may be at stake in these negotiations. Perhaps part of what allows the body/spirit distinction to persist is that it allows church to be a place of refuge from the vexations of sex in contemporary American society, the anxieties provoked by bodies. As we shall see, some members of these congregations associated sex with pain, shame, or confusion, while they associated the church with solace and clarity. They associated changing sexual rules with chaos and instability and the church with stability and timelessness. Thus, for these members, the move to legitimate homosexuality within the church threatened to disrupt this source of solace, clarity, and stability. Before we talk about changing social attitudes about sex, it is important to recognize that church and a relationship with God may help people to feel safe from *internal* anxieties.

Sex can provoke anxiety. Jerome Washington, a twenty-nine-year-old teacher and member of City Church, discussed frankly with me some of his own anxieties about sexuality.[4] Jerome was conflicted about whether homosexuality was sinful and saw himself as "coming down in the middle on this issue." For him, the controversy at City Church two years prior to my arrival had a great deal to do with people's unwillingness or inability to "confess," to speak honestly about what really bothered them. In his view, people who were against joining the RCP needed to confess that they had their own issues, stemming from their childhoods or from feelings they have had in adulthood. Jerome said:

> The church and a lot of heterosexuals in it have some confessing to do.
> It's clear to me that the church has to think about why they have been so

opposed to gays and lesbians. A lot of it is that two years ago no one was really having a very productive discussion. Productive would have been if people had said, "This is what I think, and this is why, and it has to do with this thing from my childhood, or these feelings I have, and this is why this is threatening to me." And if the Reconciling people had said whatever it is they would have to say; I don't know what that would be. But a lot of us straight people have to confess that it really threatens us, and our sexuality. If it's okay for someone else to do that, then you start thinking about things from your own life in a new light. What did that mean, back then, could that have been . . . ? And that's very threatening.

And the other side must have some confessing to do, too, though I don't know what that would be. Maybe they think they're heterosexual sometimes or something.

In the United Methodist Church, confession is an individual process between each believer and God, and it can take place during services or in individual prayer. It implies a letting go of what separates one from God, so the individual can approach God with a clean heart. In this sense, Jerome implies that some sin and untruth underlies the church's opposition to gays and lesbians.

Although few members were willing to discuss concerns about homosexuality in such personal terms, Jerome believed that many members of the church associated sexuality with certain issues about personal feelings and relationships. Including himself in the group of heterosexuals with "some confessing to do," he believed that a lot of heterosexuals in the church hesitated to move toward fully including gay people in the church because of what affirming homosexuality would imply for their own biographies.

The possibility that God endorses alternatives to heterosexual marriage can provoke the anxiety of losing an apparently timeless truth. In effect, homosexuality problematizes the timeless, "natural" truth of heterosexuality. But this was not all Jerome meant: for the church to legitimate nonnormative sexualities would reveal the complexity of every person's sexuality, that sexual identity is not the straightforward matter that the church has, until recently, made it seem for most people.[5] By invoking childhood and past relationships, he suggested that many straight people feel their own ideals of themselves threatened by the possibility that God created and endorses homosexuality.

Jerome implied that the belief that homosexuality is sinful can help to make a heterosexual identity feel stable. If homosexuality is undeniably sinful, and I am a straight member who believes that I am in right relationship with God, then those "things from my childhood, or these feelings that I have" are not threatening to my sexual identity. I can regard them as the normal transitory thoughts "everyone" has. If, however, homosexuality does not necessarily conflict with being in right relationship, then my own feelings of right relationship are not enough to secure to myself that I am truly heterosexual. Jerome's speculation about what "confessing" would be required of gay people reveals his concern about the fluidity of sexuality sending people into personal crises of identity, identities that depend, in his view, on the church maintaining theologies and doctrines that distance homosexuality from God.[6]

Sex and the Married Methodist

For many people, it is common sense that not just gay sex but sex in general is profane rather than sacred, part of the fallen, physical realm and not the spiritual. Members of these two congregations generally saw marriage as a spiritual refuge from anxieties about sex, such as those Jerome Washington described. Although different Christian movements in American history have looked in a variety of ways at the relationship among body, spirit, and sex, most of the widely popular ones have seen sexual activity as appropriate only within marriage. This is the view the United Methodists capture in the 1996 *Discipline*. Marriage is essential to making sex righteous, in UMC doctrine as well as in the everyday theologies of members. The UMC calls sexuality "God's good gift to all persons," and includes in this gift nonprocreative sex, so long as it takes place within heterosexual monogamy.[7] As we have seen, the *Discipline* asserts that "persons may be fully human only when that gift [of sexuality] is acknowledged and affirmed by themselves, the church, and society" (¶65G). The *Discipline*'s authors seem to use the word *sexuality* to mean human beings' capacity to be sexual, but they clearly state that the capacity to be sexual is only affirmed "in the [heterosexual] marriage bond."[8] In stating that the denomination does not "condone the practice of homosexuality" and considers "this practice incompatible with Christian teaching," the *Discipline* defines homosexuality as sex acts (and condemned ones at that) and thus tacitly confines homosexuality to the category of the physical. This link becomes problematic when, as we shall see, church doctrine and members assume sex to be the opposite of spirituality, the opposite of transcendence.

The vagueness of the term allows debates to persist, with both sides seeing themselves as grounded in church policy. In stating that sexuality is God's good gift to all persons, the *Discipline* opens a position from which pro-gay members can challenge the teaching that homosexuality is incompatible with Christian teaching. What does it mean to say that sexuality is God's good gift? What does sexuality mean in this context? What kind of gift is sexuality to people who the church does not allow to have sex?[9] As they ask these questions, a key task for the pro-gay movement is to dissociate homosexuality from promiscuity, or illegitimate sex, and associate it with legitimate and spiritual love, which in UMC doctrine and in these congregations is believed to be monopolized by marriage.

Although the *Discipline* reflects the work of the policy-making delegates to the quadrennial General Conference, it is not a cornerstone of daily religious practice for most Methodists. Few own or read it, and many do not know what it is. In spite of the UMC's policies on sexuality, many members' understandings of God do not lead them to see sex as something God wishes them to celebrate. In both congregations, clergy needed at some point to state explicitly the *Discipline's* stance that "sexuality is God's good gift to all persons." Few people seemed to understand sexuality as something that God had anything to do with. For some, it seemed that if they believed sexuality to be God's good gift, they saw this "gift" as something God left on humanity's doorstep in a basket and wanted to hear no more of. Few I heard from saw sexuality as similar to the other gifts God gives people, such as talents or grace, which many Christians believe they should foster and share with the world.

Members of both congregations might even concede that sexuality is a godly and wonderful thing, but that tenet would be hard to glean from simply participating in the congregations, for at both places even the matter of righteous sexuality was barely discussed. The exceptional times, when legitimate sex was mentioned in church, are instructive. At Missionary Church, an adult Bible study on "Making the Most of Your Marriage" mentioned "sexual wholeness" as part of a strong marriage, saying it "refers to the total male-female relationship, not just fifteen minutes of intercourse. Sex is a special look, a touch, the way you relate as male and female. There should be unique behavior between husband and wife that is not shared with anyone else" (Maxwell 1996, session 2:3). Clearly, the entire course reaffirmed the belief that sex is only legitimate within church-endorsed, marital sexuality. Beyond that, in teaching this lesson, leaders in the congregation seem to have endorsed the view that sex within marriage is not a matter simply of reproduction but of personal fulfillment within a marriage, by definition a relationship between male and female. This sexual component of a strong marriage was one of six subcategories under the category of "Compatibility," and received no discussion in the class.

For members of Missionary Church, proper stewardship of the gift of sexuality meant sex was to take place only between a man and a woman in marriage. Once people were married, it seemed, they would discover the bond of marital sexuality as a gift from God. The unmarried could talk about it only from the position of the uninformed, who knew nothing of what God had in store for them after they married. For an unmarried member of the class to speak authoritatively of sex would be to admit to falling to the earthly temptations of lust and promiscuity. Because sex was so little talked about, it was unclear whether members saw it has having a spiritual role in itself (which the *Discipline* suggests), or whether they saw it as a gift in that God allowed people to do this one unspiritual thing within marriage because it could lead to the spiritual experience of having children (a view which some members suggested to me). Regardless, no one asked what "sexual wholeness" meant in the class where it was mentioned, and no one asked how to achieve it. Missionary members and clergy made clear, however, that marriage was what converted the brokenness of sinful promiscuity into the promise of sexual wholeness.

City Church members also revered marriage, and believed it meant lifelong commitment and working through the tough times. Many City Church members' views mirrored Missionary Church's position, but, as with everything else, City Church was open to a wider range of opinions on sex and marriage. Not all believed that marriage was necessary or sufficient to move sex from the physical realm to the spiritual. This congregation included a number of divorced members, and while Missionary Church and many at City Church saw divorce as necessary when human sin overwhelmed the potential for a marriage to work out, others at City Church saw marriage itself as a human, and thus flawed, institution that could serve as a covenant with God, but that could also serve many other, less godly purposes.[10]

Not only did many members believe divorce could sometimes be necessary but some also did not see marriage as the necessary marker of distinction between spiritual sex and sinful sex, or purely physical gratification. For some members, same-sex relationships might join "nonpromiscuous" extramarital sex in the realm of the loving and nurturing and, therefore, godly sexual relationships.[11] Accompanying openness to different forms of sexual expression seemed to lead to a greater anxiety for many members of City Church than Missionary Church. There was less of a sense of a shared referent when people talked about sexuality being God's good gift, and less of a language was available to define the boundary between righteous and sinful sex without sounding judgmental to other members.

Some of the wide variation became apparent when RCP supporters told different groups at City Church that the *Discipline* defines sexuality as God's good gift. Alex Carter, City Church's seminary intern, believed that Christians should revel in and thank God for the gift of sexuality, rather than thinking of sex as a shameful secret to which God might turn a blind eye. In his view, sexual expression between two nurturing people was in itself a spiritual experience and a way of experiencing the love that God has for people.[12] In leading about twenty members in a Bible study group on the topic of homosexuality, Alex stated, "To Christians today, it seems we don't see our sexuality as a gift from God, but it is. Think about it. We thank God for our food; but do we thank him for our sex?" The group seemed, for the most part, pleasantly surprised by the question. Few had ever thought about it that way, and some brought it up with me in the following weeks and months as something they thought the church should talk about more.

What it meant to think of sexuality as God's good gift seemed more lost on the Young Adult Ministries' members, where the spirit/body distinction seemed more firm than it had been in that Bible study group. On a weekend retreat, the focus for discussion and meditation was love and relationships. It was a topic of great interest to the group of a dozen or so, all single except for one gay man, who had a boyfriend, and one woman, who had a boyfriend. One woman was divorced. The group that went on the retreat was largely concerned with how to find and maintain a good and fulfilling relationship. Alex Carter led the retreat, and during one of the discussions, asked us to reflect on what qualities we thought were important in an ideal partner. Group members mentioned ambition, having a religion similar to their own, a sense of humor, kindness and consideration, and a shared belief that commitment should be for life.

Alex handed out a diagram that described love as made up of a balance of three components: intimacy, the "close, connected, warm, and bonded feelings" that characterize friendship; commitment, a love that is decided on as a duty to be with and to care for someone; and passion, the "drives that lead to romance, physical attraction, and sexual consummation." He said that the church's ideal was consummate love, a love that included all three of these in some balance.

None of the retreatants had mentioned physical attraction or passion as important in a relationship or marriage. When Alex pointed that out, Winona Douglass and Keith Appleton took issue with his claim that physical passion was important in a marriage or committed love relationship. Winona had mentioned "ambition" as a very important attribute of her future husband, and I challenged her on her claim that physical attraction was not important, saying, "Ambition alone wouldn't be enough to make someone attractive to you. Since you're straight, you wouldn't be attracted to an ambitious woman, right?"

Winona replied, "Well, I'm working from the assumption that I'm heterosexual. That's the starting point."

"Yeah," I said, "And that's physical, right? So the physical does matter *somewhat*, right?"

As we went back and forth, it became clear that I was annoying her. This is not surprising in itself, in that I challenged her basic assumptions, but what was striking was that her annoyance sounded defensive, as if she heard me (and Alex) accusing her of something bad, as if physical attraction were itself bad or fallen. Later in that same discussion, the group talked about how relationships fit in with religious or spiritual life, and members tended to answer these questions with regard to whether they could go out with someone of a different religion or how to get their partners to go to church. For most of the twenty- and thirty-somethings in this group, there seemed to be no thought of sexual love being a spiritual aspect of Christian life, which was a view Alex maintained. In fact, members of the group were surprised when Alex told them about the *Discipline*'s stance on sexuality. For these members, the physical enjoyment of sex could not be mentioned or thought of as a component of a "good" relationship, at least not in a church setting. To be spiritual was to be not bodily.

Like the YAMs, many other City Church members maintained and negotiated a distinction between sex and spirituality, even if they did not uphold the normative understanding of marriage or believe that sex was contrary to spiritual life and fulfillment. Gay members confronted this spirit/body opposition when they realized that many members associated homosexuality with the physical realm. At the beginning of this chapter, we saw Brian Dodge negotiating precisely this opposition when he distinguished between "sex" and "making love." Aside from his belief that God approves of his being gay, his view of sex echoed strikingly the definition of sexual wholeness put forth in Missionary Church's Bible study course, down to the time limit.

Brian was not alone in seeing gayness as having a place on the spiritual side of the spirit/body divide. His initial critique of what he saw as other people's view of homosexuality, as out-of-context physical sex acts, echoed the distinction Linda Renaldi seemed to make when she critiqued the *Discipline*'s rule against ordaining "self-avowed practicing homosexuals" (¶304.3). "How do you say that you are not practicing something that you innately are?" she asked, drawing our attention away from what the

writers of that phrase must have had in mind when they invoked "practicing homosexuals." The passage's writers most likely intended for the "practice" of homosexuality to denote having sex with people of one's same sex.
Linda, however, saw homosexuality not as something someone practices or
performs but as something "you innately are." Just as Brian distinguished
physical sex acts from emotions and intimacy, Linda distinguished physical homosexual practices from the mental and spiritual identity of "who
you are."

Yet members like Brian and Linda rarely disrupted publicly the church's
dominant understanding of how homosexuality fit into the spirit/body dichotomy. The overarching sense that came from these congregations was
that many members saw sex as opposed to the proper church matters of
righteousness, spirituality, emotions, and the truth of who you are. Sex is
about physical bodies, while church (like godly, married sex) is about the
disembodied soul. This is the opposition Brian Dodge negotiated privately
in distinguishing a ten-minute sexual encounter from "making love." Only
in private could the body and spirit be joined.

This understanding of sex can help explain part of why homosexuality,
as an alternative to normative sexuality, causes such explosive debates in
church. In a sense, congregations generate communitas, connection between
people, by suppressing the material realities of everyday life—including the
physical markers of white, brown, and black, male and female, rich and
poor, old and young. They negate their bodily distinctions as they think
of themselves and one another as transcendent beings entering a godlier
plane. Church marriage ideally brings that communitas and transcendence
into the relationship between two people; it turns ungodly sex into godly
marital "relations."

While many members believe that traditional marriage converts bodily
sex into something spiritual, the idea of same-sex marriage does the opposite. Exposing the fragility of that which people often deem sacred, or the
strength of that which people deem profane, mixing marriage and homosexuality threatens to taint the spiritual transcendence of marriage rather
than to uplift the idea of gay sex. Gayness, for many, seems trapped in the
physical realm. Many members would say that same-sex marriage cannot be
spiritual because lesbian sex and gay sex are sinful acts. However, even some
members who did not believe homosexuality to be sinful were disturbed by
the concept of same-sex marriage. With the specter of same-sex marriage
lingering in the air at City Church, it seemed that to bless a same-sex union
would threaten something about heterosexuals' own marriages.

Although City Church did not host a same-sex union ceremony, a nearby Presbyterian congregation had. The Reverend John Doyle, pastor of that congregation, had this to say about the controversy that followed his blessing the union of a lesbian couple, two prominent and well-liked leaders in the congregation:

> To have gay and lesbian folk be able to celebrate in a worshipful ceremony, in the presence of a caring community and their God, their relationship seemed to be a threat, and that was a repeated theme. And that's an interesting theme to follow. If I'm in a more cynical mood I say, their marriages must not be in good shape [both laugh]—guess that's why they were doing that!

Some heterosexual members left his congregation after the blessing of that union. These same members who left had been content to have these women in leadership roles, content to belong to a More Light congregation (the Presbyterian equivalent of a Reconciling Congregation), and content to worship in a congregation with many other gay men and lesbians. But blessing their union was too much. Knowing of such congregational crises was part of why Senior Pastor Fred Hershey had kept same-sex marriage off the table for debate at City Church.

We can answer Pastor Doyle's question about why same-sex marriage seemed threatening to different-sex marriage if we realize that many members see same-sex sexual contact as physical or animal—the opposite of the spiritual, loving, and transcendent bonds of marriage. If the church can bless such "purely physical" unions, then traditional marriage loses the elevation that made it so special. Indeed, if marriage is supposed to be spiritual, then it is supposed to transcend bodies. Only people whose bodies do not draw others' attention, it seems, can appear to transcend them.[13] What gay people do, in part, when they demand that the church view them as whole persons and gay members of the body of Christ is to call attention to the bodies that gather when souls commune.

When people avow (or do not disclaim) their "practice" of bodily, nonmarital sex acts while demanding to be treated as "persons of sacred worth," they challenge the separation of sacred worth from the realm of physical desire. Because of marriage's role in legitimating and spiritualizing sex, when same-sex couples demand the right to marry they challenge the belief that homosexuality is necessarily physical and not spiritual. They challenge the ability of church tradition to have defined the limits of spirituality when it defines legitimate sexuality. Furthermore, insofar as the church sees homosexuality as "physical," same-sex couples and their spokespeople demand that the church acknowledge that physical bodies as well as spirits can be part of the sacred bond God creates and recognizes. Thus, gay and lesbian members' challenge to this understanding of God also challenges, in part, the way that church members rely on the distinction between body and spirit to organize their thoughts and actions. In challenging this distinction, they also challenge church members' ability to seek and find respite in the church from the physical, political world.

The Nature of Sex, Science, and Politics

When gay people *do not* seek marriage rights in churches, many members, drawing on their underlying religious views, associate gay people with all of the implications of nonmarital sex: promiscuity, selfishness, immorality, the physical. When gay people *do* seek marriage rights, however, it becomes clear that many church members see "same-sex marriage" as both immoral and an oxymoron. City Church's pro-gay members faced certain problems as they attempted to establish that homosexuality was not the opposite of spirituality. In their efforts, they often neglected the spirit/body hierarchy, and thus they inadvertently reproduced the idea that homosexuality is physical, not spiritual. Rather than frame homosexuality as spiritual, they dealt with the concerns many members had that homosexuality did not belong in the church because of its links to politics.

Most of the gay and pro-gay members I heard from insisted that homosexuality is an innate disposition.[14] This argument works to change people's minds, in part by likening being gay to being female or nonwhite, having characteristics that the church has traditionally devalued but which have, in a number of ways in mainline circles, been accepted as irrelevant to questions of moral or spiritual worth. Pro-gay members used the "born-gay" argument to turn conversations away from the question of whether homosexuality is sinful. In doing so, they attempted to frame such a question as prejudicial, like asking if being female or black is inherently sinful. For instance, City Church's Reverend Ricardo Montalvo took part in a City Church reconciliation meeting where someone asserted that homosexuality was clearly labeled as "sinful" by Scripture. He responded:

> Well, I think we need to take into account that the Bible is a living document and we need to understand it with regard to social science and medicine, and the advances they have made. And they have proven that homosexuality is natural, like being male or female, man and woman, that it's natural and people are born with it.

For Reverend Montalvo, the findings of science should help inform our understanding of God's Creation and keep us from asking whether homosexuality is sinful or not. His stronger point, however, is that the Bible is a "living document." This removes the thorny matter of conflicting interpretations of what the Bible "really" says or does not say about homosexuality.

Similarly, I asked the vocally pro-gay Ruthie Shafer, of City Church, whether homosexuality was sinful. She, too, responded with a language of science, remarking that homosexuality was "God's biological design," which, "like the cosmos," we will better understand "as technology moves forward." Ruthie sensed God's direct intervention in her life and saw much of life as deeply spiritual. Rather than seeing homosexuality as a spiritual calling, however, Ruthie's rationale for seeing homosexuality as not sinful depended on its being something science could prove to be innate and therefore "God given." The distinction is subtle, but the lack of moral volition in her model has tremendous implications for pro-gay theology.

In insisting that homosexuality is bodily, innate, and properly examined by science and medicine rather than religion, these members ignored the church's constant theme of the divide between body and spirit. While seeking to show that homosexuality can be part of God's plan, they failed to address many members' belief that an innate characteristic need not be godly. In effect, they failed to address the distance many members perceived between homosexuality and the spiritual.

Insisting on the physical roots of homosexuality entrenches homosexuality on the physical side of the spirit/body divide, rendering it the opposite of spirituality. Furthermore, as we have seen, negotiations about sexuality can seem even more unspiritual when they disrupt church transcendence, for instance, by challenging the unspoken ideals of marriage and calling attention to the bodily aspect of church membership. That challenge alone would make homosexuality seem not to belong in church. But there is even more that makes homosexuality seem unspiritual.

The church movement for gay rights challenges the idea that the church is pure, innocent, and apolitical. Each of these critiques can, from the perspective of members, make the gay movement seem opposed to the church's purpose. First, in contemporary American society, homosexuality has become inseparable from the social movements that have demanded equality and rights, or more radical changes in the social organization of sexuality. When people who were once considered antithetical to the community of believers demand equal participation, authority, and recognition in church, they challenge the imagined timelessness of the sexual norms on which many churches were traditionally built. They challenge the unspoken assumption that these sexual norms are politically innocent and transcendent. Second, they may also challenge the rules of propriety that can make a congregation into a cohesive community. As soon as someone demands to belong to the church, their sense of already having been denied that place confronts its members. Again, the democratic process, where people demand representation, appears to invade a sphere that is idealized as separate from politics.

Gay movements in the church may cast the church as political in a third way. Given the church's traditional castigation of homosexuality as sinful or even abominable, from the 1950s onward the American gay movement has had an oppositional—when not downright confrontational—attitude toward organized Christianity, especially Catholicism. This hostility was most dramatically enacted late in 1989 when thousands of activists organized by ACT-UP (the AIDS Coalition to Unleash Power) and WHAM (the Women's Health Action Mobilization) staged a civil disobedience and vocal protest at New York's St. Patrick's Cathedral. They protested then-Cardinal John O'Connor's refusal to allow safer-sex information or condoms to be distributed in any facility under his administration and his public endorsements of similar policies in the secular arena. Disrupting Mass, the protestors attempted to point out that if the cardinal could blur the boundary between church and state, then he made the church into a political actor and opened it to political critique. They dramatically broke through the line that had until then, even for nonmembers, demarcated church as sacred. They shattered, for the moment, the haven church was supposed to be for members.

Seeing this part of the gay movement, some church members may fear that all gay men and lesbians want to disrupt the sacred, that they see all of religion as fair ground for political demands and disruptions. Even some of those who paid no attention to direct action in churches spoke of challenges to church traditions as "putting God up for a vote." Some seemed to associate changes in sexual mores with chaos, politics, and secularity and not with the timeless truth of God. Changing sexual mores destabilized what seemed solid; when the church starts to change, it may seem that it takes traditional teachings away from those who have relied on them as stable and God-given truths. Thus it does not take angry direct action to threaten that worldview.

Given the terms of the debate, many in the church blamed gay people for importing politics into the church. It was common among members to see gay people as causing trouble, disrupting church members' way of life. Pro-gay members thus struggled to establish that homosexuality was not necessarily political. In doing so, they tried to show that gay members would not necessarily threaten what heterosexual members have come to expect from church: the affirmation of their way of life. In doing so, these members attempted to show that gay people could belong in church.

At the reconciliation meeting she, and I, attended, City Church member Meredith Keaton, a public interest lawyer in her late thirties, attempted to recast gay people as people who fit within the church. When a participant in the meeting asked what would change if City Church joined the Reconciling Congregations Program, Meredith was the first to respond to the question, saying:

> In my understanding there are two things. I'm on a mailing list for the RCP. We believe we're open and friendly, but being in this program, we'd be on a mailing list so that gays and lesbians would know that they are welcome here. The second thing is that we'd have access to materials and programming.
>
> Reverend Randall Ewing [pastor of a nearby Reconciling Congregation]: The biggest difference is the access to materials. When new members come for orientation, I can give them handouts from the RCP, and there's a new curriculum for church school called "Claiming the Promise," for use with an adult class. Our church just tried it out and it will be available soon. The other difference is that when gays and lesbians come to [my] church, we reach out to them.

When asked what joining the program would change, Meredith and Reverend Ewing both stressed that the RCP would give them access to resources and put their name on a mailing list. It was a standard argument in favor of joining the RCP; Linda Renaldi made that point at a different meeting, and I heard Mike Tennison make the point several times: joining the RCP would not change anything, except to provide access to resources, to give them opportunities to network with members of other Reconciling Congregations, and to print their name in a directory so that gay and lesbian people could look it up and see that City Church welcomed them.

This focus on resources belied the fact that the RCP would not begrudge resources to any congregation that requested them, regardless of whether it was a Reconciling Congregation or not. In fact, the RCP had already provided City Church members with literature, contacts with other congregations, and access to the national RCP Convocation. Clearly, the point of joining the program would be to bring the congregation into an alliance of congregations that affirmed that homosexuality was one form of God's good gift of sexuality, but rarely did an RCP supporter at City Church make that point. Rather than discuss this more controversial aspect of joining the RCP, Meredith and Reverend Ewing focused on downplaying the controversy, by comparing the RCP to a gay movement critiquing the church in a wholly different way. Meredith interjected:

> One thing that seems to be a question in people's minds that I have talked to is whether this is a radical movement, like ACT-UP or something, where they go around chaining themselves to things. I've found out that the RCP has a history of peaceful demonstration with regards to the General Conference. They had that movement that was about "the doors?"
>
> Reverend Ewing: "Open the Doors."
>
> Meredith: Right, where they, in their capacities as ushers, would open and close the doors to the room for the conference, deciding who could go in and who couldn't, and I'm told that people there all knew what that was about. So they have a history of peaceful protest, but not a radical protest aspect.

Meredith volunteered the distinction between the RCP and ACT-UP. It was not clear whether anyone recalled ACT-UP's action at St. Patrick's Cathedral, but that is not at issue. ACT-UP's direct action tactics also included shutting down the National Institutes for Health and stopping stock trading on Wall Street, tactics aimed at bringing attention to the lack of availability of drugs for AIDS and to profiteering in the health care sector. ACT-UP never injured anyone or tried to, never used bombs or firearms; however, when Meredith distinguished the RCP from ACT-UP, she stressed that the RCP was "peaceful." No one pointed out that the only violence associated with ACT-UP's demonstrations was that inflicted on ACT-UP members. Something about ACT-UP struck Meredith as what her fellow church members, if not she herself, would see as *un*-peaceful. That something must have been their direct action tactics, which threatened the daily, unproblematic life of people whose lives were not already disrupted by AIDS, as well as the belief that church-normative sexuality was timeless, sacred, and unassailable.

ACT-UP had threatened church members by challenging directly the way of life they saw as their own. ACT-UP was threatening because it was radical. An ACT-UP–like RCP would be radical in that it would challenge the *root* of antigay belief in the church; it would both call profane and make profane things that the church held as sacred. But the nonviolent RCP described by Meredith would not threaten or challenge the church. In fact, Reverend Ewing and Lorraine Eastman, a former lay leader in her fifties, immediately pointed out that many heterosexual people were involved in the organization. Following Meredith's remarks about ACT-UP, Reverend Ewing leaned on the assumption that heterosexuals would not threaten City Church members the way homosexuals did. Regardless of their beliefs, something about homosexuals was itself threatening. In fact, something about homosexuals was itself political.[15]

Meredith, Reverend Ewing, and Lorraine all tried to show at the meeting that the RCP was not radical but peaceful, and that many heterosexuals could participate in its actions. In effect, they tried to show that gay people themselves did not pose a threat to the church but sought to find a place for themselves within it, to belong. This argument sometimes explicitly addressed the question of politics, as at this meeting, but, more often, it skirted the issue of politics, as people attempted to show that gay people fit within the boundaries of church life. Yet the one thing members did not dispute about church life, its spirituality, was something RCP supporters failed to link to gay people. Homosexuality was cast as physical, or potentially peaceful and apolitical, but not as overtly spiritual.

Church, as a spiritual place, is a place where members would like to be free from politics. This was true even of those members who felt forced, by their own inequality, to make political demands for equal recognition. Even these people felt a need to maintain their innocence of politics. This is the bind liberalism can place gay church members in: like most members, many crave an innocence from politics that is impossible at this moment in history, when rights are seen as dispensed to and withheld from people on the basis of group membership.[16] Just by seeking the same transcendence and communitas as heterosexual church members, gay members could be perceived as invading and politicizing someone else's sacred space.

But many religious conservatives, especially in these two congregations, no longer saw gay people as a group but as individuals who did particular sinful things or who had particular crosses to bear.[17] From this perspective, the equation of homosexuality with politics could be blamed on gay advocates themselves, who insisted that the church's treatment of gay people parallels that of civil society. These members insisted that homosexuality was a physical difference and, therefore, a site of political exclusion. Any demand for formal equality, in church or elsewhere, drew from a language of democracy, a language of politics. Yet in much Protestant thought, at a certain level, the question of political equality is moot, an earthly concern rooted firmly in people's bodies and the world's fallenness. When people's spirits each relate individually to God, bodies can become irrelevant. Just as insisting that homosexuality is only physical will distance gay people from the spiritual, simply asserting that not all gay people are political activists fails to take into account the powerful opposition between spirit and body.

In basing claims on bodily distinctions and explicitly insisting that homosexuality is not a spiritual matter of sin or righteousness (but is, instead, a physical matter of difference) gay and pro-gay activist church members in these congregations and elsewhere insisted that physical difference already divided the spiritual realm. Or, looked at another way, they made these debates overtly political by insisting that sexual difference is physical difference. The members behind this strategy sought to move the church to recognize same-sex relationships and affirm gay people. They, no doubt, sought to protect gay people from any inquisition-like situation of having to prove their spiritual connection to God, by removing the question of whether homosexuality is sinful from debate. Indeed, they saw such a belief as a symptom of the church's traditional homophobia. But by drawing from a language of secular politics, they inadvertently established homosexuality as "political." In a community where "politics" is the opposite of everything good, the task for gay members at City Church was to attempt to distance themselves from politics.

The Politics of Sex and the Politics of Belonging

Body and spirit constitute each other, and in much Christian thought a living being must be both at once. Thus, all church members negotiate the spirit/body opposition; yet sexually unmarked church members are not seen as fundamentally physical and unspiritual the way gay, lesbian, bisexual, and other sexually marked members are.[18] Furthermore, heterosexually identified members have mechanisms in place, such as marriage, to help them negotiate the spirit/body divide and see their sexual desires and actions as spiritual. Gay members could look at their sexual desires and actions the same way, as Brian Dodge looked at his, but each gay member in these congregations, to my knowledge, had to rely on informal guidance, improvised theologies, or maybe private pastoral counseling to negotiate the divide. Few at City Church challenged the divide's validity. Gay members' own religious views tended to be shaped by the same spirit/body dichotomy that devalued them, and thus their strategies for gaining membership were limited to moving the boundary between inclusion and exclusion, rather than challenging its existence.

The lesbians and gay men I talked to at City Church all felt that they had to manage their sexual identities in order to negotiate the spirit/body divide, to feel certain that other members recognized that they belonged in the sacred and spiritual zone of the church. Insofar as members' mental pictures of homosexuality were drawn in stark opposition to everything they saw as righteous and spiritual, some gay and lesbian members found themselves struggling to show that they were not the living embodiments of sin. As they did this, however, they redrew the line between who belonged and who was excluded, a line that defied the Christian ideal of radical equality and inclusion.

Redrawing the line between inclusion and exclusion meant establishing that gay people can be "just like us." In the minds of many RCP supporters, when others believed homosexuality to be sinful, it was because they believed myths about homosexuality itself: for instance, that homosexuals participate in sadomasochism (SM), dress in strange ways, and molest children. To establish gay men's and lesbians' belonging, they sought to dispel these myths, which circulated sometimes among fellow church members and sometimes in the news and other mass media. Why consensual SM or weird clothes would be equated with molesting children is an important question. [19] In perpetuating this mythical equation, people cast homosexuality not just into the dichotomy of spirit versus body but into the related dichotomies of love versus violence and even good versus evil. Behaviors and styles that posed a challenge to the ideal in this symbolic economy were equated with violence or death.

Certainly few of the members of these two congregations expressed such an understanding of homosexuality as violent. However, there are examples of individuals and organizations in the United States that make such claims about homosexuals under the banner of Christianity. In 1992, Pat Robertson wrote a fund-raising letter expressing his opposition to an Iowa equal rights law, asserting (perhaps jokingly) that "feminists were seeking to lure women away from their families to engage in witchcraft, kill their children, and become lesbians" (Pertman 1992). Religious right videos, such as *The Gay Agenda* (1992), depict gay men and lesbians wearing leather or scanty dress juxtaposed with scenes of gay adults with children in order to suggest that gays and lesbians prey on the defenseless, impressionable, and innocent.

Many people who believe homosexuality to be sinful think much more subtly about these issues than the stereotypes presented in religious right propaganda. However, because careful and patient discussion rarely happened between people with different views on the subject, RCP proponents acted on the assumption that dispelling these myths about homosexuality would convince people that it was okay to be a Reconciling Congregation. Marsha Zimmerman, whose daughter is a lesbian, attended one of the reconciliation meetings, where she remarked: "A lot of people are opposed because they don't know any homosexuals, and they think they're all militant and march in parades and wear black leather, so what business do they have being in church?" Whether or not Marsha herself wondered what business homosexuals who are "militant and march in parades and wear black leather" had being in church, she set up a dichotomy between those who belong in church and those who do not. Her strategy in making this comment was to show that most homosexuals *do* belong in church. She implicitly accepted, however, that it is impossible for people to be, do, and wear those things and belong in the spiritual realm of church.

Terence Phillips made a similar distinction. Terence was a graduate student in his mid-twenties and made no secret, in church or anywhere else, of his being gay. Before and after church-related meetings, he often talked with a friend and fellow member about going out to clubs and meeting guys, and he presented himself in a style that was readily interpolated as gay. I asked Terence about his views on the RCP. He replied:

> From what I've experienced, I think it's a really positive thing, and I think it's something that's really needed, and I think it helps change the perspective. Everybody views homosexuals as being promiscuous; some people go so far as to say that we child molest, that we're *recruiting* nowadays, just like the army. [I laugh.] Or we have a benefit plan . . . you know, I don't get it. But I think via the Reconciling Congregations Program, if we have that kind of thing, we can show the heterosexual society that, first of all, the stereotypes that you see on TV, 80 percent of that is not an accurate representation of the gay community. Very few are flaming, you know, cross-dressers, drag queens, drag kings, whatever you choose to label people. Very few of 'em are transgender, but that's what sells. And so that's the chance. I think that with Reconciling they'll see that more people are just average next-door neighbor people. I think that's a good thing.

Terence saw the strength of the RCP as its ability to show heterosexual society that many gay people were "just average next-door neighbor people," not the stereotypical "flaming . . . cross-dressers" he saw portrayed on television.

I asked about his distinction between cross-dressers and those who aren't cross-dressers, saying:

> So why is that good? Would it be a bad thing if a bunch of drag queens started showing up at church?

Terence: That's a subject that totally baffles me. I don't understand why people do it. If it's Halloween and you're just doing something fun, I get it, but as far as the day-to-day kind of "I'm gonna be in drag today!" I just don't see it. I don't understand it. Just like there are people who don't understand me being homosexual, I just don't understand drag. I guess it weirds me out, just a little. But generally for the most part, that portion of the community wouldn't show up at church.

Dawne: Why not?

Terence: Because of the way the society at large views homosexuals. I believe that if they were to walk into any church like that, the Jerry Falwells would be like, "You're going to Hell," or "freak of nature," or whatever. I don't think people would purposely subject themselves to that by going to church.

He wrestled with his difficulty in understanding cross-dressers, recognizing that heterosexuals could express a similar lack of understanding about how he could be gay. Terence seemed to recognize that a similar "Jerry Falwell" kind of hostility that confronts them confronts him as well. Although he imagined that such hostility kept them from going to church, that hostility did not keep him from going to church. I asked about this, and he replied:

Why do I go to church? Because I grew up in church. I have a really strong attachment to church. I love going to church, actually. The spiritual side of me needs to be fed. I guess growing up, you go out of habit, but now I go because I seek guidance and answers to questions about my spirituality and how my sexuality fits into it, and on different moral issues in the day to day, [such as] how can I not feel as bad when I pass a homeless person asking for money when I know I have it. I don't give it to them because the other side of me feels they should be working, you know: "You've got enough time to be begging on the street, [you] have time to work." How can I give without going into debt myself. But that's why I go. I feel that I need to be there; I've always had a strong attachment to church, I've always been involved, that's one of the positive things I have.

For Terence, going to church answered questions about how his sexuality fit into his spirituality, as well as helped him to deal with the side of himself that could begrudge charity to the homeless. This account left open two possibilities, that cross-dressers did not have the same spiritual needs Terence saw himself as having, or that they did not have a space to get them met. Either way, as a gay man who wasn't transgendered, Terence sat on a different side of the line separating those who fit in at church from those who do not.

Elsewhere, Terence elaborated on his understanding of what church is and what is appropriate in church. He rolled his eyes as he described the gay Roman Catholic masses he had attended as *"interesting,* to say the least." He elaborated:

> I understand that homosexuals are trying to come into themselves and be comfortable with who they are. But excuse me, you do not come to church in cotton cut-off shorts like you are going to the bar to pick some- one up. You know, eeuw, you're in church, for Pete's sake! Everyone was kind of cliquish; I was the new person in. I had gone to the church for about a month, a month collective of masses, and I had gone to their little after-the-hour things. I think I met four people there, maybe, who would speak to me. And I was like, "No, this is not what I want." Especially not after the positive experience I had had before I moved to this city. With the gay Mass it was just kind of like, "This is not happening." It was really almost like going to the bars. One guy spoke to me because he wanted to *go out.* So I was just like, *no.*

Terence wrestled with his disapproval of people wearing cut-off shorts to church and showing up with same-sex dates. He said, "I understand that homosexuals are trying to come into themselves and be comfortable with who they are," which echoed his own need for church to be a place to un- derstand how his sexuality fits in with his spirituality. Terence set up an opposition between spiritual church and things that are like "the bar": in the bar, you can show up wearing cut-offs; in the bar, you hang out in cliques, unless you want to approach someone to go out. The cliquishness and bar- like atmosphere of the gay Mass made Terence feel that he was not even *at* church. Terence implied that church was for him a place where people should be friendly, not cliquish. They should approach one another, but not because they want to go out on a date. In short, the bars are isolating and sexual; church is communitarian and not sexual.

Heterosexual people in church communities not marked as "gay" may also believe the same things about appropriate church attire and have the same problems with church members not living up to their standards. How- ever, many churches do try to serve as meeting places for single hetero- sexual people. Churches that condone marriage have an unspoken sexual component; during my time at City Church, the pastoral staff talked repeat- edly about starting a singles' group, citing the statistic that 60 percent of the members were single. Whenever members of the congregation met in the church and later got married, it was announced during the Sunday service and spoken of as an especially joyous occasion in the life of the church. But this sexual economy of the church is largely unnoticed, unless its rules are violated. The spirituality so many members attribute to marriage makes even marriage appear nonsexual.

Perhaps sensing that the kind of trouble Terence thought would confront transgendered people in the church would also confront themselves, most of the gay members I spoke to (or heard about) at City Church tended not to be open about it. Even if they tended to be openly gay in other areas of life, with respect to church they said that it was not the most important thing about themselves or that it was not anyone else's business. These members sensed or feared that if other members of the church were to mark them as gay, such marking would interfere with their work as ushers, choir members, Sunday School teachers, or church committee members. Thinking about helping at the reconciling congregations task force's table at City Church's annual fair, Brian Dodge wondered what it would be like to stand, among members of his congregation, under the gay movement symbol of the rainbow flag.

> I am gay. Not a hundred percent out, or open about it. I feel comfortable in my lifestyle, but yet, I guess, I want people to accept me for who I am, not what I am. [. . .] And that seems to happen at church. And part of my goal in serving on that [reconciling] committee is to extend that churchwide, so that we accept the individuals [as] who they are. Whatever the case may be: race, sexuality, income.
>
> Dawne: So you think that doesn't happen now?
>
> Brian: I'll tell you more after next Sunday. With the City Church Fair coming up, and Mike [Tennison]'s got this thing with the gay flag. [. . .] It's going to be interesting for me to be standing under the sign of the gay flag.

When Brian asked another gay member how people would perceive that, he was told that no one who had a problem with it would think he was gay, because members who were not pro-gay tended to believe that there was only one gay person in the church, and it was Mike Tennison, not Brian Dodge.

Brian's concerns reflected a tension he seems to have perceived in his membership in the congregation. He wanted to be accepted for "who" he was (Brian) rather than "what" he was (gay), and he wanted to extend that to all members of the church. We might even see the opposition between "who" and "what" as parallel to the opposition between spirit and body. On the other hand, Brian was not sure to what extent the congregation could look beyond someone's being gay, once they knew or assumed that to be the case. To feel that he was accepted for who he was, Brian felt that the congregation as a whole could not know that he was gay.

Other gay members had similar ways of dealing with the congregation around issues of their own sexuality. James Clary, a Young Adult Ministry member, and I had a conversation about his being gay, and I asked if he was out at City Church. He replied that all of the members of the YAMs knew, saying:

> I don't try to hide it from anyone, but I don't do anything I wouldn't do otherwise. The Young Adults know and it seems fine with all of them. I mean, it was a little problem with one woman because it turned out she had a crush on me. Everyone else, though, I don't know if they know or not. I teach Sunday School with a guy who had a partner for like seventeen years who just died, and I don't know if he knows. I mean, what am I going to do, wear a flag? I'm not going to do anything I wouldn't do anywhere else. No one's going to force me to. (Reconstructed from notes)

Avoiding the spokesperson role, remaining relatively unmarked, allowed gay church members to stay outside of the equation of homosexuality with the unspiritual and the physical: when James said "no one is going to force me to" wear a "gay" sign or otherwise participate in the duty that various gay movements have established to "come out," he indicated his distance from and even opposition to those movements' strategies (though not their goals).[20] In fact, the coerciveness of the now-mainstream gay movement's strategy of mandating openness became clearer when a number of well-intentioned heterosexual liberals invoked it, because few gay men or lesbians were moved to make *themselves* the topic of debate by accepting the invitation. Avoiding being marked as gay allowed these members to feel they were part of the church and, thereby, open to experiencing church as a place to approach God.

Those members who remained quiet about being gay did so to be able to participate in the church in the way they felt called to, without having their belonging questioned. One couple was openly gay and used their openness in specific ways to show that they, too, belonged in the church. Mike Tennison and Tim Mitchell had joined City Church shortly before the infamous meeting of October 20 and were vocal in their status as a couple and their support for joining the RCP. Tim died two years later, the week before I started attending City Church and just before the congregation reopened the question of joining the RCP. Mike and Tim, a lawyer and a school teacher in their early forties, were for many people the picture of respectable homosexuality, as well as the only gay couple many of the members knew. Many members of the congregation held them up as the reason it was both good and not threatening to be in the RCP.

Glenn and Maeve MacCardle were both vocal supporters of joining the RCP, but they advocated moderation. Reflecting on an earlier time, when a young woman who had grown up there was ostracized from the church after coming out as a lesbian, Glenn said it was necessary for the congregation to make a statement welcoming everyone, including gays and lesbians. The statement was important, he thought, to let lesbians and gay men know they were welcome. To change others' hearts, however, the church would need to provide a particular type of education. Glenn remarked:

> But I think it was important to me to see that we'd rectified that situation [of the gay member being ostracized]. There was a lot of narrow-mindedness, and education does a lot to cure that.
>
> Dawne: What sort of education?
>
> Glenn: I think exposure. I think the best would be if gays and lesbians can join in normal activities and *nobody really knows.* And one of the things I try to encourage people to do is to join in church activities. We've got a couple, you know, who are ushers, and Tim Mitchell died, and he and Mike were ushers. And one guy who was really against gays, but I mean, he just enjoyed these guys and he said—"These guys, hey! They're *fine.*" Accepted them as people. And I think that exposure itself is good.

Glenn saw "education" as what was necessary to overcome the congregation's "narrow-mindedness," an education based on gay members' unobtrusive participation in "normal activities" to show those "opposed" that "they're fine" and could be accepted "as people."

Mike and Tim cultivated the image of themselves as fine people doing normal activities, but not without some ambivalence. Several months after Tim died, I asked Mike about their role at City Church:

> When you two started going, did people see you as a gay couple?
>
> Mike: Oh absolutely. They *still* push us up. That's why I wanted to usher, that's why Fred [Hershey] is still asking me to be on the head

of committees, they push us all out—"You're so *normal*," you know. That's [not necessarily right], but I can understand why they'd like it to be. [. . .] In other words, you've got these two, it used to be two, these two straight-looking people that look like normal people that we can tolerate. And so let's just use them as an example, you know, we want to attract gay people, so let's use them. That may be overstating it a little, but there's some truth in that.

Dawne: So you were the tokens?

Mike: Yeah, in a way. That's too strong a word for it. But that's not the role I want to play. That's not why I joined the church, to suddenly have a spotlight on myself. No reason like that. I don't believe that should be the basis. It's *not* a good basis—taking a person and taking something personal and taking that as their ability to contribute and get it all done.

In this discussion, Mike began to show his ambivalence about his and Tim's role in the congregation as "normal looking" gay people the church could "tolerate." He seemed critical of the congregation's "use" of them as tolerable and normal-looking gay people who could help to attract more gay people into the congregation. He believed that gay people should have full membership rights in the church: unlike those heterosexuals in the congregation he verged on criticizing, though, he did not see being gay, in itself, as a good basis for participation in church activities. He did not see homosexuality as the opposite of being a Christian, yet he set up an opposition between being gay, "something personal," and membership in the church, the "ability to contribute and get it all done."

In reflecting on City Church members' discussions about homosexuality, Mike's ambivalence became even more pronounced. As we saw in the last chapter, Mike had attended one of the reconciliation meetings, where he and Linda Renaldi had played up the congregation's ability to drop out of the RCP if it turned to political advocacy on behalf of gay, lesbian, and bisexual people. When I asked him about that meeting, Mike commented:

I was just listening with astonishment. That was at that meeting, where people were talking about going quietly, doing the educational route; how much education do we give these people?! What's gonna educate them out of bigotry, that a lifetime wouldn't do? I find it very frustrating. It's hard to be tolerant back to people like that. "I don't know. I just don't know if we should be moving on this quite so fast." Moving on *what*? Ha ha ha.

Dawne: So why didn't you express your frustration at the meeting?

Mike: Because that's not the way I do it. It doesn't solve anything; it just puts people on the defensive to argue in front of a group. It's a slow process. And it's a slow process if I'm being logical and clear, and not—what's the word I want—not *radical* about it, these people might just listen. They might accept me as a gay person more easily than someone else.

Here, Mike related a sense of ambivalence about "education" in the church about homosexuality.[21] On the one hand, he was frustrated with the congregation's need for "education," wondering how effective education could be against what he saw as members' "bigotry." On the other hand, he was aware that by presenting himself as "logical and clear," and not radical, people might come to realize that there is nothing about being gay that makes someone inherently unsuitable for membership in the community of believers.

For these and other members, participating in church was not a wholly transcendent experience of vanishing earthly boundaries but one where they regularly considered that church members would question their right to be part of the church. Were the church the place of unconditional love and equality before God that members idealized, no one would be or feel subject to such questioning. In spite of their different modes of self-presentation, these gay members all sought to debunk the stereotype that cast them as the embodied opposite of church itself. Whether quiet about being gay or directly affirming it, these members all lived within the rules of church membership, to actively produce their own belonging by highlighting the ways that they resembled other members, those members whose belonging was not subject to question. To prove and feel that they belonged, they could not challenge the very system of categories that constantly threatened to cast them, and others, out.

These members' experiences show that belonging confers belonging; when the group recognized a member as belonging, the member felt more transcendent and experienced the group as transcendent, far more so than when a member's belonging was in question. Such issues of belonging did not go unnoticed by gay members. One day, the Reverend Cory Jacobsen and I had a conversation about such social boundaries. Cory was a gay pastor at a local congregation who did a great deal of work for the RCP and who was familiar with City Church. He talked about people in his congregation or other places who told him, or implied, that he was "one of the good ones." I said I wasn't sure what to say because no one had ever accused me of that. He said, "You're okay, Dawne. You're one of the good ones."

It felt good to hear, but then I remembered he was just trying to make a point. "If someone actually said that to me, they'd be mistaken, I think," I replied. "They'd have to be thinking I was *like them* in some way that I'm probably not."

"That's what it is," he replied. "They're saying that I'm *like them*. That's what would make me one of the good ones."

In the symbolic economy established and reproduced in these congregations, difference itself fell out of the realm of the spiritual. Difference became the realm of bodies. When members sought to move the boundary of inclusion, to allow in those gay people who otherwise conformed to the church's spoken and unspoken traditions, they ended up treating the church's established way of life as something that should not change. They treated the church's established ways as spiritual and unchangeable—and not only the church's ways of sex, marriage, and worship but sometimes even the church's established ways of dress and comportment.

Belonging in the Spiritual

The spirit/body opposition pervaded church members' thinking, echoing through other divides, such as those between hetero- and homo- and between belonging and exclusion. In one sense, proponents of the pro-gay Reconciling Congregations Program sensed that the opposition's reservations about the RCP were really fears about the church being taken over by people who were different from them, people who would change church from their idea of what church is and should be. One tactic they used, then, was to try to show that gay people were not different from them, but the same. But why should difference be so threatening in a congregation such as City Church that prides itself on its diversity? As Marsha, Terence, and the people who upheld Mike and Tim as model gay church citizens revealed, there was indeed a concern that gay people were inappropriate in a church context, a belief that had to be challenged by showing that not all gay people were *like that*. This problem reveals a tension in the church itself.

Church members strove for the church to match their ideal of love and welcome to all humanity, a place where God's abundant grace could be found, even if the rest of the world showed little. Any standard of boundary maintenance struck most members of both congregations as entirely inappropriate behavior for a church. As Ruthie Shafer pointed out at one of the reconciliation meetings:

> Well, anyone who sees it as us and them is wrong. [. . .] We have to
> learn how to love. That is our mission as Christians. One thing that's
> harder for me is to love those who disagree with me. It's difficult to
> accept, but we must learn. This is not a club, it's a church. It's not about
> who you want to socialize with. If you want a community, go to your
> community center. [Scripture] says the world will know we are Chris-
> tians by the way we love each other. The church should be a leader of
> love in the world

For Ruthie, and indeed for most other members, church was ideally not a
place to pick and choose who gets in; it should be a place to show people the
unconditional love God has for all of humanity. When gay men, lesbians,
and bisexuals demanded equality in the church, they brought to light the
tension that existed around that belief.

In some instances, the congregation at City Church defined who it was
by defining who it was *not*. Social scientists observe these distinctions happening universally in more or less visible ways, but it happened overtly on
one occasion that came to my attention, when an usher spotted a homeless-
looking person in the sanctuary during the service and asked him or her to
leave.[22] And it happened when members pictured drag queens and wearers
of shorts or black leather as inappropriate for church. In these circumstances,
the boundaries of church propriety were explicitly invoked, as when Marsha
asked, "What business do they have being in church anyway," and when
Terence said, "You're in church, for Pete's sake!" Although both of these
members asserted that some gay people do belong in church, their stand
took the form of transplanting the boundary between inclusion and exclusion, rather than uprooting it.

But that is only a part of the problem gay people posed in the church.
It was not simply that the church excluded gay people for being different.
Rather, gay people challenged the unobserved but pervasive heterosexuality
of the church. They disrupted the belief that the one-man-one-woman marriage endorsed by the church was the timeless, natural, and universal form of
human sexual expression and that it was uniquely spiritual. They challenged
the church to renegotiate what (and whom) it categorized as physical and
what (and whom) it categorized as spiritual, and because so many members
saw them as firmly entrenched in the physical, they held the potential to
challenge the very idea that people could not be both spiritual and physical
at once.

Homosexuality is also associated with the physical not just because it is "sexual" but also because it is political. Church members wished to be free from politics, but regardless of the desires of some gay members and their supporters, the gay rights framework of the RCP *is* political by its very nature. By this I mean that the pro-gay movement in the church demanded for its beneficiaries equal rights such as those of marriage and ordination, and that it was based on an analysis of the church's power to shut some people out, to decide who gets the benefits of membership. In this way, gay church movements were political because they recognized that the church is not only a sacred institution but also a social one.

More fundamentally, gay men and lesbians seeking membership in the church involved themselves in politics because they challenged the church to bring to light unspoken systems of authority. Who determines what counts as appropriate is a matter of power, as are the rewards that go to those who, for whatever reason, comply with those rules. In congregations where certain people were accustomed to having authority behind their views, they may have associated that authority with the experience of being part of a church.[23] By challenging some members' experiences of church, gay people could seem to challenge the foundation on which traditionalists had built their relationship with God.

Interestingly, even as they challenged one component of church sexuality, they affirmed and sought to be included in the other. Gay members had two distinct ways of being gay in City Church. One was to be like Mike Tennison and Tim Mitchell, to take on a role of near tokens and risk being the subject of religious and political debate and of being scapegoated for causing all the trouble involved in it. The other option was to stay quiet about being gay, to try to blend in with the membership and do what people go to church to do, to try to stay out of the political fray. Some walked a line between both, attempting to stay out of both politics and the closet by only revealing what they saw as their "personal lives" to those they knew and trusted.

RCP supporters at City Church were limited in what terms they could use to make their case. They could argue that gays were the same as everyone else, or, as we shall see, they could argue that gays needed compassion; but they could not argue that being gay was itself a morally good thing. Pro-gay members never suggested in these congregational debates that being gay is a calling from God. They never argued that choosing to live as gay was akin to choosing to live as Christian, that it was a moral choice commanded by God and righteous in its submission to God's will. This argument is not unheard of in a Christian context. It is possible for someone to identify as Christian and believe that homosexuality, bisexuality, or transgenderism can come to people as God's particular will for their lives.

For instance, at a national conference of the RCP, I attended a seminar on sexuality, and our "homework" one night was to find people at dinner and ask them what it meant to them to say that sexuality is God's good gift. I sat down with two women who were heavily involved with the RCP, Erica and Liz, both ordained ministers and both lesbians, and in this conversation with me, they answered in a way no one in my two congregations would have. Erica remarked: "When we repress part of who we are, we are repressing what God calls us to be. We should strive for a world—and it's a sign of our separation from God that we are not there—where people love and accept each other and ourselves as we are called to be."

Liz later remarked, "For me, it's healthy to be in relationships as a lesbian woman. I am at my best when I'm in relationship." Erica and Liz both believed that God intends for some people to be lesbian, gay, or bisexual, that it is "healthy" for them and helps them to be at their best. But instead of saying people are born that way, Erica implied that just as God *calls* some people to the ordained ministry, God calls some people to be "in relationship" with people of their same sex, a calling where one may exercise one's Christian volition and choose to take it up. This language was absent at City Church. Why? Because it would have made clear to all that people on different sides had radically different understandings of God? Because they themselves did not see homosexuality as something God could call people to?

If the question at hand was "Is homosexuality sinful?" then the members we have heard from can be seen to answer that question either yes or no. Yes, because Scripture clearly says it is sinful, or no—but why not? The members we encountered who believed homosexuality to be sinful all spoke a great deal about volition; the gifts God gave people to choose to live morally, that human beings are not simple robots but have volition. From this perspective, human beings are all born with a predisposition to sin; the essence of transcendence is to choose a better way of life.

Pro-gay members were a little shakier when it came to the question of volition. They assumed that gay people just *are* gay, whether because they are born that way or because they just are for some other reason. They saw sin as that which separates people from God, and they accepted the testimonies of those gay friends and relatives who said that being gay was how God made them. But in basing their belief that homosexuality is okay on the assumption that it is innate for all gay people, they disallowed those gay friends and relatives from even expressing the possibility that positive choices had a role to play in the formation of their identities.

In the remarks we have seen, there was little discussion about why a person would be gay; pro-gay liberals saw questions about the origins of homosexuality as themselves antigay. And they were partially right; such questions are often based on the ahistorical assumption that heterosexuality is natural and that homosexuality is a deviation. But in refusing to address the question of origins, these members also avoided the question of volition. Instead of assuming, as many feminist and queer theorists do, that heterosexuality and homosexuality are both problematic historical constructs, these members attempted to see them both as "natural." By attempting to foreclose the origins question, pro-gay members avoided dealing with the question of moral volition. By arguing that homosexuality is natural, they did not respond to the main concern of those who saw homosexuality as sinful—the question of moral choice. In seeking to naturalize it with a language of bodies, they opened the door to its being denaturalized with a language of sin and volition.

Pro-gay members found it difficult in the context of these church debates to say that gay people can choose to be gay, and that that is a good thing in God's eyes. They found themselves unable to argue (or perhaps even think) that God calls some people to be gay, to say that God demands that some people choose to live as gay, the way they believe God calls or demands that people take certain jobs, marry certain individuals, become ordained pastors, or sing in a choir; the way God calls or demands that Christians choose to live as Christian. In their silence, they denied that homosexuality might be a social good, that God might call people to challenge the ideologies of heterosexuality and the nuclear family that have come to dominate Western, and especially American, society. When they argued about the semiotics of sin rather than the goodness of being gay, they appeared to lack a moral compass. Furthermore, in insisting that homosexuality is biological or genetic, in denying that God can demand that some people choose to be gay, they posited homosexuality as bodily and separate from God. And many members on both sides of the issue saw separation from God as the very definition of sin.

The sociologist Jack Katz (1999) shows how emotions are people's reflections on their bodies in the environment. For instance, he analyzes "road rage" as the built-up frustration at not being able to express sufficiently the violation of a driver's personal space. I agree with Katz that emotions are felt in our bodies, but church members think of bodies and emotions as separate. In fact, we might say that by putting physical sensations to language, we remove them from our bodies; we make them social or spiritual.

To the extent that church members associated homosexuality with the body, openly gay members highlighted the fact that church members go to church in their bodies, and not just with their souls. As they did so, they brought out the physical and other material distinctions that separate peo-ple into hierarchies, and the reality that those hierarchies do not disappear when people walk into the church building. They highlighted the exclusions that have developed within the church, even as it seeks to reach out to the world. They are challenging the church to come up with a new basis for transcendence, one that does not depend on a spirit/body opposition, one that can acknowledge hierarchies and address them, rather than render them unspeakable.

If gay men and lesbians seem too political to simply belong unproblem-atically in church, the task for the pro-gay movement is to find a way to cast them as belonging. Arguing that Scripture does not condemn homosexuality is too direct for a prolonged conversation within many congregations, where such an argument can threaten some members' relationships with and iden-tities in God. To avoid conflict over Scripture, pro-gay members have tried arguing that gays were created that way by God, given innate drives toward members of their same sex; but this chapter has shown that such a framing recasts homosexuality as physical and, therefore, in the logic we have seen, as political. Members have come to another way to try to reconcile these dif-ferent positions and defuse conflict: the truth that comes through feelings.

chapter SEVEN

The Truth of Emotions in Everyday Theologies

When church members saw marriage (or something else) convert sinful sex into a spiritual experience, feelings came into the picture for them—"having sex" became "making love." In these congregations feelings have come to represent truth— not only the truth about sex but, as there is no truth without its guarantee in the divine realm, the truth about God. As we sat overlooking her garden, Missionary Church member and school librarian Jessica Lake shared with me an argument she once had with God, when God had called her to have a child out of wedlock. She found this perplexing given that she had not previously thought God would want this of her or, for that matter, anyone. She told me the story of a man she had hoped to marry:

> He came into my home and for a year I argued with God, because God told me—and I know the only person *I* told was my sister. I said, "Karen, every time I pray, God is telling me he wants me to have a child and it's gonna be a girl." But, I thought, "God can't possibly want me to have a baby until we're committed and legally married." And one day, it was, do you remember the book, *The Thornbirds?*
>
> Dawne: Sort of, I remember that it exists.
>
> Jessica: Yeah, in the book this priest and this girl have an illegitimate son who becomes a priest himself; his name's Dane. He's very up and coming and has achieved all that his priest father wanted to achieve by being at the Vatican. One day he's out swimming when two girls get into trouble, so

he goes out and saves them and then he is out in the water and he's struggling. He says, "Why am I struggling? Lord, if this is my time, then what more could I want than to be with you?"

And that came to my mind, this secular book, came to my mind, and I thought, "God, you know what I am thinking about this. You couldn't possibly want to bring a child into this relationship unless we are married. And you know how I feel about it. But," I said, "if this is your will, okay!" I swear, like that [snaps fingers], that second, there was some little sperm floating around in there that got zapped, you know? And sure enough, we had Tammy. I struggled, I really struggled. I still did not want it to happen.

I remember it was almost a year later and I was reading in the Bible, and it was something about Mary. And when she was told that she had conceived—and here she was engaged to Joseph, he could have divorced her—God said, "I sent my son down. I could have made Him a king. I could have waited until Mary and Joseph were married, but I didn't. Why do you think you're better than God?" And I really was humbled. I was like, you know, "It is, it's your will and it's your way. What purpose this serves, I don't know. But it's up to me to either submit to you, or not." [Pause.] "And thank you for saying something that helps me just put this away and not deal with it anymore."

In Jessica's story, God touched her life in ways she could never have imagined. God told her she was going to have a daughter, even though she knew it was sinful for her to have sex outside of marriage. Then God touched her again, showing her through Scripture that Jesus could have been made a king but God chose to come to the world as a humble child conceived out of wedlock, and that she too could give up her struggle and know that God's purpose would be served. Scripture told Jessica that sex outside of marriage was contrary to God's will. But Jessica experienced God communicating to her in other ways—through a novel.

Members could disagree over Scripture, but they had other avenues for seeking transcendent contact with God. The Protestant account of the trinity—God the Father (or parent), Christ the Son, and the Holy Spirit, sometimes known as Creator, Redeemer, and Sustainer—allowed members to communicate with God personally, as individuals. When members such as Jessica heard God's inspiration or guidance in their lives through feelings, moments of clarity, or intuitions, many of them saw that as the work of the Holy Spirit. When a member felt that God touched his or her heart, he or she might feel him- or herself to be a part of the great fabric of life in Christ. This feeling came about because the member perceived him- or herself in direct contact with the divine. Such a feeling naturalizes the truth the person learns in that experience of feeling. But at this historical moment, it is probably more than coincidence that this most transcendent religious experience was the one that was the least negotiable. Those who knew and worshipped with Jessica would have trouble openly disputing her feeling that God wanted her to have a child out of wedlock, regardless of what they knew from Scripture.

This chapter looks at the emotional component of everyday theologies; it explores how members who seek transcendence may turn to the experience of personal emotions, which is rhetorically more difficult to contest. In our society, we see feelings as a special and almost sacred form of knowledge—a form rooted in the body and therefore seemingly more "real" and natural than abstract rationality. We can regard feelings as indisputable; an effective way to silence argument is to close a potentially controversial statement with "but that's just how I feel." The cultures of psychotherapy and self-help in recent decades have helped make people into subjects who identify with or against their feelings, who take emotions seriously, and who, in many contexts, work to develop a language to articulate them.[1] Yet we retain an ambivalence about the truth of feelings, because they cannot be verified and because so many factors can make them seem elusive or irrational. This ambivalence may come into play whenever people invoke a language of emotion, but it is unlikely to spark controversy, because it seems rooted in one individual's experience.[2]

When an event shapes a person's knowledge of God, that event might be interpreted in many ways. This need to interpret creates problems when people want God's message to be clear, unmoved by social influences, and unaffected by individual interpretations. Regardless of this ambivalence, emotions have come to represent their own special kind of truth. Members, both liberal and conservative-evangelical, often talked about how they knew God's will in terms of the truth of personal feelings—transcendence itself is a feeling, after all.[3] When members relied on their own emotions to talk about God, they sought, in part—and possibly unconsciously—to stave off contradiction, but this use of the language of emotion brought with it a paradox. Personal feelings could force members into ever more polarized positions, because each side could perceive the other as immature, fearful, or misguided—lacking the ability to discern God's true message.

Part of what makes the language of emotion special in our society is that we find it hard, if not impossible, to express the grandest and most profound emotions.[4] Feelings strike us as grander, indeed, transcendent, when we are incapable of articulating them. Thus, sometimes even when we could articulate them we choose not to for fear of seeming not to feel them at all, by appearing unromantic or cold, for instance, reducing a feeling such as love to "mere words." Our inability to express some feelings makes those feelings appear to transcend the earthly in a way few other human experiences can. However, the fact that people find it difficult, and can even resist trying, to put feelings into words can be more or less strategic as well as accidental. Expressing something in a language of emotion forecloses debate, and therein lies its rhetorical power.

Emotions are not new to Christianity by any means. But in turn-of-the-millennium American society, they have come to seem essential, even within noncharismatic religious traditions where emotions were once suspect.[5] Because feelings serve as an incontestable form of knowledge, church members sometimes use them, unintentionally, in their effort to avoid conflict and debate, to make their church experience feel transcendent. Paradoxically, the language that seemed most transcendent could create the deepest and most profound divides between people.

Emotions and Epiphanies

Church members learn about God the way they learn about everything else in the world: others can guide their interpretations, but ultimately what they know comes from their own social experiences. God acts in their lives, and other occurrences shape their interpretation of God's message. Members' desires to transcend the earthly and human realms lead them to extrapolate from their own experiences; they often saw their experiences as versions of God's universal message. Yet wanting to know the eternal God often meant insisting that God's message does not depend on human experience and that others' experiences, if they lead to different beliefs, must not be divinely inspired. Here we look at the comments of three members, one from Missionary Church and two from City Church, that show how different members' emotional experiences appeared to them as God's message about the appropriate Christian response to homosexuality. By simultaneously using and denying personal experience as a way God can communicate, members generated the conflicts they most wished to avoid. Members in these congregations seemed closed to the possibility that God might tell different people different things. They saw the social influences on others' beliefs, but not on their own.

For instance, Missionary Church member Tina Harrison saw God at work on her through her marriage. Her experience with distance from God shaped her view of what God intended for a gay friend of hers. She explained to me how she knew God's desires for her in her life, in seeing what made her own marriage work more smoothly. In her experience, submitting to God's will made her life better. She explained:

> Oh, I don't like the word "submit," because I'm a controller, so I always thought that was ridiculous. And I guess I thought maybe [the Apostle Paul] was a male chauvinist. Because I used to always have an attitude, and I thought most men were male chauvinists. I think that's because my grandfather dumped my grandmother when my mother was fifteen, so I had a lot of bad feelings. [. . .]
>
> When I was about twenty-seven I went on something called Tres Días, the United Methodists call it the "Walk to Emmaus" (a three-day walk to develop church leadership). I just had a whole new change in my concept, because there were several men there who spoke, and who spoke with such love and respect for women. Then I went through a study called "Christ in the Home." It was all about the roles of men and women, and the neatest thing about submitting is that if you look at Christ, he is equal to God, because he is God. Yet, he is not inferior, because he did what God asked him to do.

Tina's experiences in Christian programs showed her men's love and respect for women, and provided her with the new understanding that submission does not require inequality. She put these lessons to use, and she found that submitting to her husband added joy to her life. She continued:

> Ephesians 5:21 says, "Submit to one another out of reverence for Christ." Originally I had memorized that for all *men*. Because it already says, "Wives submit to your husbands." But then it's like, "Oh! I figured out, it's for *Tina*. Tina is to submit, because Christ submitted to the cross and everything else that he did." So it's a way of me learning to serve others and not focusing on the way that my husband should treat me. It's a paradox. When you start focusing on doing things that Christ would have you do, be more service-oriented and loving, you get more of what you want, you get more joy. If I'm this demanding type of a wife, and I used to be more like that, I never got what I wanted. So, I really had a big change when I was twenty-seven.

These experiences shaped her understanding of how God's word makes life better for her, even if it seems at first to conflict with her own mother's life experience and the goals of contemporary political movements, such as resistance to male chauvinism.

Tina's conversion from secular feminism to a deeper understanding of Christianity improved her life. She felt greater joy and started to get more of what she wanted, paradoxically, when she stopped making demands, when she became more loving and less self-centered. This experience seems to have shaped her understanding of homosexuality and how it is sinful; she remarked:

> The whole point of church is to help people accept Christ as their savior. When I became a Christian, I didn't change overnight, and I wouldn't expect that a gay person would either. I would expect that if they accepted Christ as their savior, then they would slowly begin to see the selfishness. Because the thing about adultery or homosexuality is that all sin is sin in God's eyes. If I tell a little white fib, God does not draw close to me, because he doesn't partake in sin. If I am involved in adultery, God does not draw close to me then; I have shut my communication off with him. But the difference with a little white lie and adultery is that adultery has *major consequences.* And homosexuality does too. It has a lot of major consequences. It hurts people. I can't talk very knowledgeably about that, because I'm just where I am. But all I know is that's why Paul comes down so hard on that, because they're very self-centered—all sin is very self-centered—but more significant sin impacts and hurts others.

Tina knew how sin could be selfish from her own earlier refusal to submit to her husband and family. She could thus extrapolate; knowing that sin is selfish, she could say that homosexuality is a sin because it is selfish and hurts others. This tautology caught her when I asked how homosexuality hurt others, and she responded:

> How does homosexuality hurt others? [Pause.] You want me to tell you all the many ideas I have in mind? [Pause.] For one thing, number one, I think, it hurts themselves. I've known a lot of different gay people, and I've never seen one of them truly happy. [Pause.] It hurts family members a lot, especially my dad; if my brother were to say that he were gay, that would be very hurtful to my dad. And that's not to say that my dad is right, but that what my brother had done would be hurtful to my dad. Does that make sense?
>
> Dawne: What if—

> Tina: But it's also hurtful to the gay person when we don't accept
> them, so I'm not just saying it's a one-way— it's a two-way—thing.

Here, Tina shifted among languages—from a language of biblical injunc-
tion, to a language of harm, then to a language of personal happiness, as
she sought to explain what she knew to be true about homosexuality. These
shifts point to each language's failure to account for why homosexuality was
sinful.

Tina did not believe that God laid down arbitrary prohibitions; she explained that lying and adultery are sins for a particular reason: their harmful
consequences. She asserted that homosexuality hurts people too, thereby using harm as the standard by which to ascertain sin. But she could not think of
a satisfactory account of homosexuality hurting people. She tried two. First,
she said, homosexuality hurts its practitioners, by preventing them from
being truly happy. Then, she said, homosexuality hurts people by offending
them. She recognized that that offense hurts the rejected person as well as
the person who is offended, but she still blamed homosexuality, rather than
the rejection of it, for the two-way street. Her language of happiness seemed
to provide the most reliable terms on which to build her view that homosexuality is sinful, given that her own joy was partly what let her know that she
understood God's plan when she submitted within her marriage. Following
this logic, she suggested that people can know they are doing God's will when
they are *truly happy*.

Tina's knowledge of Scripture combined with emotional experiences to
let her know God's will. City Church's Linda Renaldi would have disagreed
with Tina on the question of whether homosexuality was sinful, but she too
expressed a certain clarity that came from emotional life experiences. Recall
from chapter 3 that Linda had the question of homosexuality clarified for her
when a member of the congregation, in her story, lunged across the table at
her friend and condemned him.

Many members who believed homosexuality to be sinful might think
that Linda had rejected Scripture wholesale, or wished to contextualize it
out of relevance. Such a view would be mistaken; rather, Linda drew from
her experience to interpret which part of Scripture had the most relevance
to Christians, something theological conservatives do as well.

For Linda, an uncritical acceptance of the scriptural prohibitions on homosexuality, taking them to mean that homosexuality is sinful, amounted
to "brainwashing," which she saw herself as having undergone. Yet she used
a literal interpretation of Micah 6:8 ("Do justice, love mercy, walk humbly
with God"), which the Reverend Parnell often pronounced as a benediction

at the end of the service, to guide her on the question of which side of the controversy she should take. Seeing the nonmerciful and not humble pronouncements of someone who believed homosexuality to be sinful and lunging across the table at her friend gave Linda all she needed to make whatever struggle she had had before into "a no-brainer." Her experience with Christians who believed homosexuality to be sinful, and with a gay man who behaved in ways that seemed to her more Christian, convinced her of what side to stand on. These experiences shaped her understanding that Scripture is not antigay, that it teaches justice, mercy, and humility.

Given City Church's emotional history of these debates, we can read in Linda's comments an emotional experience as well. The member who had said homosexuality was sinful at the meeting Linda spoke of did not, in Linda's account, offer a level-headed and compassionate account of scriptural interpretation to make her or his point. Linda's experience at this meeting must have been emotional—angering, frightening, and painful. Emotion plays a role in epiphany, even epiphanies that can be talked about in slightly more dispassionate terms years later.

Linda portrayed that meeting as catalyzing a transformation in her views of God and sexuality. Her fellow church member Tony Pitcher did not recount any such dramatic experience, but he also showed how emotions can shape people's understandings of what God expects of them in terms of justice, mercy, and humility. About the debates over homosexuality within City Church, he remarked:

> When we get down to it, it's about personal issues around sexuality. You see a group of people who, historically in our society, have been and still are stigmatized, and society has in general a hostile viewpoint towards gays, and I have an inherent discomfort with that. The reason that I come out where I do on this issue is that inherent discomfort, that feeling of "that just doesn't seem Christian to me," is more powerful than any feeling of being sexually threatened by acknowledging homosexuality exists.
>
> We had this [controversial all-church] meeting two years ago, and then a year later my brother comes out to me. He lives down in Texas and the church that he was involved with was a very conservative church, or traditional, maybe I should put it that way, a *traditional* church. He's estranged from the church and estranged from his faith, because he believes that he's sinning. And that bothers me, I mean, it bothers me a lot. And I'm *sick*, really, to see this.
>
> Dawne: So he *believes* that he's sinning, or he believes that the *church* thinks that he's sinning?

Tony: He's conflicted. He is who he is, [he might say] "This is who
I am, and you know what, I'm all right, this is how God made me and
that's okay, but if I have sex with anybody, then I'm sinning. Of course,
I sin other times too, but I know I'm going back to it. I'm not repenting
of my sin. I'm not giving it up. I'm not struggling against it." And for
somebody who had acquired a strong faith that was very important to
him, it's a big thing to lose. So, it's less academic than it was two years
ago. I don't feel any different than I did then, I just feel more strongly
about it.

For Tony, the fact of his brother having come out to him as gay did not
change his mind, but it made his feelings about the church's traditional
stance all the stronger. For him, knowing how important faith was to his
brother, and knowing that his brother was estranged from it in order to be
"who he is," made the church's traditional stigma and hostility seem all the
more unchristian, because they drove a Christian away from the church,
accentuating his "inherent discomfort" and making him feel all the more
"sick."

Tony, Linda, and Tina had all had concerns about social justice. But
whereas Tina's beliefs about male chauvinism were challenged by her understanding of Scripture and her experience of men who respected and loved
women, no such challenge came to Linda or Tony. On the contrary, both
of them had experiences in the church that convinced them that the traditional church position on and treatment of gay people was unconscionable
and unchristian. Epiphanies and emotions led them in different directions,
as they all sought to grow closer to God.

Tony pointed to another trend as well, that people find it easier to see
the influence of social or psychological factors on other peoples' religious
views (or their own past views, which place those with similar views as less
developed than themselves), than on their own present views. Tony observed
the secular, psychological concerns about sexuality that people raised in their
objections to joining the RCP, but somehow he saw his own political commitment to the underdog, his own discomfort, as Christian rather than secular or psychological. Similarly, Linda observed the "brainwashing" to which
the church had subjected people, but only after she could see herself as no
longer brainwashed. Tina could see the psychological reasons that she might
have been a "female chauvinist," having to do with her grandfather's actions, but not the psychological reasons that she might now value wifely
submission.

These members all saw something timeless in God's will, which meant that they had to see something timeless in their own understandings of God's will. Thus, they could posit their detractors as both akin to their own past, less mature or less aware, selves and as unable to see God's timeless truth because of social and psychological factors. In their desire to see God's will as unshaped by social factors, they created two opposed camps—with each side seeing its own views as transcendent and the other views as earthly, there could be no way to "agree to disagree." Each side would have to hope for, and possibly work for, the day that the others would see the light.

Each of the people we have heard from referred to emotions in his or her accounts as well. Tina referred to the joy that allowed her to embrace submission, as well as the happiness she believed practicing homosexuals, on the other hand, could never truly have. Linda's experience of seeing her friend attacked came to her as a moment of clarity. Tony referred to discomfort and feeling sick as how he knew something was not God's will. Each of these members experienced God's communication to them through their emotions. Emotions here served as a way of knowing, but a special way. Unlike scriptural interpretations, historical traditions, or political analyses, our assumptions about emotions dictate that emotions cannot be challenged. We experience emotions as difficult to express, and this reticence makes them seem truer, because they cannot be known to another except through the subject's attempts to convey them. Emotions are not very open to debate; after all, it would be difficult to argue that Tony did *not* feel sick. In a context that sees debates as the undoing of transcendence, as the very process that roots people among the earthly and base, emotions seem particularly transcendent.

God as Feeling

While emotional experiences can appear to members as epiphanies, furthering their knowledge of God's will, at another level religious truth itself is, for many church members, an emotional truth. This section explores two ways members on different sides of this issue talked about God in chiefly emotional terms. For liberals at City Church, religious truth might be experienced as what Immanuel Kant called an oceanic feeling—the sublime feeling of the vastness of God's Creation.[6] The sublime experience of God's vastness informed liberal members' stance on homosexuality, as well as their beliefs about those who thought it was sinful. On the other side of the issue, many who believed homosexuality to be sinful felt God's presence as the comfort and safety of children in their father's protective arms, safe from the contemporary world's dangers. In both perspectives, God's vastness was known through feelings, but these members differed as to *which* feelings they associated with God.

For liberal City Church member Ruthie Shafer, faith was about transformation of the heart. As she described her theology, she explained that she experienced her spirituality in terms that she said could be called being "born again"; however, she was hesitant to use that term for fear of misleading people into thinking she supported many of the political and theological stances associated with conservative born-again, evangelical movements. Ruthie believed that when someone decided to make God the center of his or her life it would lead that person to experience a transformation of the heart, to be open and learn to "love, in a Christlike way." She elaborated:

> At some point in life we *all* are forced to make a choice. First, for those
> people who choose a path that takes them someplace other than their
> highest self, they will not ultimately be fulfilled or satisfied with their life
> experience. Second, they will not be able to go through that process of
> transformation of the heart and be open and learning to love and be with
> others. There's a sort of closing off, it's hard to put into words because it's
> a very intuitive sort of experience that I've had, but I do believe that to
> be the case. And I believe that that is some of the stuff that Christ talked
> about in the New Testament. You know, the who you are, not what
> you do of the Old Testament. The spirit you bring to the world, and the
> connection you have, is what, in fact, defines you as a human being. Not
> your occupation, not how much money you make, not how much power
> you have, or the kinds of people that you associate with. It is, in fact, who
> you are, what's inside of you.

For Ruthie, one experiences God through loving other people, through experiencing the wonder of God's Creation, through loving in a Christlike way, through following a path that takes one to one's "highest self," being open, and having "connection."

The evangelicals we have heard from would agree with her completely on that point. However, following this understanding, Ruthie did not believe homosexuality to be sinful. In fact, she saw any such judgment as closing people off from God. For Ruthie, different forms of sexuality were merely one way the vast "genius of God's Creation" contributed to a humanity that is "alive and healthy and exciting." People do not always understand the genius of God's Creation, in her account, but just as we have learned more about the planet and the universe, we can learn more about humanity's variation with the help of science, which God has also guided and helped people to understand.

In her analysis, to live in wholeness, love, and connection to creation—both human and cosmic—people cannot judge portions of creation to be wrong. To do so would be to limit themselves from God's "extraordinary" design and to close themselves off from God, by closing themselves off from God's love. She elaborated:

> The most wonderful thing that Christ brought us was the understanding that we are *all* one. So, regardless of how awful another person may be, I *cannot* be separate from that person. If you look at the story of Christ, even if you only take it allegorically—I personally don't, it's more than that, and the reason for that is because I have had some uniquely divine miracles in my own life, okay, so I have seen some truly extraordinary things happen, and I believe that they were directive in my own life; in other words, I am not walking this path alone. Nor are you. Do not believe that anyone is walking a path alone. [. . .]
>
> Within the context of that faith, we are only here for a moment. *This* is not It. *This* is a piece of It. So, if you don't have that faith, then I cry for you, or for anyone else in the world, because then the world is going to continue to be a horrible place for you and anyone else who lives in it, and there is no hope then. But within the context of *that* faith, there is great hope. Because you *can* do that. You can *choose* to love, regardless of what someone else chooses to do. *Your* love, *your* faith, is not relational in that way. You do not derive your values from what someone else chooses. So within that process, if you look at the people who have had the greatest impact upon us, you will see that they are those who rose up to lead in that way. [. . .]
>
> I think that it's not just this issue [of homosexuality]. Our only life's work is to spend the time, to allow ourselves to just take a deep breath, and love. And I think there are a lot of people who, in a certain way, find that trite when I say it, because if you just take the words, they're not very meaningful. You have to take it within the context of love, some pretty extreme life experience. I mean, I can show you better than I can tell you. Like, the movie would be a lot better!

For Ruthie, God is love, God is the life force, God is expressed in the vast diversity of creation. To know God is to open your heart to that vastness, to choose to practice love in everything. God's power is with those who choose to live in that kind of love, and people who have it, others know. For Ruthie, God's unifying love defines life, it *is* life, and to seek separation is to experience, as we have seen her say, "a living death."

City Church member Edie Litvanis's understanding of creation resembled Ruthie Shafer's. She, too, saw God as a universal source of life, a universal commonality, a commonality expressed through the vast diversity of creation. She summarized her beliefs by saying, "God is our diversity and God is our commonality." I asked her to elaborate, and she remarked:

> Each of us, in trying to make everybody the same, goes against the whole idea of creation. Yes, God created male and female, but also in terms of eye color and hair color and skin color and all of that. That diversity has to be honored and respected, and I don't think it is. In our culture and many other cultures, we tend to be attracted to people just like us, just like ourselves. And we close everybody else off and judge them. I find myself being in awe in terms of God's diversity, even in terms of walking down the street in the morning to work and noticing the shapes of people, the colors of people, that people are happy and sad—that's incredible. No two people are alike. I think people are still very afraid of sharing a lot of their uniqueness, their range of differences. So that's why I think diversity has to be allowed and accepted and encouraged, and not just tolerated—to be welcomed, and encouraged.
>
> Too often, even [in] congregations you get a profile, and everybody wants worship to be a certain way and retreats or activities to be a certain way or a certain flavor, and people can get a false sense of comfort. Not a false sense, but become comfortable in that, and then not really risk trying anything different or seeing anything differently. And I think that's what life is about: experiencing it in all of its diversity and all of its potential, while recognizing that within that diversity there is a seed that connects us together.

For Edie, God is universal connection and perfection, as well as the creator of human diversity. God puts a different "seed" in each person, which should be nurtured and allowed to blossom. This seed seems to be part of what other members call identity, the sense of who a person is, each individual's uniqueness, *whom* God creates each person to be. For Edie, these differences were "what life is all about," and for people to suppress these differences, for family and culture to inhibit the seed's growth, goes against God's purpose in creation. For people to say that one is better than the other or preferred over the other, according to Edie, "seems to put us in a position of defining . . . the way life should be," which should not be people's role, but God's.

In Edie's view, people go against God's whole plan when they succumb to fear and seek out a feeling of comfort. When people state which way is preferred, better, or normal, this amounts to "judging" others, which, in her view, was God's job. Judging others is a way of closing ourselves off to difference, to uniqueness, and, thus, to the diversity of God's Creation and perfection. To Edie, closing "everybody else off" results from fear and phobia and falls short of God's perfection, which is connection among people.

Edie described the sense of "false comfort" that comes from groups of people, even congregations, when they want everything to "be a certain way or a certain flavor." As she clarified her statement, comfort comes from not "trying anything different or seeing anything differently." This comfort, in Edie's view, comes from denying "what life is about." Life is about "experiencing life in all of its diversity and all of its potential," finding connection within that diversity rather than suppressing it. Thus, Edie differentiated between the comfort she saw people finding in congregations and the connection that she saw as the wonder of God's expansive creation. The appropriate emotion concerning God was one of awe; to search for a sense of "false comfort" was to try to make God small.[7] This view of comfort directly opposed another view, which saw comfort as precisely what God wanted for people.

To others, the theology expressed by Ruthie Shafer and Edie Litvanis is too vague, allowing too much room for an "anything goes" kind of sentimentalism that has little to do with the righteousness God demands. These other members of the two congregations also saw feelings as an essential way to know what God wants from people, but those feelings must be structured and guided by close readings of Scripture as the infallible word of God, as well as the guidance of other Christians in a community of faith. Although some members of City Church would no doubt agree with this view, I heard it elaborated most thoroughly at Missionary Church.

A number of Missionary Church members drew from Charles Stanley's writings. In his 1992 book, *The Wonderful Spirit-Filled Life*, Stanley understands the primary source of truth for Christians as Scripture "understood in context," with the help of knowledgeable Christians, guidance from the Lord, and the peace of mind that comes with proper understanding of the will of God. The most important indicator of God's will, according to Stanley, is the Bible. When Christians read the Bible, Stanley says, they can be moved by the Holy Spirit to understand God's will, to see something in it they have never seen before, which gives them a new peace of mind when they interpret it correctly. That "peace of mind" bears looking at.

Missionary member Betsy Meisensahl invoked Stanley in describing the
peace of mind that comes to the believer who interprets Scripture correctly.
I told Betsy about a conferencewide meeting of the Confessing Movement I
attended, where the executive director of the national movement, Pat Miller
(her real name), addressed the crowd. Pat told the story of how she came
to be the executive director of the Confessing movement, starting from the
moment when she and her husband considered leaving the UMC because of
its debates over homosexuality. She then heard about the Confessing movement's executive director position and flew to a neighboring state for her interview. The evening of the interview, she was in her hotel room and turned
to the Bible for guidance and solace, praying that God's will would be done,
whether that meant she should direct the organization or not. She said, "As
I opened up the Bible, I opened right up to Paul saying women should not
speak in church!" She paused. "So I just kept on reading!" The crowd shared
a hearty chuckle at the joke.

This seemed to me an example of dismissing the literal word as it appeared in Scripture (something pro-gay members are often accused of), so
I asked several people, including Betsy, to explain to me how such a joke
would not be seen as dismissing the Bible. Betsy understood my confusion.
As we saw in chapter 4, Betsy resolved this problem by saying that it comes
down to God's work on the individual believer's convictions, which change
based on what God reveals to them. God "forms our convictions to be in line
with his." Given that "all Scripture is God-breathed," it was her conviction
that God's injunctions on homosexuality apply today.

On the other hand, Betsy tentatively said that she did not believe that
women should be banned from speaking in church. She remarked on the experience she had with a woman clergy member who "spoke the truth" from
the pulpit and showed her that such a ban could not be God's will. Experience
had countered her reading of Scripture on this issue, but she would have to
work through other issues one at a time.

So how did she know that homosexuality was not another case of a
prohibition written for a different time and culture, like the ban on women
speaking in church? Here, Betsy articulated the difference between women
speaking in church and homosexuality as "a gut feeling," personal "conscience," and what "we intuitively believe or not." In her view, as believers
developed in their faith and relationship with God, the Holy Spirit could
change their gut feeling, their intuition, to make it more "in line with what
God believes." In the end, Betsy's feeling of comfort made all the reasons
she had given for people to be confused by Scripture irrelevant.[8] Betsy had
always believed that homosexuality was sinful, and since she began to live

in relationship with God, nothing had come to change her mind. She "just [knew] that's right." Furthermore, if someone came from the perspective that homosexuality was acceptable, and were truly walking with God, seeking him, reading the Bible and praying Betsy said, "if indeed, it is wrong, he will change their mind, or change their heart."

Although she seemed to express some openness to the possibility of a new message from God about homosexuality, Betsy was confident that homosexuality is sinful because God had done nothing to change her mind, as she believed he would change the mind of a Christian who had always thought homosexuality was acceptable. But was Betsy open to the possibility of God changing her own mind? I asked her: "How do you know? If God were to tell you something that seems improbable to you, like 'actually, homosexuality is just fine,' how would you know? What would make you believe that?"

She replied:

> That's a good question! My first inclination would be to keep reading!
> [We laugh.] I mean, honestly, my first inclination would be to keep
> reading, you know, maybe that's not what he's telling me. Knowing what
> I believe about God, if that's something he's trying to change my mind
> about, it'll keep coming up. It'll be something that sticks in my mind,
> and it'll be something, maybe all of a sudden there'll be news stories
> about this. I'll pick it up in magazine articles, and I'll be overhearing it
> in conversations. It'll just keep coming up in one way or another. Until
> I open my mind about it and start to think, okay, maybe this is true. Or,
> okay God, you want me to do this?

In this passage, Betsy explained how God would speak to her to tell her to believe something that wasn't already "ingrained" in her conscience. It would keep coming up. She would suddenly see news stories about it, overhear people talking about it, see it mentioned in magazines. God would not let her forget about it.

She compared God's potential revelation on the question of homosexuality to a revelation that she was to become a missionary and pack up and move away, remarking:

> Like, if he called me to go be a missionary, something that I cannot
> imagine, it's like, "You want me to pick up everybody and move . . .
> and what about my husband? I'm supposed to be submissive to him!"
> And, if [God] wants me to believe something or me to do something,

it's gonna keep coming up. And I'm not gonna feel settled until I deal
with that. Until I come to where he's trying to get me to on that. So if
homosexuality is acceptable in God's eyes, you know, I know that we're
not to be judgmental, but if he wants us to accept that [. . .]

If indeed God finds that acceptable, I think indeed he will make that
an issue. Maybe he's doing that by having this, you know, Reconciling
versus the Confessing movement, and making it more of an issue in
churches. Personally, it's not a big issue for me. I think if it's something
that he wanted to make acceptable, it would *become* a big issue. And
that's why I said, if you're heading in the right direction, I think God
can confirm that, you'll be more settled. If you're going off in the wrong
direction or fighting against what he wants you to believe or to do, then
it'll just keep coming at you, like pestering. It'll keep popping up.

Betsy imagines that God *could* call her to go against the scriptural mandate
of submission to her husband.[9] She would not want to believe it, but she
would not "feel settled" until she "deal[t] with" God's command, regardless
of the call to submission. Feeling settled was, for Betsy, a major indicator of
doing what God wanted her to do. "If you're heading in the right direction,"
she said, "I think God can confirm that [. . .] you'll be more settled." Feeling
settled, not fighting against the conscience she had had her whole life, these
are goals of faith in God and effects of following God's will. Betsy knew she
was living God's will because she did not feel that homosexuality was an
issue.

In Betsy's understanding, God could communicate to his followers by
giving them a feeling of being settled or at peace when their beliefs and
actions are in accordance with his will. Betsy knew that her belief in the
sinfulness of homosexuality was in accordance with God's because she felt
no conflict about it, no discomfort, and it was not an issue in her life. In this
view, someone who had always thought homosexuality was acceptable, were
she or he walking with God, would not have this feeling of settledness until
that person's views came into line with God's.

This understanding of settledness would be completely subjective were
it not for its proponents' belief in the primacy of the Bible. They believed
that God does not change from what he inspired people to put in the Bible.
However, as we have already seen, how people understood the Bible also depended on what was already "ingrained," as Betsy Meisensahl said, in their
consciences. To make sense of the Scriptures in today's world, people must
interpret them. No one who spoke to me about the matter disagreed. However, for a community of believers to recognize someone's interpretation as

true to Scripture and true to God's intentions, members needed to adhere to what that community recognizes as the spirit of the text; they could not stray onto what appeared to be their own subjective paths.

In explaining faith, Betsy's fellow Missionary Church member Pete Vogel highlighted what he and his faith community saw as some of the boundaries of acceptable texts:

> [In school when we talked about religion], the whole thing was, if you want to have a relationship with God, it's a leap of faith, because you can't hear him, touch him, see him, and all that. So, but you jump into faith because if, ta, [then] da da, da da, da [intones an if-then statement]. Now I'm asked, "Pete, just jump into acceptance of gays, lesbians, hetero—," well, you know. But I'm being told to jump, but no one's saying the whys, other than, "It didn't work out. I just feel like there's a different identity for me. This is the way that God designed me. And so I read a passage in Scripture . . ." And *that's* my leap of faith? Well, how did they get past Romans 1?
>
> When people tell me that Ruth and Naomi were lesbians because they had this deep love, that's not— *I'm not gonna jump.* [. . .] And so, for me, I'm saying to the gay and lesbian community, what's my reason for jumping? Why should I abandon my beliefs? Offer me some evidence beyond me just saying, "It didn't work out," or "I really love this person," or, "This is the first person I've really had intimacy with." I could easily say, "Well, right now I'd love to have extramarital affairs," or something like that, but that doesn't mean it's right. We want so much freedom, when really freedom's not always in our best interest.

For Pete, believing in God and believing in the need to live in relationship with God were questions of faith: "You can't hear him, touch him, see him, and all that." Believing in God does not require evidence: "So, but you jump" because—why? Pete filled in the reason for "jumping" into faith with meaningless syllables, which he intoned in an if-then rhythm. You "jump" and have faith in God because, presumably, *if* you don't accept Jesus as your savior, *then* you will not have eternal life. However, we cannot know, for certain, that Pete meant that.

Now, however, Pete felt he was being asked to "just jump into acceptance of gays, lesbians, hetero—"; he almost slipped into saying "heterosexuals," and perhaps he was really correct that the issue on the table for debate was the existence of *marked* sexual identities, including marked heterosexuality. Because he stopped himself from saying "heterosexuals," we can assume he meant to refer to gays and lesbians. He was being told to jump, but no one offered him any "whys," any evidence that he should accept that homosexuality is not sinful. The only evidence people offered him was their own subjective feelings, backed up, in his view weakly, by one passage in Scripture. None of the people asking him to jump had given him a way to get beyond Romans 1.[10] To make that leap of faith would be to jump into the unknown, or worse, while faith in God was a jump into the certainty of God's eternal care.

Again, we see that a sense of settledness, a sense of comfort and peace, knowing that to maintain the beliefs one has always had is in keeping with God's will. The logic seems to follow this path: (a) If I feel settled about my belief in something, then (b) that thing is God's intention. Therefore, (c) it is God's will for all, and (d) whatever I see as contradicting my belief in this thing is not God's will for anyone. This logic posits that if God gives Pete or Betsy his approval with a feeling of settledness, then God cannot give someone with whom Pete or Betsy disagree the same approval via the same feeling of settledness.

Pete knew that faith is all that is required to believe in God, yet he demanded evidence in order to change those beliefs. None of the evidence people had given him was sufficient. When people attempted to show him the merit of understanding the biblical prohibitions of homosexuality in context, directing him to the "horrifying things that were happening" in the Old Testament, he understood those horrifying things in the context of God creating an identity for his people. The Old Testament must be understood in context. An account of the covenant between Ruth and Naomi, which indicates that they were "lesbians," failed to convince Pete; he found such an interpretation preposterous.[11]

For Pete, nothing in the bigger picture, which for him was about the Old Testament God's creation of an identity for his people, nor in the specifics of the text, would serve as evidence that would make him "jump." But as Pete had established already, "jumping" had nothing to do with evidence. Jumping was a matter of faith. For him to "jump" would mean, in his explanation, to "abandon" something. What would he be abandoning?

In Pete's view, certain people feared God's narrow road of sexual morality; these people were like children who failed to know what was best for them. Pete had seen among his friends and others how often nonmarital sexual experiences created feelings of being used, hurt, and broken; seeing the emotional wreckage after couples broke up convinced him again and again that "promiscuity" was contrary to God's plan, and the identity God wants for his people. He explained: "God does have a plan, and the plan scares people because it says that the road is narrow, and we live in a society that does not like narrow roads, and we want to shatter things like that and just have freedom. For me, the promiscuity is the freedom." Although Pete made it clear that he did not see himself as better than those who had sex outside of marriage, the fact that those who did so often became "tainted" by heart-breaking experiences helped him to see God as forbidding certain sex acts in his role as a protective parent. Pete elaborated:

> I believe God says "A man and a woman" not to be rigid, but to protect us from the hurt, the brokenness, the taintedness. Does that make more sense?
>
> It's not that God is being so cruel, and so narrow-minded, and so un-politically correct, but it's just that he can *see* the brokenness that has been passed, that is just laying ruins everywhere. But we so often want to neglect it and forget about it and go on to our next relationship, and hopefully, it will be better. And it leaves us broken, but then we don't just wait for that special relationship, but we move on to another relationship and explore that one, and maybe it is between a man and a man, just because maybe this one will work. And it may or may not. And so, to me there is this *freedom* and this current of promiscuity that only further increases the likelihood of a tainting experience, of brokenness.

For Pete, homosexuality was not only a form of nonmarital sex but was also a symptom of humanity's sinful ways. Sinful ways created the brokenness that drove some people away from the one-man-one-woman marriage God intended for everyone.

Although others we have heard from looked directly to Scripture to know that homosexuality is sinful, Pete went a step further. He drew from scriptural prohibitions but placed them in a broader context of God's intent for people. While some of the pro-gay people we have heard from believed that God intended for people to experience God's love through the awe-inspiring diversity of creation, Pete believed that God intended for people to feel the awesome security of being safe in God's arms, as children in heavenly peace rather than children running amok and in danger, indulging immature desires for what feels like freedom. Pete, like City Church's Edie Litvanis, saw fear as pulling people away from God, but their understandings of God were virtually opposite. Whereas Edie saw fear at work in people's desire to make God's Creation seem less awesomely and terrifyingly vast, Pete saw fear at work in a different way. He said, "God does have a plan, and the plan scares people because it says that the road is narrow, . . . and we

want to shatter things like that and just have freedom." For Pete, people fear
the narrowness of God's path, and this fear drives them from the security of
God's shelter. It takes courage *not* to jump out of God's arms, to stay along
his narrow path.

Through his explanation, Pete made it clear what would be at stake for
him in "jumping" into acceptance of homosexuality. To jump into a new acceptance of sexuality would challenge his whole understanding of God's way
and, thus, his whole understanding of God as the figure who laid down the
law to protect his people from being "shattered." His faith in God included
his faith that sex must only take place within the marriage of one man and
one woman. In other words, central to Pete's faith in and identification with
God was Pete's faith in and identification with one-man-one-woman marriage. That is why the understanding that Ruth and Naomi were "lesbians"
was preposterous to him.

Homosexuality and the Holy Spirit

For many members of the two congregations who believed that homosexuality was sinful, to entertain a new understanding of sexual rules would
necessitate taking on a new understanding of God. Although such members of City Church as Ruthie and Edie seemed, at one level, to see the
hand of God as "naturally" denaturalizing human assumptions, Missionary
Church's Betsy and Pete saw God as the ultimate naturalizing force. They
believed that God wished for them to feel settled. They believed that God
wished for them to feel at peace with their own consciences. They believed
that God wished for them to move through life unburdened by baggage,
feeling whole rather than shattered. They believed God's way is best, and
around matters of sexuality, it is simple to understand, even if it might at
first seem confusing.

The Christian writer Charles Stanley (1992) also sees direct communication with God, through the Holy Spirit, as enabling Christians to know
God's will. Stanley writes:

> The Holy Spirit is constantly working to reveal the thoughts and truth
> of God. He does that by opening the minds and hearts of believers so
> that we can understand the thoughts of God as we have them recorded in
> Scripture.
>
> Have you ever had a verse of Scripture jump off the page and affect
> you in a way that takes you totally by surprise? Have you ever read a

passage that is very familiar to you, but you gain new insight from it? Have you ever been in a pressure situation and from out of nowhere a verse comes to mind that brings you comfort or renewed perspective? Or how about those times when everything is falling apart and you throw open your Bible and BAM! There it is—a verse tailor-made for your situation.

When these things happen, they are not coincidental. More than likely the Holy Spirit is at work—illuminating our minds, opening our eyes, infusing our hearts with the specific truths we need for the moment. (211)

For Stanley, as for those who read his books at Missionary Church, the Holy Spirit can come to a Christian through Scripture to illuminate a situation, to tell them just what they need to hear at the moment.

I suspect that these members, following Stanley, would have trouble believing that the Holy Spirit could work in that way to tell someone that homosexuality was not sinful. Yet others recount experiences that sound remarkably like Stanley's description, including Reverend Cory Jacobsen, a gay pastor involved with the Reconciling Congregations Program.

Stanley would say that because God forbade homosexuality in the Bible, he will never want anyone to be a practicing homosexual. However, we have seen that even Stanley's evangelical readers can have more complicated understandings of how to read Scripture. Believers interpret problematic Scriptural passages (such as those about adultery, women, slavery, dietary restrictions, and blended fabrics) in light of other passages in Scripture, as well as a wide range of nonscriptural circumstances. The same could be said of Cory's epiphany.

As we discussed the UMC's ban on ordaining "self-avowed practicing homosexuals," Cory said:

> "Self-avowed practicing": well, I am both. I think it's insane some of the ways people try to get around it, to deny themselves. We are sexual beings. I have seen [gay clergy] do a lot of different things to get around it; when they deny it, or try to, they're not experiencing the love they can. To be Christian is to be loving. I believe you can only lead people as far as you've gone. Some people can try to project what it would be to be fully loving, but that's not it. To be Christian is to be loving, and that means fully loving [including having the love that you experience in deep intimacy with another person]. (Reconstructed from notes)

Cory Jacobsen did not make the traditional distinction between brotherly love, godly love, and erotic love. For him, love is love, and God desires oneness with people the way people desire oneness with each other.[12] He added:

> In my own personal closet, in my own homophobia, I heard people saying
> I was wrong, but I couldn't hear them saying I was okay. There's a study
> about when different people come out, when they have their first experi-
> ence, when they feel good about it. And the average age that people feel
> good about it is thirty. Well, here I am! And I know God made me this
> way, and he's not surprised that I'm this way. (Reconstructed from notes)

Cory had struggled with himself, his desires, and his faith until he heard God speaking to him through Scripture. Then he came to a sense of peace.

About his experience reading Scripture, Cory said: "Psalm 139, that's one of my top five or ten passages for understanding this. Reading that one time, it came to me. I am not a surprise to God. God knew me before I was even born, knew my desires and needs before I did. I may have surprised my parents, and myself, but not God." Cory had struggled against his feelings of attraction to other men, and he prayed about them until one day he read Psalm 139 and it moved him. Verses thirteen to sixteen of this psalm read:

> For it was you who formed my inward parts; you knit me together in my
> mother's womb. I praise you, for I am fearfully and wonderfully made.
> Wonderful are your works; that I know very well. My frame was not
> hidden from you, when I was being made in secret, intricately wrought
> in the depths of the earth. Your eyes beheld my unformed substance; in
> your book were written all the days that were formed for me, when none
> of them yet existed.

Cory told me he heard God speaking to him through this passage. Through this psalm, God let Cory know that although he may have surprised his parents and himself with the revelation that he was gay, he did not surprise God. For someone who believes that being gay is a gift God gives some people, it takes no great leap to see being gay as part of Cory's frame, his substance, the days that were written for him. In fact, City Church members read this passage in one of their Bible studies on homosexuality (Osterman 1997).

Were Stanley not committed to the belief that homosexuality is sinful, he might say that when Cory prayed about his own self-hatred and conflicted desires, and searched out God's wisdom through Scripture, the Holy Spirit led him to Psalm 139 and "BAM! There it [was]—a verse tailor-made for [Cory's] situation. . . . More than likely the Holy Spirit [was] at work—illuminating our minds, opening our eyes, infusing our hearts with the specific truths we need for the moment." Stanley would not say that, but Cory would.

It is interesting to note that even while Cory relied on Scripture to affirm his homosexuality, as well as his theology of God as love and Christian duty as that to love, he also relied on a lack of volition. Cory remarked, "God made me this way, and he's not surprised I'm this way." For Cory, the knowledge that he had no choice about being gay, that God knew Cory would be gay before he was even born, helped to provide the peace of mind he needed to know he was walking with God, that God knew his desires and needs, and knew them even before Cory did. In Cory's view, he was not rebelling against God but being the person God always knew he would be, "wonderfully made."

The Divisiveness of Common Feeling

Cory felt settled. My point is not about whether homosexuality is sinful, as Charles Stanley would say, or not sinful, as Cory Jacobsen would say. My point is that the experience that Stanley describes is available to members regardless of their theological position on homosexuality. Any member might experience that sense of settledness that Stanley attributes to a person in the right place with God. Similarly, any member might believe that people whose beliefs differ from theirs are bound by fear or immaturity in faith. Both Pete and Edie attributed others' divergent theological views to fear. Both sides can use the languages of emotion to characterize themselves as at peace with their creator of the universe, while positing that those who disagree with them are experiencing the opposite of peace, whether it be fear, smallness, or shattering.

A language of emotion is not easily refutable. As people sought to know how God expects them to deal with the challenges the gay movement has issued the church, a language of emotion served as a way to seal people's understandings about their theological knowledge. This is not to say that members were cynical in their use of the language of feelings. To the contrary, they really felt settled, awestruck, peaceful, or afraid at times. Their experiences with God, and their earthly concerns, do threaten to overwhelm or to shatter them at times. Coming to a sense of peace with God and humanity is what religious people see themselves as having and nonbelievers as lacking. As Ruthie Shafer said, "If you don't have that faith, then I cry for you." What members involved in these debates fail to realize is that their experiences are not limited to those who share their views of who or what

God is, what God expects of people, or what sin is. Members of these two congregations show us that people with widely divergent theologies can experience God with a similar richness.

Although languages about Scripture are subject to counterinterpretations, languages about the individual interventions of the Holy Spirit, about transformations of the heart, cannot directly be challenged to a speaker's face. When a speaker employs such a language of emotion to describe how God has spoken to her, detractors are left with little ground for critique. To a believer who knows God has spoken to her personally, detractors can only seem disingenuous, misguided, or ignorant. Meanwhile, the detractor sees the speaker in the same terms—and not ignorant of just anything, but ignorant of what it is like to be at peace with God.

When members addressed debates using a language of emotion, their emotional experiences with God came to be the only evidence suitable for determining what is right. These languages gave extra credibility to those who could tell the most passionate and moving stories about God's miraculous power in their lives. These stories were supposed to bring people together, to share the wonder of God's promise, but when used in debates, these languages cast a speaker's detractors as profoundly ignorant and fearful of God's love. Detractors were implicitly portrayed not as different, or even wrong, but as fundamentally incapable of transcending the world and approaching God.

Using the languages of emotion this way can further obscure an already obscure fact, that emotions themselves, even "gut feelings," are products of social interactions. Anthropologists have shown us that in different societies people experience completely different emotions and can assign different values to emotions that appear to be natural and universal across societies.[13] As we become socialized, we are taught which sensations to interpret as pain, joy, or something else. Even the range of sensations we experience are in large part conditioned through social interaction. The people we have heard from really felt "at peace" or "sick"; feelings *are* real. However, to assume too unreflectively that these feelings are God's pure way of speaking to people would be to attribute to God whatever people experience as a result of their interactions with other people. Many members believed that God works through other people. But feelings do not automatically transcend earthly life, as they too are shaped by people.

Languages of emotion appealed to members precisely at the moments when they wished to stay out of political-seeming debates and controversies. These languages seemed to transcend the earthly divisions that plague the church and secular society alike. Because of the high stakes involved, these languages divided people more deeply and profoundly. Different experiences in life lead people to hear different messages from God, but when members assumed that only their own feelings represented truth, they effectively shut out those whose experiences differed. In denying the social and earthly element of their own faith, members created the divisiveness they sought to escape. The desire for transcendence and freedom from politics strengthened some of the very political divisions the church decried, because the stakes in differences of belief were heightened.

At the same time, because so many people see emotions as pure and as distinct from politics, the language of emotion has, in fact, led to great changes in church policies and responses to homosexuality. In particular, a narrative around gay people's pain has served as the bridge gay people have needed in order to belong in church. However, as the next chapter will show, basing membership on pain tends to constrain gay members within the church rather than free them to be equal members.

chapter EIGHT

Gay Pain and Politics

I f feelings can help people to get around politics or conflict, then it makes sense that showcasing feelings could depoliticize homosexuality. Nancy Cook was a fiftyish married woman whose community development work stemmed from the twentieth-century theology she learned and lived during the Civil Rights movement. At one of City Church's reconciliation meetings, the discussion turned to whether homosexuality was innate, and therefore God-given, or whether it was a Christian's duty to preserve social order by following religious codes. Nancy responded by sharing her own thought process, how she had moved from the point of thinking that homosexuality was ungodly to thinking of it as God's intention for some people and one of God's miraculous ways of surprising people. At the meeting, she interjected:

> I, too, was at a point of thinking about society collapsing; I had feared that we would be saying "anything goes." About God's intentions for us I was thinking, "If people choose to reject God's plan for us, to reject the creative ability God has given us, then they are rejecting God." But then I came to think about the *pain* that homosexuals must be feeling, all the rejection that comes from the social structure. And, I just saw the movie *Priscilla, Queen of the Desert;* [it] is really shocking to see the pain people are in that makes them feel they have to do such *wild* things just to be able to say, "This is who I am."[1]

For Nancy, the question had been whether homosexuals rejected God by rejecting their reproductive "creative ability," or whether homosexuals were constituted as gay by God (saying, "This is who I am") and then rejected by society for being how God made them. Here, Nancy suggested that what helped her to change her mind was observing the pain that people were in, that they had to do such "wild" things.

Witnessing gay people she perceived to be in pain changed Nancy's mind about homosexuality. Although members who believed homosexuality to be sinful and those who were pro-gay diverged widely in their reasons for welcoming gay men and lesbians into the church, both spoke frequently of gay people's pain. Regardless of their views, the theme of gay pain helped members to see gay people as belonging in church. In spite of members' differing intentions, this common thread produced similar results.

Members used a language of pain to attempt to negotiate the terms under which gay members would be brought into the church. Given the overwhelming belief in the importance of Christian love and compassion, it comes as no surprise that a theme of relieving pain figures prominently in current moves to include gay people in the life of the church. This theme of gay pain figures in both sides of the debate: some recognize gay pain as what needs to be cured so that gay men and lesbians can overcome their homosexuality, while others recognize gay pain as the reason the church needs to affirm that homosexuality is part of God's good gift of sexuality. As we shall see, however, when members attempted to use languages of pain to disengage homosexuality from politics, they could end up denying that gay people have volition and that they might have a reasoned and adult perspective on their lives with God.

Healing the Homosexual

Although thinking about religion and homosexuality together might first bring to mind Christianity's history of intolerance, contemporary American Christianity is also positively associated with comfort and healing. Christianity has traditionally stressed God and the church's positive roles in offering aid to the poor and needy, relief to the ill, guidance for the wayward. Regarding homosexuality, there are two ways the church members I studied extended this theme of healing. One includes homosexuals, while recognizing homosexuality as sinful; and the other includes them by redefining homosexuality as part of God's gift of human sexuality. Both views included a notion of a pain particular to gay people. How pro-gay church members envisioned and sought to heal gay pain is the subject of the next section.

The present section examines Transforming Congregations and their supporters, those who saw homosexuality as pathological and sinful and viewed it as a symptom of the damaging pain of real or perceived dysfunction or abuse.[2] In this view, homosexuality—along with drug addiction, alcoholism, pedophilia, and promiscuity—is a pathological problem for which the church can offer healing through Christian counseling and support.

The ex-gay movement, represented most visibly by the umbrella organization Exodus International, consists of small, local para-church ministries that work with people who seek healing from homosexuality, and the parachurch ministries find allies in church movements such as Transforming Congregations. These movements work closely together, frequently sharing and reprinting information in their respective newsletters' news, commentaries, and testimonies sections, and inviting speakers to each other's events. For instance, former Exodus president Joe Dallas (his real name) spoke at a Transforming Congregations conference that I attended, where he taught members about the gay movement and presented the perspectives of his ex-gay therapy clients and his own experience as an ex-gay man.

Dallas talked about three types of homosexuals that members of a Transforming Congregation might encounter as they try to do God's work on this issue. In his ex-gay typology these included: "the militants," who he saw as a relatively small group of those who "back a political agenda to normalize homosexuality" and do not "tolerate opposing viewpoints"; and the more common "moderate" and "repentant" homosexuals. His account of how to deal with the militants revealed his understanding of the place of politics in the issue of homosexuality. Mentioning the 1989 ACT-UP demonstration in St. Patrick's Cathedral as but one example, he told the audience that such "intolerant" gay militancy can tempt Christians (who, by his definition, must all believe homosexuality to be sinful) to either shrink from the argument, or to attack back, acting like the bigots they are accused of being. To respond in either way, he warned, would be for Christians to let gay militants control them. He advocated a third way, a way of showing love while standing firm in the truth that homosexuality is sinful. In the talk, he hoped that an unwillingness to attack militant gay people might come from understanding "what often fuels the rage," that is, from understanding the militants' pain. In effect, he defused militants' politics by attributing their critique to pain.

Dallas began by explaining that he agreed with many pro-gay advocates insofar as they claim that most gay people do not choose to be gay, that they discover in childhood that they have feelings that might make them different. When they hear other kids throwing around slurs, whose definition they do not even necessarily know, these children may come to think that these slurs describe them, and come to feel that they themselves are bad. In his view, the ensuing insecurity and school-yard bullying shape their developing psyches. He explained:

> And the child often feels very awkward, very unwanted, very different. And very uncomfortable and very unsure of himself or herself. Now, you remember the school yard. What is one thing that is absolutely unforgivable in the schoolyard environment? Insecurity. The feeling of not belonging, being different. And so when the child or young adolescent enters into that environment, with the feelings of either inadequacy or ostracization or intimidation, what do the other kids do? Do they gather around and say, "Oh my goodness, you seem to be dealing with gender insecurity and same-sex issues. How can we affirm you?" No, the little monsters peck 'em to *death!*
>
> Imagine the sense of helplessness. Having feelings you didn't ask for. And feeling as though if you did admit those feelings to *anyone*—family, friend, priest, parent—you could meet with repercussions that might border on and/or include violence. The sense of the unfairness of it all, the desperate attempts to change it on your own. "If I date. If I buy *Playboy* magazines (or *Playgirl* magazines, whichever is appropriate in the self-induced healing process). If I pray hard enough. If I fast. If I wish it away. If I pretend." The number of relationships that are started and then stopped, and the number of friendships that are started so often on false premises, and the lies and the excuses and the fears and the self-doubt and the self-*loathing.* (Dallas 1998)

In Dallas's understanding, the roots of gay rage are found in the childhoods and adolescences of proto-gay people. In his view, the deep and profound roots of gay militancy could be found in childhood pain and self-loathing.

Dallas skillfully and compassionately accounted for the rage of militant gay activists, showing how childhood ostracism and later fears of rejection and violence build up into a dismal whole, relieved only when similar people appear on the scene and allow celebration and fearlessness. His account remained entrenched at the level of individual feelings and perceptions, where "ill-advised or stupid or contemptuous remarks" from religious people—as well as violence and threats of violence—did not amount to an actual population of people who were "the enemy." Rather, some people can "come to be seen" as promoting "intolerance and bigotry and homophobia." His use of the passive voice helped him to construct an account where no one was really responsible for gay people's perceptions of the world as antigay. In Dallas's account, homosexual militants are wrong, but their mistaken impression is understandable because of the intense pain of coming to terms with feeling attraction toward people of one's own sex. For Joe Dallas, having compassion for militant homosexuals meant "respect[ing] the rage," which he attributed to "something very deep and very profound."

In this narrative, feelings of fear, insecurity, helplessness, ostracism, being pecked to death in the school yard, became "forms of pain" that develop into the rage of gay political activists. Curiously, this view neglects to account for the vast majority of *hetero*sexuals produced through or resultant from this teasing.[3] Dallas, however, interprets these "forms of pain" to create only homosexuality, while he silently naturalizes heterosexuality. Dallas hoped that his account would encourage his audience of Christians who, like himself, believed homosexuality to be sinful, to see these militants not as enemies but as people who need to hear the truth with love and compassion. He hoped that understanding militants' childhood pain and fear would help his audience to be more "unwilling to attack" militancy in a like manner. For Joe Dallas, understanding militant gay activists' pain, seeing in them the hurt children they once were, might make them seem less threatening to Christians and more loveable. When gay activists attempt to frame organized religion's or the nation's belief and ensuing actions around homosexuality as political, Dallas hoped that Christians would respond to them the way loving parents respond to hurting children.

Members of the two congregations I studied echoed Dallas's understanding of pain, as well as his use of child imagery, to make homosexuals seem less threatening, while naturalizing their place in the church hierarchy. For instance, seeing homosexuals as children also helped City Church member Ron Wilson to think of how to deal with the gay adults entering his congregation as it moved toward joining the RCP. Ron struggled to reconcile his understanding that homosexuality was sinful with his desire to welcome gay people into the church. As we saw in chapter 3, he saw the Bible as clearly stating not only that homosexuality was wrong but that Christians must love one another. He welcomed the person who agreed that homosexuality was sinful and struggled with it in her own life, but he had greater problems welcoming the unapologetic gay person, the one who challenged his understanding of right and wrong by asserting that homosexuality was not wrong.

Ron modeled his love for homosexuals on his love for his children. If his children were to run off and threaten to do something dangerous, it would be his job as a parent to "help them not to do it." The same would be true for church members who run off "willy-nilly," engaging in "harmful actions."

Like Joe Dallas, Ron envisioned homosexuals as children, and thus found them less threatening while accounting for their failure to conform to proper "adult" sexuality.

At Missionary Church, Pete Vogel also used the imagery of childhood, as well as the language of pain, to figure out his Christian response to homosexuals. Like Joe Dallas, Pete wished to extend compassion to gay men and lesbians by understanding them as living in a state of pain. Also like Dallas, Pete looked to gay people's childhoods to find the origins of their pain, and saw childhood pain and mistreatment as leading to a reactive desire to take on a gay identity. In an interview, Pete explained to me his problem with the pro-gay movement—that it relied on the belief in a "gay gene" to legitimate the belief that gay people cannot change. He illustrated his understanding of gay and lesbian identities by sketching a three-tiered pyramid.

The large bottom tier of the pyramid consisted of those people who identified as gay or lesbian because of sexual abuse, date rape, or some other abusive situation. He recalled seeing a movie where a college student was raped and then fell into a campus group whose members insisted that her aversion to men was because she was a lesbian. This example for him illustrated what the gay movement was about—seeking to up its numbers while neglecting people's needs for healing. In effect, he argued, the gay movement preys on the abused who are psychologically susceptible targets.

A middle tier represented the proportion of those gay men or lesbians who were not abused (as Pete saw it) but who became gay as a result of being teased or tormented because they were nonmasculine boys or nonfeminine girls.

A small square on top of the pyramid represented those who might not be gay because of any painful experience but because of a "gay gene." Pete was not ready to concede that this category existed until science could prove it, however. Pete knew that it was possible for gay people to find healing from their homosexuality; he had met or heard from ex-gays himself. No one had yet been able to prove to him that there were other gay people who could not change and did not need healing from their homosexuality; to him, this was only a theory.[4]

In Pete Vogel's view, the gay movement denies the existence of ex-gays for political reasons, because of the threat ex-gays would pose to the popular "gay gene" theory. The ex-gay movement naturalizes homosexuality with a language of pathology, so to see it naturalized in any other model, such as with a "gay gene," threatens to delegitimate or denaturalize it by equating it with politics. He remarked, "Why don't we just celebrate the ministries that are happening and the movement of ex-gays? But the problem is we want so much to sanctify the gay-gene theory, that something like an ex-gay is a direct threat." Within both of the larger tiers of the pyramid, Pete believed, political movements (from both sides) capitalize on people's pain. He saw the church (those who believe homosexuality to be sinful) participating in this battle over gay people by insisting that homosexuality is sinful while not offering the support gay men and lesbians need to become ex-gays. He saw the gay movement, on the other hand, as snatching these victims up and giving them the comfort of an identity and a sense of belonging, but one that the Bible clearly says is sinful.

Not wishing to be seen as bigoted (that is, political), Pete made it clear that he did not have anything against people who identify as gay or lesbian, saying:

> For somebody who comes to me and says, "Pete, I don't care about a gay gene, this is really who I am; this is who God made me," I don't hold any condemnation of them. Because to me, "Hey, I don't blame you. You're a pawn. You're a pawn. You've been burnt, probably from the church. And we as evangelicals have created a place, maybe, where you don't feel safe, which is sad."

Pete described gay political leaders as trying to increase their numbers, disallowing any option besides living as gay, refusing to allow that some people may need to find an ex-gay style of healing from whatever caused them to turn to homosexuality. He saw gay men's and lesbians' pain—their having been "burnt"—as putting them in a position to be used as pawns by political actors fighting to up their movements' numbers and prove their point. (And he thought that these battles waged in the name of politics might be responsible for the suicide rate among gays.) Pete saw being gay or lesbian as a direct result of the hurt, betrayal, and "baggage" that follow from sexual sin in the world. Recognizing gay people's pain allowed Pete to be willing to befriend them, and indeed he had made gay friends. It also allowed him to naturalize his own heterosexuality as *not* rooted in pain. His problem was not with gay men and lesbians, people he defined as pained, but with those who manipulated them and denied that they could find healing; such people he defined as political.

The Power of Pain

Like those who believed homosexuality to be sinful, pro-gay members also saw the church as providing healing for homosexuals. In this view, however,

homosexuals needed healing from the world that devalued homosexuality
and discriminated against gay people. Pro-gay members wanted the church
to be a haven for gay people, a place where they could be recognized as wonderful creations of God. However, to make gay people even seem to belong
in church *as gay people* in the first place, while maintaining church as that
haven, pro-gay members found themselves having to dissociate homosexuality from politics. To break that equation, members sensed that the church
must see gay people's "pain."

Given the disdain for politics in the church, comments on what might be
seen as political or oppressive situations or policies in other spheres needed to
take another form. At one of City Church's reconciliation meetings, participants brought issues of social justice to the antipolitical camp of the church
by expressing them in terms of pain. The discussion began on the topic of
what it would take for the church to actually welcome gay men and lesbians.
After a bit more discussion, the topic moved on to gay people's need to be
"patient" with the church as it attempted to undergo a change of heart and
mind. Gordon Voller, a white man in his fifties, compared contemporary
debates over homosexuality to the Civil War, seeing both as situations that
caused wounds:

> The Civil War was 130 years ago, and the Methodist Church hasn't done
> a whole lot in that time to heal the wounds left over from that. Some
> wounds take longer to heal than you might expect. Second, I have friends
> who are United Methodist ministers who think they are as devoted and
> loving as you think you are, and who think we are dead wrong on this
> issue. So, just because we all seem to be of fairly like mind is no reason to
> think this is a simple issue. This is not an easy issue, it's very emotional.
> Third, I think we have all the pieces. This is the right place [to become a
> Reconciling Congregation], this could work here, but I'd hate for us to
> use such strong medicine that we kill the patient. The body of this church
> shouldn't be destroyed over this issue. It could take a long time. We need
> to be more patient.

In this comment, Gordon framed what some in the church call "justice
issues" in terms not of oppression and power but of more individual-level
phenomena. The Civil War, in Gordon Voller's comments, resulted in
"wounds."

What are wounds? They are injuries that can be perceived immediately,
which require attention to heal properly. A wound is known immediately
from the pain or disorder it causes the wounded person. The strength and

immediacy of the stimulus is real. A wound does not require analysis; the wounded party has clearly been wronged, even if the wound was inflicted accidentally. Any wound hurts all victims equally, the way that a bullet in the leg hurts all soldiers the same.[5] In Gordon's analysis, some of the wounds of the Civil War still had not healed. By using a language of wounding, Gordon removed himself from the position of having to assess any systematic imbalances of power that may have been at stake in or resulted from the Civil War, or in the contemporary church's beliefs about homosexuality or treatment of gay people. Just as a doctor is required by oath to treat everyone in need of care, regardless of their social position, so too must the church, in Gordon's analogy, disregard social position when treating the wounds of society.

For Gordon, the issue of homosexuality was complicated by too many emotions to allow the church to take action hastily. Gordon admonished patience for those who wanted the church to change its policies too quickly, saying that the Civil War was a long time ago, while the issue of homosexuality was, in his version of church history, much younger. His call for patience was a call to stop demanding change and to allow those who are "just as devoted and loving" (that is, not hateful) as RCP proponents to have their feelings too. He admonished RCP supporters to respect the feelings of those who opposed the goals of the RCP, including their devotion and love. Otherwise, the people who would make the church welcoming to gay men and lesbians (the medicine) risked destroying the church (the patient).

In the discussion, Gordon Voller's comments drew a response from Alex Carter, the congregation's seminary intern, who interjected:

> Well, as a student, I am required to take a course on the history of the denomination. I *have* to learn this. [This is said in a poor-me tone, and people laugh supportively.] So it wasn't till 1930 that the church pulled back together over [the issue of] racism. [. . .] Okay, so after that the church was split over the decision to ordain women in 1955. So, only three times has the Council of Bishops, this governing body of our denomination, split amongst themselves within the denomination, and this is what really put these issues into perspective for me. They split over the issue of racism, over ordaining women, and now over gay and lesbian concerns. A group of fifteen bishops signed a document saying that they don't support the *Discipline* on this.[6] And so it really seems that when we have these splits is when progress happens. [. . .] As a student, it's interesting to see how social justice comes about. But as a human being, it's painful to see things be so slow.

Alex thus responded to Gordon's call for patience, and it was clear that he felt an urgency in responding to that call. Such patience as Gordon called for, Alex implied, allowed injustice to persist. Although Alex reframed the issue of pain, his analysis of this injustice shared Gordon's tendency to make the church's debate an issue of concern to individuals, rather than about spiritually disenfranchised and oppressed groups. As he recounted church history, he recounted it in the form of a story of himself, being required to learn this history, then feeling his own individual emotions as a result of his learning.

As a seminary student, Alex said, he was required to learn about the lengthy processes of social change in his church, and thus he could see the parallels between this and other cases of gross injustice. For instance, his studies put him in a position to see slavery and the denial of ordination rights to women as parallel to the case under discussion. As a student, Alex had to think about spiritually disenfranchised and oppressed groups such as African Americans and women. As a student, Alex found it interesting to see historical parallels, such as in the Council of Bishops' own internal divisions. And as a student, these historical parallels showed him that the situation at hand was indeed a case of gross injustice on the part of the church, a case where the church was guilty of using God's word to enforce humanity's unjust hierarchies. Rhetorically, Alex legitimated his engagement of political and corporate issues in the church by accounting for it with his requirements as a student—he didn't *choose* this line of argument, so he was not out to make trouble.

Alex did not assert that the church's slow progress in achieving justice accommodates injustice. As we have seen, such a political remark would not cohere with the transcendent claim Alex was trying to make. Rather, he called it "painful." Situations that might call for an analysis of power in other circumstances here called for the healing of wounds or the palliation of pain. And it is "as a human being" that one feels this pain. Alex seemed to invoke the group's shared humanity to stir their compassion for the pained, while gently showing Gordon that having patience with RCP opponents was not necessarily the most compassionate way church members could deal with the issue.

Later, I spoke with Alex about that meeting. After a lengthy discussion of pain in the church, he made a wish, saying:

> I wish some things would be said at those meetings. I wish someone
> would show up and give witness to what the church's stance on homosex-
> uality can do. Stand up and say, "Because I thought I was so unworthy,

I lived this life of many sexual partners, and not feeling like I was worth doing it safely, and now I have HIV or AIDS."[7]

Alex wished that gay people would give witness to their own pain, in this case, the incontrovertible pain of AIDS or HIV, believing that such a witness would make church members see what he saw as the results of their beliefs and actions. He hoped that seeing such a demonstration of the painful material results of church beliefs would inspire members to feel compassion and change.

At the beginning of this chapter, we saw Nancy Cook at a different reconciliation meeting making the move Alex had hoped to see, but not on her own behalf. Instead she spoke about having seen a movie, *The Adventures of Priscilla, Queen of the Desert*. In an interview with me later, she elaborated on her analysis of the film. Nancy tried to work out the meanings and origins of the "shocking" things she saw gay people doing, framing shocking behavior and dress as the pain of difference and exclusion. She compared the outrageous performances in the movie and in the New York and San Francisco Pride parades to "Black is Beautiful," later positing gay outrageousness as a means for people to construct more positive self-images, combating the negative images that said to gay people, "You're a walking sin; you're an abomination." She reinterpreted such outrageousness as a way to help gay people compensate for the negative things society says about them, to find "healing," and to realize that "Christ's death was for *everyone*," and God's Creation is all "very good."

Nancy hesitated to articulate her own shock at such outrageous displays. She struggled to be accepting, and, indeed, she brought to our interview a copy of a sermon she thought captured the essence of Christianity, Paul Tillich's "You Are Accepted" (1948). In Nancy's understanding, shock was not an appropriate emotion for a Christian to feel. To be Christian, she needed to feel more empathetic and accepting. She adjusted her feelings by calling into awareness the context of a society that feeds some people—in these examples black people and gay men—negative self-images that make them feel bad about who or how they are. What helped her to make this move was understanding the *pain* underlying gay people's outrageous displays. Here, gay pain inspired Nancy to change her mind about the sinfulness of homosexuality; in effect, pain legitimated otherwise "shocking" displays of homosexuality. Gay pain seemed, to her, truer than her earlier notion that God commanded every human being to reproduce.

If we draw from her earlier comment, we can see that her new understanding moved her to understand gay people as painfully rejected by society, rather than themselves actively rejecting society, or God. Nancy supplemented what she had believed to be the timeless truth—that God created people to reproduce—with another truth. If they are in that much pain, she seemed to say, it can't be their conscious choice. She characterized homosexuality as "the struggle that didn't go away. The guy . . . *had* had a wife," suggesting that a gay male character in the movie had tried to conform, but even with his struggle he couldn't help but be gay. Even the public and political outrageousness of some Gay Pride parade contingents were not "political," in her view. Parade participants were not defiantly rejecting; they were painfully rejected. The anger and defiance of militant gay movements, including movements that actively rejected dominant norms, became a symptom of pain, and pain became truth. In her analysis, because society's nonacceptance caused gay people pain, society (and Christianity) should accept gay people as they are.

Even though Nancy disagreed with Joe Dallas and Pete Vogel on many points, all three saw gay people's pain as something that made gay people seem less threatening. For Pete, gay people's pain meant, "Hey, I don't blame you. You're a pawn," and, as he remarked later, "Let's have lunch, let's have a friendship." For Nancy, it meant that gay people were just trying to foster a positive self-image. Nancy saw society's prejudice as the source of gay people's problems. Joe Dallas and Pete Vogel similarly recognized that once someone identifies as gay or lesbian, even Christianity's traditional stance may have, in Pete's words, "burned them." Each portrayed gay people as unable to make their own conscious political choices, and it was this inability that rendered them unthreatening and deserving of compassion. Dallas saw gay militants' rage as rooted in their childhood pain and fear; this helped him to "respect the rage." Pete saw gay people as pawns, being used by a political movement that does not have their interests at heart; this understanding allowed him to befriend gay people, to have lunch with them. And Nancy understood the shocking things gay people do as a way to dramatize their difference, to improve their self-image and feel fabulous. Thus, she came to understand homosexuality as something other than a rejection of God's plan. In all three cases, this language of pain countered the threat of homosexuality denaturalizing church members' grounding assumptions about sexuality.

Alex Carter wanted gay people to witness to their own pain and suffering. Nancy Cook showed how such a testimony can be effective, in that understanding gay people as being pained moved her to understand homosexuality as one of God's surprising gifts. Although issues such as HIV/AIDS policy, discrimination, and general anti-gay beliefs have, in other contexts,

led to political protest and public expressions of anger and outrage (for instance, the Stonewall riots and ACT-UP demonstrations), in the church these
issues must be dealt with in less "polarizing" and "divisive" terms. Instead of
looking at another person and accusing him or her of acting unjustly, in the
"militant" style Dallas talks about, in the church such complaints must be
addressed at the level of individual pain. And as a popular Protestant hymn
goes, the church idealizes "the fellowship of kindred minds," as members
"share each other's woes."

The Truth of Feelings and the Value of Pain

As Nancy Cook testified, one strength of the language of pain is that it can
change people's minds about whether homosexuality is sinful. Similarly, Joe
Dallas and Pete Vogel showed how a language of pain could defuse the threat
gay people might cause some people, inspiring love from those who wish to
help gay people to become sexually normative. As this section shows, pain
also worked by defusing potential conflicts—pain abstracted the person experiencing it, taking away his ability to make legitimate political demands or
authoritatively analyze the workings of power. Thus, the language of pain
was well suited to a realm whose members constituted it as free from politics. Churchgoers avoided what City Church member Mindy Reynolds, in
chapter 3, called "bad [political] thinking," by feeling bad, by feeling pain.

When a member wished to bring to light an oppressive situation, it was
not enough to simply express a concern in the language of pain. Church
members needed to be sincere. Hence Alex Carter's wish that someone with
the undeniable pain of HIV or AIDS would testify to the church's role in
making her feel worthless and that her life was not worth protecting. They
must manage their emotions, coming to actually feel what they *should* feel.
If a church member wished to stop feeling angry at, alienated by, or impatient with the church, to recoup it as a place of communitas removed from
the world of human divisions and politics, he must not simply express such
bad feelings in the language of pain, but *feel* them as pain.

We have already seen how the feeling of communitas, of connection,
of being at peace, could be produced through church rituals. Belonging to a
church produced other feelings as well, some that people might more or less
consciously adjust, others that they experienced as visceral and uncontrol-
lable. Thus, Alex Carter did find it painful to see people advocating patience
in the face of what he perceived as injustice. Other members really felt pain
at the thought of their gay siblings and friends being shut out of the church
or deemed especially sinful because of their homosexuality. And Pete Vogel

really felt pain at the thought of a rape victim being denied the possibility of healing by political actors (though he did not see the rapists themselves as political actors). Strikingly absent from the debates at the time of my research at City Church was the testimony of gay people themselves sharing their pain; rather, gay men and lesbians in the congregation tended to keep a low profile. Some reasons for this reticence will soon become clear.

In the absence of lesbians and gay men from the congregation who were willing to witness to their supposed pain, others were occasionally invited in from neighboring congregations to speak. For instance, City Church had an adult Sunday School class that focused on marriage and other committed relationships, where the teachers invited various married couples, widows and widowers, parents and kids in blended or mixed-race families, and others to speak about their relationships. One Sunday the guests were Becky Lee and Jane Redmond, a lesbian couple who were members of another United Methodist congregation. They spoke chiefly about what a regular, normal couple they were. "We're not activists," Becky said. "People talk about a gay lifestyle. Our lifestyle is boring. We have a bird feeder, a house to clean; we have to mow the lawn." With such remarks, they distanced themselves from some people's perception of lesbians as "activists" with a nonnormative or perhaps outrageous lifestyle, describing their own lifestyle as "boring."

As outsiders, Becky and Jane could perhaps afford not to mince words about their church's beliefs and treatment of gay men, lesbians, and bisexuals, and themselves in particular. Among the couple's remarks were some very pointed comments about the current debates about homosexuality. For instance, Jane commented about the Christian "love the sinner, hate the sin," philosophy: "We've had members say they love us, they 'love the sinner, and hate the sin,' or however they put it. But you know, really, that's a hateful thing to say. You tell me you love me, salve your conscience, and then leave me to go home and lose sleep. It's just hateful." Here, Jane rejected the entire premise of the belief that homosexuality is sinful, calling the "love the sinner" philosophy "hateful" because of what she saw as its self-centeredness, its insistence that homosexuality is sinful, and its refusal to listen to the experience of those who, like her, understood it as simply part of who God made them. Similarly, Becky commented that their relationship was made stronger by their church's hostile treatment, saying they were "bound by a common enemy—the church—that's trying to break us up, that tells us we're part of the fallenness of humanity."

In spite of their uncompromising language with regard to the church, Becky and Jane expressed their anger in nonconfrontational terms. Jane said

"It's just hateful" with downcast eyes, so that whatever anger she may have felt did not confront her audience directly. She remarked, "It's painful to have the church stop being the home it's been for us." Whether Jane somehow "really" felt anger but expressed it in terms of pain, or whether she "really" felt pain, is not at issue. In all likelihood she probably felt both. But to do what she and Becky had to do, to naturalize their demands for equal treatment in the church, she had to express pain at the treatment she had received at the hands of the church.[8]

Elsewhere in City Church, proponents of the view that homosexuality is sinful were able to echo back RCP supporters' use of pain language to distance themselves from politics. Ron Wilson, who had been a member of City Church for decades, believed that his understanding of homosexuality as sinful followed from "traditional Christianity." When City Church's original pro-gay reconciling congregations task force recommended that the congregation join the RCP, he felt that he had been "attacked," "hurt," and "dismissed" by the clergy and members of the congregation. Meanwhile, others in the congregation had implied that his belief in the sinfulness of homosexuality was motivated by something other than a desire to be closer to God. He recalled:

> Well, the thing that got most strongly to me was an article in the newsletter which I understood to say [. . .] that anyone who did not think church should instantly and completely be opened to all homosexual people in every way was deliberately trying to kill the church. That was one of the most hurtful things that has ever been said to me under any circumstances.[. . .] Now that's the way I interpreted the article in the newsletter. I have tried to forget as much of the detail of that article as I could, because it hurt, dreadfully.

Clearly, Ron never believed that he intended to kill the church; he believed himself to be upholding God's word. Yet he did not describe the statement as "absurd" or "off the wall," nor did he describe it as "aggravating." Rather, he described the statement as painful, "one of the most hurtful things that has ever been said to me under any circumstances." When things in the congregation got adversarial, Ron responded to the accusation that his goals were not godly by feeling and expressing pain. By expressing pain, Ron positioned himself as the victim, the person wronged.

Ron attempted to show that he was motivated not by worldly concerns but by God. He summed up his opinions briefly by stating his desire that the congregation find a way to resolve its conflict over homosexuality without alienating or hurting anyone, and his statement was expressed in terms of pain. He continued:

> The thing that's most important is to find a way to minister to the families of homosexuals, to welcome them. I know that it's hard for the homosexuals, that they feel beaten on. But there must be some way [for the church] to be loving without making other people feel beaten on, or that they're being dragged into it by their hair. They say your rights end where my nose begins. The problem is how to accommodate people, how to be welcoming and allow the [congregation's pro-gay] reconciling committee to do the work they feel they need to do, without hurting others [those who hold the more "traditional" view of homosexuality as sinful].
>
> I am sure there must be homosexuals in the church, and they are welcome here. One of the things people said two years ago was that we do welcome everyone already. They are welcome here. If there are two people of the same sex who love each other and live together and have a private life, that's their business. That doesn't bother me. It's when they drag other people into it, when they become blatant, become open about it, that it causes problems.

In these comments, Ron established that he cared for homosexuals, that he understood their pain and feeling "beaten on." He then broadened the scope of who counted as a victim, suggesting that the problem with homosexual couples' demands of the church is that they made "others feel beaten on" and "dragged into it by their hair." In using violent imagery to describe the actions of the homosexuals, he subtly shifted the terrain of debate. While he saw homosexuals claiming a position of righteous victimhood based on their pain, he pointed out that they, too, could cause people to feel pain. Ron effectively blurred the clear delineation of right and wrong, comforting and wounding, that RCP supporters had created in invoking gay pain. He thus denied a central premise of the pro-gay movement's use of pain, that understanding their pain should cause the church to change. In his view, homosexuals could likewise inflict pain, on more traditional church members such as himself.

Christian Pain and the Suffering Servant

It was not pain, per se, but talking about it that naturalized moral authority in the church. Ron Wilson's struggle to inhabit the moral authority of the pained in this debate reflected not only a desire to blur the righteous position of the gay movement but a Christian tradition of privileging the weak, the downtrodden, the oppressed. The language of pain demands that people respond with compassion, but pain is also an appealing language for Christians because many see it as a key theme in the teachings and life of Christ, the suffering servant. Members were reminded again and again that Jesus taught that the "meek" are blessed, and that the first among humanity will be last in the kingdom of heaven.[9]

Ruthie Shafer invoked this theme when she recalled part of what brought her to advocating the goals of the RCP, including the painful death of her dear friend Lucas, who was gay. Lucas had died from complications of AIDS, but the physical pain of his illness had been compounded by people's abusive treatment of him. This experience transformed Ruthie and changed her understanding of Christianity:

> The allegorical tale of Christ, he suffered and died, okay? And I think the truth for all of us is that if we choose that path we must understand that's exactly what's going to happen to us. We are going to suffer from it, if we stick to our values of love. There are going to be those that don't understand, don't wanna understand, don't choose to understand, don't want to be part of it. Those that want to control you, want to hurt you, and that you do not have to let yourself go because of it. Instead, you will be transformed in that process in ways that you can't know, can't understand. They may resist it, but they will be transformed. There's nothing more engaging than a loving person who's at peace and has a sense of self. I don't care how bad you are, it will really throw your stride off.
>
> This is very hard for me because, you see, I spent three years before I talked about this particular experience with my friend. I felt that human *rage*. My instinctive reaction was to hurt back. I had to really spend a great deal of time with myself. I spent literally days in churches, at the waterfront, in libraries, reading, praying, reading, praying, reading, praying. My instinct is that there had been some really awful things that had been perpetrated, and it's beyond protecting my friend, he's gone. It's retribution.

Ruthie related her experience of pain, seeing it as part of what it is to be Christian, a way of deepening her conviction not to respond to others with "human rage," but to be transformed and possibly transform others with love and a sense of peace. Likening her own suffering and her friend's to an allegorical reading of Jesus' suffering and death, she thus envisioned pain not as a disempowering weakness or loneliness, such as that of the pained child or outcast, but as the lot of Christ and of those who walk in his footsteps. She thus placed pain within the realm of Christianity, rather than outside of it. Though she differs from Joe Dallas in her understanding of what it means to love another (and what it means to suffer), they agree that Christians should ideally respond to suffering people not with retribution but with love.

Ruthie characterized her feelings around her friend's illness and death as a human instinct to hurt back, to seek retribution toward those who had hurt him. "But," she continued:

> I cannot be a Christian and live that way. I can't live it out, and I can't keep it in my heart. I have to find another way to use that experience and the energy that comes from the pain to make the difference. I don't know what that will be. You know, I may never know what that is. That's the other side of faith. [. . .] We are not given the right to know that everything we do will have some wonderful consequence that we get to see on a big screen at the end. So I have faith that if I take the gifts God has given me, including that experience, and use it, as best I can, in whatever inadequate way I may have, that something good may come of that. [. . .] Things will unfold in a pathway that is unique to your process. So as you go through this, or other things that you may be dealing with in your life, you can then relax and have comfort. You don't have to process every day; you don't have to worry every day, because it's not you, you're not the god, God is. As long as your heart is in the right place, God *will* do the rest.
>
> If you had told me during the time I saw what my friend, my wonderful Lucas, went through, there would come a day when I would have a forum where I would be able to address it in a public way that would be positive, that I would actually be sitting in a coffee shop talking to a researcher, I mean, I couldn't have imagined that. All I knew was the pain. But there's more beyond that. The pain and the anger are the beginning, the planting of the seed.
>
> Our only life's work is to spend the time to allow ourselves to just take a deep breath and love.

For Ruthie, not only vengeance but goal-oriented action fell beyond the realm of Christian action. A Christian should not impose her own goals but simply take a deep breath and love, having faith and taking comfort in the knowledge that God will use her for good. Ruthie saw pain as bringing people to the place where they could see what it means to show Christian love and a greater understanding of God. In her view, the pain of gay people and others could be the transformative process that showed them how to love. She thus reproduced or reified gay pain, paradoxically idealizing it even as she denounced the church that caused it. Those who never suffer, she implied, may not know how to be Christlike; pain and anger plant the seed of Christian action. Yet even while Ruthie believed that pain played a transformative role in Christianity, she still believed that the church should be a place of comfort and healing for the pained.

The Politics of Pain

There are a number of reasons that the language of pain appealed to members. First, many people, gay and otherwise, really did feel pain because of the way they felt the church treated them or because of the conflict in the church. Furthermore, by inviting people to experience compassion, the pain argument actually worked to change people's hearts and minds about what steps the church should take. The language of gay pain helped many heterosexual church members, regardless of whether they believed homosexuality to be sinful, to see gay people as seekers of compassion rather than as threatening troublemakers. They could use a language of pain to help the church by making it more open and compassionate (however defined) to homosexuals, to help them in Christian love.

A language of pain, gay and otherwise, also helped members as they created an image of the church as a haven, a place of comfort from the pain and politics that forced people to think of themselves as rooted in earthly bodies. Seeking a transcendent haven from worldly conditions is part of what it means to members to seek closeness to God. Casting oneself or one's allies as pained helped to frame the pained persons' goals or desires as apolitical. Most members understood politics as distinct from emotions. Seeing gay people or others as caught up in emotion allowed them to seem free from "political" motivations.

In their focus on feelings as truth, they reflected the "therapeutic ethos" sociologist James Nolan (1998) identifies. Nolan argues that in response to the societal shifts of industrialization and bureaucratization throughout the twentieth century, Americans have come to seek truth and comfort in the self, in speaking the language of feelings. Although Nolan focuses on the therapeutic ethos in state institutions, he suggests that in a world where few other sources of truth can be agreed on, the self is all that remains: "If one is discouraged from appealing to religious symbols or even to divine reasons in the classical sense, one is left with one's own feelings" (1998, 5). The debates we have examined here show that even where religious symbols prevail, the self can be seen as a source of truth. After all, these debates make abundantly clear that even religious beliefs and symbols are the products of everyday theologies, that even God can be argued about—and arguing about God can disrupt members' experience of God. Compared to Scripture, feelings are harder to dispute.

Not just any feelings rang of "truth," however. As we saw in Nancy Cook's account, church members recognized the language of pain as a language of truth. Why pain? Pain seems to be something you can only know when you feel it; it isn't open to outside interpretation. Pain seems natural, yet it is something Christians are called to both revere (for example, Christ on the cross) and to alleviate. To harm another is wrong, perhaps even Pilate-like, but to feel pain can be almost sacred. Because of the truth value of pain, and because members idealized the church's role of showing compassion to the needy and giving relief to those in need, pro-gay church members could think and speak of gay people's pain as the reason the church must be open to them. Seeing God as a universal redeemer and sustainer, they could see pain as the opposite of God's intent. In spite of the Christian theme of the suffering servant, healing and comfort from pain seemed to have become part of what it meant for church members to desire to know and worship God.

When church members envisioned gay people as pained or childlike, they held them at a social distance, defusing any threat they may have posed to the church's normative worldview. In the languages of those like Pete Vogel and Joe Dallas, who believed homosexuality to be sinful, gays and lesbians were seen not as adults with different experiences of God, life, and sexuality but as children or victims whose special pain rendered them socially distant and in need of special treatment until they could find "healing."[10] By positing gay men and lesbians as victims or children, they produced a distance, insulating themselves from the possibility of learning from the very people they sought to welcome. As they welcomed certain repentant gay people, they disallowed the possibility of a gay identity; they hoped and prayed that the human being underneath the pain and artifice of homosexuality could find new life—a life free from the shackles of homosexual sin.[11] None of this is surprising; given their belief that homosexuality is sinful, these members found a way to reconcile that belief with the desire to make the church more open.

For those who believed homosexuality to be "compatible with Christian teaching," the language of pain was, in fact, a slightly different language. For pro-gay members, the language of pain worked in a more complicated way, because it drew not only from the therapeutic ethos but also from the politics of identity. We saw this in comparisons to abolitionism and "Black is Beautiful" and the women's movement. Here, gay men's and lesbians' pain figured as another example of what literary critic Lauren Berlant calls "subaltern pain." She remarks:

> Subaltern pain is not considered *universal* (the privileged do not experience it, they do not live expecting that at any moment their ordinarily loose selves might be codified into a single humiliated atom of sub-personhood). But subaltern pain is deemed, in this context, universally *intelligible*, constituting objective evidence of trauma reparable by the law and the law's more privileged subjects. . . .
>
> In this political model of identity, trauma stands as truth. We can't use happiness as a guide to the aspirations for social change, because the feeling of it might be false consciousness; nor boredom, which might be depression, illness, or merely a spreading malaise. Pain, in contrast, is something quick and sharp that simultaneously specifies you and makes you generic: it is something that happens to you before you "know" it, and it is intensely individuating, for surviving its shock lets you know it is your general survival at stake. (1999, 72)

For Berlant, subaltern pain has come to register as a certain kind of truth. In identity politics, actors base their claims in the pain said to be caused by the failure of American political ideals to recognize marginal people—those at the bottom of American hierarchies of race, gender, sexuality, and the like—as full citizens of the American, or church, ideal. As the political theorist Wendy Brown (1995) points out, in such a political model group members often make the pain of exclusion central to their identities. They can end up positing pain as the only legitimate source of social critique.

Furthermore, as the cases we have seen demonstrate, outsiders can focus on the pain itself and neglect the critique altogether. Feelings do not have exactly the same role in church as in secular politics, however. Church members often speak to one another in terms of emotion. Yet just as with Transforming rhetoric, when pro-gay Christians invoked gay people's pain, they turned gay people into unthreatening figures whose difference could be seen as a matter of pathos, not rational political critique. As Nolan points out, therapeutic language can have unintended consequences. These consequences might explain why lesbian and gay church members, who wanted to be accepted for "who" they were, might be selective in disclosing "what" they were, lest their personhood be defined as essentially pained.

Feelings do not form a solid basis for moral argument because, as we have seen, they can point to multiple truths. The literary critic Elaine Scarry analyzes the political and ethical ramifications of pain's inability to be confirmed or denied, remarking, "To have pain is to have certainty; to hear about pain is to have doubt" (1985, 13). In other words, because the actual feeling of pain cannot be remembered, the person hearing about another's pain can never know for certain what the other feels. Drawing from that doubt on the part of the hearer, Lauren Berlant asks: "What does it mean . . . when the shock of pain is said only to produce clarity, when shock can as powerfully be said to produce panic, misrecognition, the shakiness of perception's ground?" (1999, 58). Pro-gay Christians relied on a language of pain to demand the comforting and welcoming of gay people, but in doing so they failed to address the fact that those who believed homosexuality to be sinful saw pain itself as the pathological cause of homosexuality. Many pro-gay advocates found themselves unable to counter this argument.

An argument from pain failed to make the pro-gay case for other reasons as well. As chapter 7 showed, many members saw comfort, not pain, as what indicated right relationship to God. What is pain if not *dis*comfort? How could people in perpetual pain, associated with their state of being, be in right relationship with God in this framework? Second, when members used pain to show that gay people belonged in the church, they made gay membership contingent on that pain. Gay people who were not in pain were still effectively equated with political self-interest. If gay members must continually experience and demonstrate their pain, then their belonging in church must reflect a quest for healing and comfort from the very pain that makes homosexuality seem compatible with church. In effect, righteous homosexuality, even as pro-gay members envisioned it, demanded either a quest for healing or constant suffering.[12]

Even as the proponents of this language sought equality for gay members of the church, the language of pain foreclosed the option of being a whole gay member shouldering no particular burden because of being gay. Thus limited by a language of gay pain, gay members were not allowed to transcend their worldly position and still "just be" gay. In this symbolic economy, their gayness continued to root them in the earthly.

The Perils of Pain and Politics

When I participated in the congregations of City and Missionary United Methodist Churches, I sought to learn how different members understood homosexuality in relation to their own timeless truths. As members shared their thinking with me one-on-one and in groups, their negotiations revolved around so many sources of truth—science, health, happiness, care, justice, righteousness, pain, and so forth—that the various truths threatened to denaturalize each other. Thus, these debates revolved around what members defined as opposed to all of these truths: politics. Church members' repeated distancing from the "political" suggests that their understanding of the world was shaped by the knowledge that politics was the opposite of their ideals.

Homosexuality itself has been equated with politics in these debates for a number of reasons: because of its apparent roots in the carnal body, because the pro-gay church movement has at times drawn from a secular language of rights, because these debates brought to light the hierarchies that inhered in the church, and, most important, because homosexuality threatened to denaturalize many members' foundational assumptions about heterosexuality, sin, and the nature of God's Creation. To welcome gay men and lesbians into the church, people on both sides of the homosexuality issue sought to distance the members and potential members from politics by using a naturalizing language of emotion, specifically a "pain" supposedly particular to homosexuals.

My thinking about this project has been strongly shaped by the school of thought known as queer theory, which looks at how the processes of defining sexuality tacitly shape realms of social life that seem utterly asexual (Epstein 1994, Seidman 1996, Warner 1993). Following that logic, this might have been a study of how notions about sexuality naturalized beliefs about God and creation. But I ended up observing something different, something even larger. Sexuality is not alone in this naturalizing role; in this study, we have seen how the definition of politics, even more than sexuality, tacitly undergirded the debate and served to foreclose certain possibilities. In this case, the language of politics worked to foreclose the possibility of being a gay and unpained member of a congregation. While we looked in chapter 6 at what distinguished sex from other topics for congregational debate, I have shown throughout that central to congregational debates about homosexuality was the process of defining God's transcendent truth in contrast not only (and not necessarily) to homosexuality but in contrast to the repudiated category of politics.

We have seen how church members built and maintained church as a place free from politics: a place to transcend the bodily limitations and markers that divided people; a place to commune with God and others and to feel one's place in the world; a place to know that no matter how painful, stressful, cynical, or cruel the world might be, there was something greater, something stable and reliable, something that made ultimate sense. They sought in their everyday theologies to build and maintain church as that zone of transcendence. They fused together beliefs that threatened to denaturalize each other. Rather than let that happen, they rejected denaturalization itself, by agreeing to repudiate the opposite of all of their ideals: "politics." Yet in seeking to create church as a transcendent haven from politics, members inadvertently reasserted the (political) hierarchies that structured daily life. This is the paradox of avoiding politics.

Repudiating Politics

Politics, be it civil or theological in nature, does not need to be how many members defined it: selfish, dehumanizing, and materialistic. This is why some members, at both congregations, participated in politics *as* Christians. In spite of their vast differences, they believed that people working together to confront issues of power and privilege in society could make the world a more humane and moral place. Yet in both congregations, these more politically active members found themselves negotiating a way to do what they believed God required of them without alienating their fellow members,

many of whom saw church as a haven from politics.[1] They were not alone
in this effort to avoid politics. Working to translate their efforts into unthreatening terms was itself a strategy (a "political" strategy) for changing
relations of power and privilege. Nonetheless, in the big picture of American
political culture, many people define "politics" as threatening rather than as
noble or inspiring.

This repudiation of politics is not arbitrary; another category could not
easily replace politics in its repudiated role. Politics was repudiated in these
congregations to the extent that it denaturalized, or threatened to denaturalize, people's foundational assumptions—the assumptions around which they
organized the world and their places in it. In effect, it was not simply that
politics served as the opposite of members' ideals; rather, members defined
as "political" those things that threatened to *denaturalize* their ideals.

What ideals need to be maintained and what seems natural can change
over time. For instance, sociologist Robert Wuthnow points out that in the
1980s, during the Reagan era, Americans came to idealize "a positive attitude," which meant rejecting collective action that seemed to distract from
individual rights and motivations. The positive outlook he describes emerged
in a context of individualism so deep that even political leaders who sought
to foster an attitude of individualism were seen as not individualistic enough,
too "political," because of their attempts to mobilize people (1998, 108).
Wuthnow sees this trend's legacy in the spirituality of the 1990s as well,
where people reported finding spiritual solace in such individual activities as
jogging in the woods. It seems that for the joggers, even the age-old "natural
rights of the individual" has been supplanted as a naturalizing discourse. For
them, perhaps, only Nature itself will do.

Other sociologists have found people defining politics as something to
avoid. Examining parents' volunteer groups, antidrug groups, environmental activist groups, and recreational dance groups, Nina Eliasoph (1998) finds
again and again what I observed in these two United Methodist congregations: across the board, people defined politics as the opposite of whatever
they held as ideal, be it care (an antidrug group), personal efficacy (volunteer
groups), or fun (recreational dance groups). Even environmental activists
might one-on-one tell Eliasoph that they believed in the need to create a
better world by challenging powerful and polluting corporations but as soon
as they had the opportunity to make a public statement they had to express
their concerns in terms of self-interest as concerned parents. To further their
political goals, I would add, they had to naturalize their goals in terms of
self-interest. In the dance group, some white members told Eliasoph about
their antiracist views, but in the group they found it impossible to criticize

racist jokes within the legitimate ways of talking (Eliasoph 1999). It is taboo to denaturalize another's assumptions, even if those assumptions seem wrong.

This definition of politics bodes ill for American representative democracy. Just by looking at the news, we can see this treatment of the category of politics as a catch-all for the negative. For instance, in 2002 the *Los Angeles Times* contained several accounts of people using the charge of politics or political motivations to delegitimate their opposition. These included (1) a letter to the editor arguing that for the paper's editorial staff to criticize the Bush administration's failure to warn investors about Enron's impending collapse seemed "more the product of political motivations than sound reasoning";[2] and (2) the Los Angeles police chief, in an address, accusing the mayor and police union of placing political motives over human life, saying: "You as council members and the commission in the future will have to determine how many lives should be lost to accommodate a police union as payback for its endorsement of the mayor and to accommodate a small number of community activists who want the Police Department at their beck and call." He then went on to say, "The true question is how much emphasis is placed on the value of life over political agendas."[3]

Even politicians can use the moniker of "politics" to delegitimate things. In September 2002, as the Bush administration prepared to go to war against Iraq, Senate Majority Leader Tom Daschle commented on a speech by President Bush, saying that a partisan "politicized environment" would "diminish, minimize, degrade the debates on an issue as grave as war." Citing the Republican president's comment that "the Democratic-controlled Senate is not interested in the security of the American people," Daschle called for an apology to Democrats in the Senate who were military veterans and to the American people, saying, "That is wrong. We ought not to politicize this war. We ought not to politicize the rhetoric about life and death."

Although "politics" means something slightly different in each of these three cases, it is used in all three to accuse someone, even politicians, of treachery. In the first case, politics is the opposite of reason (and honesty); in the second it is the opposite of valuing life; and in the third it is the opposite of taking life and death seriously. In the last example, the senator effectively casts the decision of whether to "preventatively" invade an autonomous nation as not a "political" question, defining "politics" as pertaining to partisan infighting, not important questions of power and privilege.

Similarly, sociologist Joshua Gamson (2001) finds that news media treated a politician caught with a prostitute not as a moral transgressor but as an indicator of what kind of people go into politics. Such media portrayals send a message to readers and viewers that politics is not something for decent people. Such portrayals might reflect, or produce, a political culture where, as the political scientist Robert Putnam (2000, 47) points out, roughly three-quarters of Americans do not trust the government to do what is right, and where 57 percent agree with the Harris Poll statement "The people running the country don't really care what happens to you," in contrast to the 66 percent who *rejected* that view in 1966, during the Vietnam War and in a period of numerous race riots. This antipolitical language has the effect of subverting public democracy, which is based on the ideal of universal political participation.

Searching for Hope, Not Pain

Many people might, like City Church's Keith Appleton, find depressingly dehumanizing my assertion that people cannot escape politics, that we can neither escape the politics that is part and parcel of any language/discourse that makes the socially constructed really real, nor can we escape the civil politics of a democratic state. Many might agree with Keith's view that politics is a "humanity killer." But such a view supposes that politics has to be as dehumanizing as people have made it and that the realms of linguistic power and civil politics are somehow avoidable. If we see human society as necessarily "political" then we can recognize, negotiate, and challenge hierarchies of power and privilege. This need not depress us.

In the 1970s, the feminist slogan "The personal is political" mobilized women who had seen their unhappiness as a personal problem, drawing them together in consciousness-raising sessions to see such issues as discrimination, rape, depression, and domestic violence as political, as collective issues stemming from a structure of patriarchal domination. This movement responded to sociologist C. Wright Mills' (1959) call to see the relationship between individuals' "troubles" and social "problems" and to demand social change. These feminists were radical and angry but propelled by a sense of hope. People were changing society for the better, and they could change it more.

We are not so hopeful anymore. Nowadays, we might say that an ideology of "The personal is personal" (that is, the personal is apolitical) has replaced the old slogan. The persistence of hierarchies and domination, even within those optimistic New Left movements, has made meaningful change seem slow going. As Lauren Berlant (1997) discusses, the frustration people feel at the persistence of injustice and the failure of ideals has created a backlash. In our era's dominant liberal individualism, despite all the data we have come up with to show that social structure objectively exists, power is now seen as a personal attribute, which means that power is even freer to operate without oversight. We see it as a sign of mean intentions rather than a structural fact. People who wish no ill to others find themselves hurt when someone accuses them of having power. Discussions of politics can quickly degenerate into contests to see who is less empowered, and who is meaner, who is hurt by whom. As Wendy Brown (1995) points out, leftist activists can find it easier to foster resentment of others' privileges than to overthrow social hierarchies and disrupt the languages that legitimate those hierarchies. In Berlant's analysis, a politics of resentment has contributed to political exhaustion in America.

In the congregations I visited, church members and leaders sought to replace exhaustion with hope, and restrictive identity labels with transcendence. These congregations maintained themselves as the opposite of what members called "politics." But many of the same hierarchies and conflicts that they found in secular life appeared within their church as well. Although congregations (though not only congregations) tend to be more communitarian, more loving and accepting, and more gracious for many of their members than American public life is, some of the same dynamics that exist in American public life exist in congregations. Indeed, debates about homosexuality are both profoundly political and profoundly spiritual, yet their political nature is one of the factors members used to argue that the debates should not be taking place in church at all.

The people we have heard from here sought to transcend the earthly and the political and to build communities based on shared beliefs about that transcendence. They also sought to build hope into their communities, with an ethic of compassion. At one level, compassion, "feeling with" another, implies the radical equality of communitas. But when people already live in a hierarchical relationship to one another—as when some have the discretion to decide if others can join their group, share their rights and privileges, or even truly know God—compassion does not require equality.[4] In fact, as we have seen, it can reinforce inequality.

The compassion we have seen can reinforce established inequality at a number of levels. First, if one member can only be understood or welcomed into a community by demonstrating pain, that member is not free to experience and express the full range of human possibilities. Second, if someone is defined by his pain, an emotion known through physical cues and understood to be caused by the failings of the earthly and imperfect realm, then that earthliness becomes essential to the way others perceive him. Transcendence is impossible for him. Meanwhile, the person granting the compassion retains the authority to determine whether the pain is genuine and what the speaker of the pain deserves in response.

These results of a politics of emotion can be found in government as well. While a language deemed "political" has become illegitimate even among politicians, people in government have found that, as is the case in these two congregations, a language of emotion can legitimate and naturalize certain moves. James Nolan (1998), for instance, finds a language of therapy and individual feelings shaping policies in the areas of welfare, education, criminal and civil law, and even legislation. He points out that while liberal, therapeutic approaches to problems of education, law, social work, and the like (how to build self-esteem, how to make people feel efficacious) can help some people, they do not bring people together as a community; these approaches do not remedy the modern world's isolation of people. Nor do these programs increase individual liberty; state actors retain the power to determine who is healthy, who belongs in society, just as heterosexual church members retained the power in this case to determine who belonged in their congregations. The people I observed drew from this liberal move of seeking relief for the pained, and produced unintended consequences similar to those Nolan observes.

Pain may be a person's ticket through the door, but a language of pain does nothing to challenge the unequal authority structured into people's relationships—in this case, by church tradition and policies that establish that certain statements about members' relationship with God shall not be given credence. If liberals wish to abolish the church's established inequality between heterosexuals and others, focusing on gay pain is not going to achieve that. In fact, the language of pain can further entrench inequality in a Christian context, where heterosexually identified church members can feel all the more transcendent by exercising their apparently Christlike ability to show compassion for others less fortunate, even if their misfortune is simply to be seen (by church members themselves) as rooted in the realm of the physical.

The ethic of compassion, certainly a laudable ethic, can accompany individualism and hierarchy as well as community and equality.[5] If one believes that *politics* is what needs to be avoided, retreating to the self may not even help. Personal identity and feelings have become overtly politicized for people who have not always perceived their identities to be relevant to conditions of power. The identity politics of the past several decades has advanced the ideals of equality for those America has left out—including women, people of color, sexual minorities, disabled people, and those who fall into two or more such categories. And we have seen that not only identity but feelings as well have been implicated in these politics. Identity politics derives its strength from collective pain and wounds.[6]

This is not to say that pain is not effective in politics. It has been very effective, no doubt in part because of its ability to address aspects of a social problem and create feelings of public virtue while retaining social hierarchy. Sentimental texts that told of the pain and "indelicacy" of slavery inspired much of the abolition movement by focusing on the shared humanity of slaves and free whites.[7] Likewise, seeing someone in pain can make that person, and those she or he purportedly represents, seem more human and deserving of compassion, as we saw when Nancy Cook spoke of her change of heart in watching a movie about drag queens.

When people use the language of pain in politics, they risk perpetuating hierarchy and further isolating people, and there can also be broader unintended political effects as well. The politics of emotion has contributed, of late, to a political climate where being a victim, being wronged or pained, is what gives people a right to challenge the way things are; victimhood has become *the* righteous position from which to make political interventions, the only political position that is not immediately suspect.[8] This state of affairs pervades contemporary American culture.

Within this climate where politics must be based on personal emotions, activists and advocates find themselves with few options. Speaking openly of politics makes them look cynical, even inhuman, in the ways that we have seen. Yet when they repeatedly seek to play on American feelings of guilt by dramatizing the pitiable victims of politics, they risk seeming trite and running up against a wall of public emotional exhaustion and wariness of being manipulated. Thus it becomes ever less possible to speak about the realities of power at all. Political questions seem inhuman unless they are couched in terms of individual emotions—and people find constant demands for their compassion exhausting. This exhaustion makes even feelings seem to be an unsatisfactory haven from politics.

Again we revisit the question: Where can people find a haven from this political cynicism and exhaustion? Can it be provided by the metaphysical or the church? For many of the people we have heard from here, religious participation has become, among its other functions, a place to search for a haven from heartlessness—from cynicism, selfishness, worldly and material concerns.[9] In answer to a question with which I began this project, debates about homosexuality are so explosive in these contexts because they bring to light the ways that church might not automatically provide a haven from the world's problems. Power and privilege can pervade any group of people, whether they come together for secular or sacred purposes (or a mixture of both). Church members do not transcend earthly life simply by virtue of being in a congregation.

Attempts to escape or avoid politics by using a language of emotion can lead to emotional exhaustion. Part of what is so exhausting is that only addressing "pain," a symptom, leaves its causes to run rampant, like taking narcotics for a broken leg while doing nothing to reset the bone. Pain language can be effective, but it also has a price. Rather than simply addressing the endless onslaught of symptoms, we need to turn to a less exhausting and more hopeful approach. We might address the root problems that cause all the pain, as well as the anger, disgust, outrage, and despair. This is hardly a new solution. To address what is wrong with society, we could try ways to revitalize the public spaces in which we might talk about our different visions of what a better society would look like.

Addressing Fundamentals

The theoretical literature on pain and politics can help us to critique pain-based arguments such as those I observed in these two congregations. On the other hand, these congregations have something to tell us about politics as well. Debates about homosexuality (or racism, sexism, and so on) disrupt the image of religion as a haven from politics, but that is not the only reason these debates are so volatile. As we have seen, these debates are hardly about homosexuality at all. They are about sin and love, body and spirit, right and wrong, belonging and exclusion, community and power. Homosexuality sits at the nexus of so many fundamental issues because people have projected onto it the negatives of so many things they value, not out of conscious choice, but at the level of their grounding assumptions. Homosexuality is certainly not alone in this position—other sites of difference have taken this role in the past and present, and yet others will in the future. Part of the reason homosexuality has this role at this moment is that it touches on issues of contemporary concern: struggles between science and morality, changing family patterns, identity politics. In focusing on homosexuality, people can avoid focusing on the fundamental concerns that are really at stake. In this way, focusing on homosexuality is even more of a distraction than focusing on emotions.

We have seen how, in these congregations' debates about homosexuality, questions of religious belonging and duty have distracted people from the more fundamental moral questions of right and wrong. For instance, when Mark Montero (in chapter 1) asked if the RCP's goal was to say that gay relationships were equal to heterosexual marriages, no one present could just say yes. In fact, no one could even address his moral arguments in moral terms. They spoke instead of health, science, compassion, and choice (and lack thereof), but not whether it were sinful to have sex with people of one's same gender. Why was it so difficult for pro-gay members to address a moral critique of their position in terms of what they felt was morally *right?*[10]

Debates about right and wrong expose the differences that exist in places where people most want agreement and concord, such as in church. But more fundamentally, when people force each other to debate morality, they can frustrate each other terribly and denaturalize each other's sense of the world. We all build our worldviews around questions of right and wrong; we get our senses of who we are, what we take for granted, what just *is*, what makes the socially contingent feel really real. This is the case whether, for instance, our sexual morality idealizes sexually liberated promiscuity, or one-man-one-woman marriage, or something else. And regardless of our views on any particular moral issue, someone (like an ethnographer) poking around in anyone's life asking "why" about things that just *are*, like a four-year-old who asks the same question over and over, can prove exasperating. Being challenged about the "why" of what we take for granted by those who actively *disagree* with us can be even more threatening.

Even though many members sought to avoid these central questions, others insisted, and rightly so, that at the heart of these debates are different understandings of right and wrong. Fundamental questions about right and wrong strike a nerve because they form the very roots around which people build their worlds and selves. Even those of us who "know" that there is no ultimate truth still organize our worlds around some principle we take to be unquestionable, even if we do not acknowledge it. Individual freedom, equality and justice, the right to do what one wants, rational self-interest— these are all naturalized grounding assumptions that work the same way as naturalized assumptions about Christian duty.[11] We can choose to be intentional about what assumptions we wish to naturalize, to acknowledge them and openly consider their ramifications.[12]

To challenge people, anyone, on these grounds exposes those root assumptions—those things that we desire to hold as beyond question—to the scrutiny of the outside world. Such exposure can traumatize us the way we are traumatized when something cold strikes the nerve of a tooth. But such pain can show us the weak spots in our grounding assumptions, places that need attention, so that we do not inadvertently affect the world in ways we do not intend. Engaging in such assessment and rebuilding may involve change, but it need not be devastating change. Members on all sides of church debates about homosexuality could benefit from such examinations, but these examinations require trust that people won't trample over one another in pursuit of their own goals. They must be able to trust that rather than scapegoating stereotyped images of one another, they will respect one another as equals, even in times of mutual pain and struggle.

I learned from members of these congregations that addressing fundamentals is difficult and threatening, but I also learned that it is necessary and possible. Communities such as congregations may come to model how people might address questions of power and morality without dehumanizing one another. One of the things most disruptive of my own worldview was when I realized at my first RCP seminar, the one where I found myself sobbing uncontrollably, that the participants struggled actively and daily (or at least weekly), one on one, with people whose worldviews differed from their own, fellow members to whom they were committed. These members suddenly struck me as living on the front lines far more than my fellow activists and I, who protected ourselves from engagement with the enemy with leather jackets, the anonymity of city life, and sometimes with self-righteousness.[13] I still believe in showing anger when I feel it is called for, and I still believe that direct action can be a productive political strategy. What I learned from the people I studied here was that people on all sides need to be clear about where their anger comes from and direct it productively by struggling and negotiating with other people on their terms.

People need not constantly engage those whose worldviews they do not share, or find reprehensible. We all may still need time to retreat, to focus, to be with others with whom we find hope, affirmation, and sustenance.[14] When we do so, however, we should do so with a clear idea of what we believe and what distinguishes us from those we call "other." None of us ultimately gains in the long run by creating dehumanizing stereotypes at which to vent anger and frustration. We can be angry enough at actual people.

As we have seen, seeking to avoid politics does not protect people from them. Political issues will demand discussion as long as some members of any community are denied access to the ideals they share with their community. The right to be believed when one testifies as to God's power in one's life, the right to receive the church's blessing for answering God's calling—these are the rights gay church members seek, to this day, when they seek affirmation in the church. They seek the same transcendence all members seek. As long as the church denies them these ideals, the church will have to contend with the results of the power its members exercise in this denial.

Members who insist that they know what God can or cannot will others to do or be, and to whom church tradition grants the authority and power to legitimate their views, exert power and thus act politically. So do those who

challenge that traditional authority. That is why politics must not be imagined as separate from questions of spirituality or morality. As long as gay
members and their allies refuse to speak the church's language of morality,
they will never effect the changes they seek in the church. When someone
argues that homosexuality is inherently sinful, gay members and their allies
need to assert that homosexuality is good in itself and not just a condition
that cannot be helped. Gay people and their advocates need to not stereotype those people who disagree with them, nor avoid dealing with the issues
they bring up by changing the subject. Instead of seeking to dodge questions
of morality, they might engage those who challenge their worldview. They
might assert that homosexuality *is* a moral good.

Where can people turn for a haven in a heartless world? If there is no
haven after all, the answer should be clear: the world itself need not be so
heartless. Rather than retreat from politics into individual feelings and isolated experiences of self, we need to deal with the inequality that issues
of power and privilege bring to light and demand their redress in a humane, communitarian, and moral way. By examining religious groups, we
can see what people seek to get away from in their flight from politics. At
one level they wish to avoid denaturalizing the assumptions around which
their worlds are built. At another level, they wish to avoid the cynicism, the
calculation, the self-interested side of politics. And they wish to avoid it by
connecting with other human beings.

In secular American life, no less than in religious life, we need to learn
from these debates, to rethink why we so often seek havens from politics. Instead of treating political questions as an excuse to be inhumane and selfish,
we need to see them as entirely relevant to issues of duty, morality, community, and love. We need to hold politics accountable to our ideals, and we
need to open questions of right and wrong to discussion, to be explicit about
our grounding assumptions. To bring morality into political discussion is
not the same as erasing the separation of church and state. In fact, to do so
is simply to acknowledge the unspoken moral claims on which state actors
already base their decisions.[15] After all, morality is not the sole province of a
particular religious group, or even of religion. We all have ideas of right and
wrong. What does it mean to be free to enjoy life, liberty, and the pursuit
of happiness? Who should have that freedom? What common grounds exist in spite of the tremendous political differences that permeate American
society?

With this vision, I am calling for an intensification of public politics,
but one that would allow discussions of power and privilege to address, at
the same time, human connection, community, and justice. These things

have not always been separate, nor do they need to be. Just as in congregations, when someone suggests that particular kinds of sex are immoral or
sinful, those who disagree should be able to argue that those forms of sex
are morally good, and to explain why. When someone suggests that state-
sponsored welfare breeds immorality, others should interrogate the terms
that define that morality and articulate the moral vision that sees it as moral
and sensible for society to support all of its members. And when our democratically elected Congress votes to bomb or to impose sanctions on another
country, people should demand that they explain their moral reasoning; and
if our representatives fail to do so satisfactorily, we should use the democratic process to put a stop to it. The left, as well as the right, should be able
to articulate such views and back them up with reasoning based on its notions
of right and wrong.

When church members disagree over the meaning of Scripture, they can
turn to feelings to know what God demands, what is eternally true. When
they disagree over what God can communicate through such feelings, they
can doubt that the other really knows God at all. It is impossible to find
transcendence among people with whom you disagree about fundamental
truths. The question then is to what extent members—of particular religious
groups or the larger society—can find a sense of community and transcendence without denying it to others.

Notes

Introduction

1. In October 2000, the Reconciling Congregations Program changed its name to the Reconciling Ministries Network. The RMN mission statement says: "Reconciling Ministries Network is a national grassroots organization that exists to enable full participation of people of all sexual orientations and gender identities in the life of the United Methodist Church, both in policy and practice." At the time of my research (1996–1998), the RCP mission statement focused specifically on gay men and lesbians, and sometimes bisexuals; although the movement was open to transgenderists, no bisexuals or transgenderists identified themselves as such or had their concerns discussed regularly in the discussions and debates about homosexuality that I observed. It is for that reason that this book focuses largely on debates about gay men and lesbians.

2. "God" is capitalized when I refer to the proper name given by most members of the congregations I studied.

3. This tradition draws from Durkheim ([1912] 1965), Berger (1969), Turner (1969, 1974), and Geertz (1973). The best statement I have read of the relationship between social science and religion is in Berger's (1969) second appendix. There, he makes clear that the sociology of religion makes no claims about the nature or existence of the divine; it only examines what people believe about it.

4. According to a 1997 survey by the University of Michigan Institute for Social Research.

5. This notion has been most clearly elaborated by Hunter (1991) and Wuthnow (1988).

6. This approach draws from "grounded theory" (Glaser and Strauss 1967), which posits that social theory should be developed from the ground up by comparing different groups of people and generalizing from comparisons of specifics. Some examples of this approach in the

sociology of religion can be found in Ammerman (1987, 1997), Becker (1999), Chaves (1997), Eiesland (2000), Finke and Stark (1992), Neitz (1987), C. Smith (1998), and R. S. Warner (1988).

7. Burawoy (1998, 1991) defines the extended case method in contrast to a grounded theory approach to ethnographic research. For Burawoy, the purpose of ethnographic research should not be to approximate objective survey methods but to inform and expand existing theories by making them account for an increasingly broad range of observed circumstances.

8. See, for instance, Ammerman (1987, 1997), Becker (1997, 1999), Demerath and Williams (1992), Eiesland (2000), Neitz (1987), Smith (1998), Warner (1988), and Williams and Demerath (1991).

9. See, for instance, Ammerman (1987, 1997), Eiesland (2000), Finke and Stark (1992), and Nietz (1987). Notable exceptions include Dillon (1999), who examines how members can belong to a church and oppose church doctrine in her study of American Catholics who are pro-choice, gay, lesbian, or supportive of women's ordination; Chaves (1997), who explores the symbolic meanings of church doctrine with respect to the ordination of women; and Wilde (2004), who explores the effects of Vatican II on Roman Catholicism.

10. Specifically, pre-nineteenth century power was based in a sovereign model, the king. Since the nineteenth century, power has begun to operate more through modern institutions (prisons, hospitals, clinics, armies, schools, etc.) that "democratize" power by instilling discipline and conformity in each individual.

11. I use the term *language* to mean precisely what Foucault means by *discourse*, but I stick with my term for the sake of clarity. The term *discourse*, like *language*, has multiple meanings, and even within the field of sociology, scholars use the term in different ways. The term can thus have the effect of obfuscating the very workings of power it was meant to illuminate. It should not be forgotten, however, that I see all languages as modes of power.

My thinking on these questions has been shaped in large part by post-structuralist feminists such as Joan Scott (1999) and Judith Butler (1990, 1993), who see language as systems of categories that are central to the workings of power. Scott has a particularly clear statement of this perspective in her introduction.

12. See, for instance, Goffman (1986) and statements on frame analysis in social movement theory such as Benford and Snow (2000) and Snow et al. (1986). Whereas Goffman's concept includes the ways language acts on people, frame analysts often focus on the more intentional linguistic strategies people employ.

13. The sociologist Ann Swidler (1986) is often interpreted as saying that culture works as something people consciously manipulate, though, as she makes clear, she sees culture as shaping how people can think about their worlds, themselves, and their relationships (see also Swidler 2001).

14. See Epstein (1994), Rubin (2002), and Weeks (2000). A few sociological examples of this earlier work include McIntosh (1968), Gagnon and Simon (1973), Plummer (1975, 1981), and Weeks (1977).

15. See, for instance, the papers in Abelove et al. (1993), Warner (1993), and Lancaster and di Leonardo (1997).

16. I discuss more broadly assumptions about nature in religious conceptualizations of sexuality in Moon (2002).

17. The sociologist Kathryn Fox (1999a, 1999b), for instance, uses Foucault's framework to show how education and therapeutic languages are used in penal institutions to craft new subjects rather than simply punishing wrongdoers.

18. See, for instance, Angelides (2001), Diamond and Quinby (1988), Hartsock (1990), Hunt (1992), and JanMohamed (1992).

19. Among sociologists with this approach see, for instance, Alexander and Smith (1993), Ellingson (1995), Jacobs (1996), and Steinberg (1999).

20. The sociologist Jyoti Puri (1999) also moves to apply this Foucaultian conception of power to the everyday in her study of Indian women's understandings of gender and sexuality. Because she uses interviews alone, however, she focuses on the role of state-level discourse in the construction of people's understandings of themselves, rather than the way power is reproduced in interactions.

21. Although the literature on this point is very large, Clifford and Marcus (1986), Collins (1989), and Smith (1987) provide some major explorations of the limits of ethnography in producing "truth."

22. The anthropologist William Reddy (1997) makes such a point with reference to how language works against the ambiguity of emotions.

23. The first view is widely implied but not generally stated outright. The second view is most clearly put forth by Finke and Stark (1992).

24. In spite of the many scriptural passages that have been used to justify slavery as godly (see Swartley 1983).

25. This is one move in the school of thought known as structuralism, and it can be found among theories of religion in, for instance, Durkheim ([1912] 1965), Berger (1969), and Turner (1969).

26. This is a later move in the trajectory toward French post-structuralism as found in Saussure ([1915] 1983) and Lévi-Strauss (1966).

27. See Halley (1993).

28. When certain persons are not categorized as citizens, for instance, they can suffer the effects that come from being denied a right to vote and seek government protection. The gravest material consequence of these categories, however, is death. Butler (1993) refers to the ever-unsolved murder of a Latina transsexual prostitute. Similarly, Patricia Williams (1988) refers to the priest at the 1987 funeral of the eleven-year-old black-Hispanic New York City boy who was mauled to death by polar bears in the Brooklyn Zoo, who said that the boy had not died in vain since his death saved him from a life of crime.

29. See Becker (1997). Church and politics have not always been deemed fundamentally antithetical; R. Stephen Warner (1988), in his examination of the transformation of a Presbyterian congregation, shows how this very relationship can change.

30. See Scott (1991) for more on this use of experience.

31. This passage was reconstructed from memory in my field notes, though in this case, it is a particularly jarred memory. I discuss this incident further in Moon (2003).

Throughout the text, excerpts from field notes were reconstructed in my notes, while interviews were generally taped unless otherwise noted.

32. The ex-gay movement has been in existence since at least the mid-1970s and consists of many small ministries loosely organized under an umbrella organization, Exodus International. It is an ecumenical Protestant movement that sees homosexuality as a sinful result of dysfunction and that seeks to help "transform" homosexuals through a combination of Christian salvation and therapeutic support. See Moon (2001).

Chapter One

1. *The Book of Discipline of the United Methodist Church* [1996], ¶65G. This passage retains much of the wording first drafted in 1972, at the UMC's first General Conference after the merger of the Methodist and Evangelical United Brethren churches. In 1966, the passage was revised, after much contention, to forbid "homosexual unions," from taking place in UMC buildings and being performed by UMC clergy. While this amendment was subsequently moved to a different section of the *Discipline*, I refer throughout this book to the 1996 edition, which was current at the time of my research. See Wood and Bloch (1995) for more on the UMC's General Conference.

2. In case the dangers of sex are not clear enough, the authors invoke a special concern for the protection of children from the dangers of sexual abuse and exploitation. Unlike their descriptions of the other dangers of sex, the authors do not elaborate on the consequences of the sexual abuse of children. They thus allow the image of abused childhood to speak for itself, an emblem of the horrible damage and destruction humanity can suffer when sex does not keep its place. Rubin (1993) explores the Western ideology that posits sex as dangerous, exploring cases similar to this where nonviolent and consensual sexual variation is categorized with violence and danger to social order.

3. It is for this reason that many of those I discuss in this book do not refer to such categories as bisexuals or transgenderists. Some people involved in the pro-gay movement in the UMC believe that the church should be open to everyone, regardless of gender and sexual identity. However, even many of these members, speaking to church groups they see as more conservative, will disregard transgenderists. Bisexuality, on the other hand, was not talked about very much as a sexual orientation in its own right but was more often seen as a sign of confusion or transition from a straight self-misperception to a gay self-acceptance. Both bisexuality and transgenderism challenge the clear distinctions many liberals in these congregations wished to maintain between homosexuality and heterosexuality.

4. The literature on this topic has become vast, but it includes Foucault (1978), Freud ([1962] 2000), Marcuse (1966), McIntosh (1968), and Weeks (1986).

5. The names of congregation members are pseudonyms.

6. Later chapters will explore the ways members define sin.

7. Eiesland (2000) points out that many members join or affiliate with congregations for various services they need, and that they tend not to hold much denominational allegiance. Wuthnow (1988) also discusses the lack of denominational allegiance among contemporary American church members, showing how members can search for a congregation that they feel comfortable in rather than simply going to the nearest congregation of their lifelong denomination.

8. Scholars such as Bellah et al. (1985), Habermas (1987), Hochschild (1997), and Putnam (2000) draw from the sociological tradition of Weber, Durkheim, and Marx to see modernity and/or capitalism as atomizing.

It should be noted that here the word *American* refers to the ideological monolith that is constituted in the process of describing itself as "American," and thus, when I use this word, I am talking about people to the extent that they are not excluded by and do not contest the term's meaning. Members of these two congregations, for instance, are not all necessarily born or naturalized American citizens, but for our purposes here they fit into the category of American (and many officially recognized citizens are not always considered fully "American") to the extent that they do not challenge American citizenship ideology and to the extent that they participate in American political culture.

9. Also see Hout and Fischer (2002).

10. Also see Finke and Stark (1992) and Eiesland (2000).

11. Herein lies a different problem with such cultural appropriations. While Wuthnow points to the "inauthenticity" of people finding solace in religions in which they were not raised, I would add that for people to see Lakota practices, for instance, as more "natural" and "timeless" than the practices of their own culture reproduces a certain colonialist exoticism. As Povinelli (1997) points out with regard to Australian liberal conceptions of "authentic" Aboriginal tradition, such views deny members of these marked categories the possibility of changing, freezing their identity in dominant cultural fantasies.

12. The UMC's population is surpassed by the Southern Baptists, whose 1999 statistics placed them at 15.8 million members.

13. ¶304.3 reads: "While persons set apart by the Church for ordained ministry are subject to all the frailties of the human condition and the pressures of society, they are required to maintain the highest standards of holy living in the world. Since the practice of homosexuality is incompatible with Christian teaching, self-avowed practicing homosexuals are not to be accepted as candidates, ordained as ministers, or appointed to serve in The United Methodist Church."

¶65C reads: "We affirm the sanctity of the marriage covenant that is expressed in love, mutual support, personal commitment and shared fidelity between a man and a woman. We believe that God's blessing rests upon such marriage, whether or not there are children of the union. We reject social norms that assume different standards for women than men in marriage. Ceremonies that celebrate homosexual unions shall not be conducted by our ministers and shall not be conducted in our churches."

¶65G is quoted at the beginning of this chapter.

14. These are the generally more liberal denominations, such as the Presbyterian Church (U.S.A.), the Evangelical Lutheran Church, the Quakers, the American Baptist Churches in the U.S.A., and the Disciples of Christ. The Episcopal Church also has a strong pro-gay movement; the Unitarian-Universalist Association and the United Church of Christ have been at the forefront of changing denominational policies around homosexuality.

15. Exodus International is the largest organization in the ex-gay movement and serves as an umbrella organization for many local-level transforming ministries that are not affiliated with a particular church or denomination.

16. As of 2000, there were about 150 Reconciling Congregations in the United Methodist Church nationwide, out of over 36,000 United Methodist congregations. There are also about 150 Transforming Congregations, but these were from several denominations.

17. The UMC is organized much like the United States, with a General Conference where representatives from the entire denomination meet every four years to work out denominational policy. The UMC's regional level of organization is the Annual Conference, which is analogous to state governments in the United States. The Annual Conferences have yearly representative meetings to carry out more local-level business.

18. See, for instance, Bellah et al. (1985), Hochschild (1997), and Putnam (2000).

19. Wuthnow (1988) describes the divides that pervade much of American religious life and which have split denominations apparently down the middle. He points out that liberal and conservative Methodists, for instance, may have far less in common with each other than a liberal Methodist might have with a liberal Presbyterian, Catholic, or Jew.

Chapter Two

1. Burawoy (1991, 1998) describes the methodological value of this approach in his account of the extended case method. Rather than attempting to minimize our own participation as ethnographers in the field, Burawoy argues that we should use our role as outsiders to engage people to learn about how they make sense of their world. This method of research differs from that described by Glaser and Strauss (1967), who suggest that ethnographers can be neutral observers, neglecting outside knowledge.

2. On reading this, a friend from Missionary Church said I would not have to disrupt my whole life; I could let Christ into my heart right where I was. Imagining this possibility exemplifies how languages produce identities. To speak, truthfully, the language of letting Christ into my heart as this friend spoke it, I would truly have to become a different person.

3. I draw this definition of transcendence, as feeling part of something bigger, from Peter Berger (1969).

4. That a nonbeliever would experience such a feeling need not come as a surprise to Christians. Willimon (1990) relates the story of John Wesley, founder of Methodism, whose life was changed through a revelation he experienced at a meeting he had not wanted to attend. Before that meeting, where Wesley's heart was "strangely warmed" with faith in Christ and in his own salvation, when he was in turmoil about his faith, a university teacher advised Wesley "to get that [dry and contemplative] philosophy of yours out of your system . . . preach faith till you have it." In Willimon's words, "Sometimes it's possible to *act* as a Christian before you *think* like a Christian" (1990, 98).

5. These concepts are described by Durkheim ([1912] 1965), as well as Turner and Berger.

6. For instance, Matthew 22:34–40: "When the Pharisees heard that he had silenced the Sadducees, they gathered together, and one of them, a lawyer, asked him a question to test him. 'Teacher, which commandment in the law is the greatest?' He said to him, 'You shall love the Lord your God with all your heart and with all your soul,

and with all your mind. This is the greatest commandment. And a second is like it: You shall love your neighbor as yourself. On these two commandments hang all the laws and the prophets.' "

7. See Berger's (1969) appendix 2 for a useful account of the distinction between the sociology of religion and religion itself.

8. Members seek a wide range of things in going to church. The sociologist Penny Edgell Becker (1999) did an extensive study of all of the congregations in one town and found four different congregational models, which reflected members' different desires in and reasons for going to church. Whether a member desires a "leader congregation," a "community," a "house of worship," or a "family," however, all are seeking some connection to the transcendent truth of God.

9. Wuthnow is in good company in observing changes in the way society is structured. See, for instance, Skolnick (1991), Stacey (1991), and D'Emilio and Freeman (1988) on changing family forms. See Williams and Demerath (1991) on the separation of church and state. See Fraser (1989), Pateman (1988), and the papers in the Landes (1998) volume on separate gendered spheres.

Chapter Three

1. This view reflects what members cited as Methodist Church founder John Wesley's tool for understanding God's will, the Wesleyan quadrilateral: Scripture, tradition, reason, and experience. At City Church, this quadrilateral was often invoked by the senior pastor and others, though not everyone gave these four components of God's will the same weight. At Missionary Church, I heard no mention of the Wesleyan quadrilateral.

2. In this way, people's social and economic experiences shape their theologies. Many believe that their understanding of God is just plain right and has nothing to do with their economic or social situation, but given how widely Protestant and even United Methodist theologies range, those members may at least wonder how it is that others have come to believe so very differently. Luker (1984) makes this case in her discussion of different sides in the debate over abortion.

3. Genesis 19:1–29 is the story of Sodom. When two angels visit Lot's house, the townsmen come to the house and demand, "Where are the men who came to you tonight? Bring them out to us, that we may know them" (verses 4–5). Lot meets them at the door and says: "I beg you, my brothers, do not act so wickedly. Look, I have two daughters who have not known a man; let me bring them out to you, and do to them as you please; only do nothing to these men, for they have come under the shelter of my roof" (verses 7–8). The men of the town do not listen to Lot and approach the door to break it down; the angels strike them blind so they cannot find the door. Then the angels tell Lot to gather up his family and flee to the hills, so they will be saved when God rains sulfur and fire on Sodom.

The book of Leviticus lays down God's law. Leviticus 18:19–23: "You shall not approach a woman to uncover her nakedness while she is in her menstrual uncleanness. You shall not have sexual relations with your kinsman's wife, and defile yourself with her. You shall not give any of your offspring to sacrifice them to Molech, and so profane them in the name of your God: I am the Lord. You shall not lie with a male as with a woman; it is abomination. You shall not have sexual relations with any animal and defile yourself with it, nor shall any woman give herself to an animal to have sexual relations with it: it is perversion." Also see Leviticus 20:13.

I Corinthians 6:9–11: "Do you not know that the wrongdoers will not inherit the kingdom of God? Do not be deceived! Fornicators, idolaters, male prostitutes, sodomites, thieves, the greedy, drunkards, revilers, robbers—none of these will inherit the kingdom of God. And this is what some of you used to be. But you were washed, you were sanctified, you were justified in the name of the Lord Jesus Christ and in the Spirit of our God."

Other frequently cited New Testament passages concerning the sinfulness of homosexuality include Romans 1:26–27 and I Timothy 1:8–11. Although these six passages seem to constitute the main scriptural argument against homosexuality, some support their argument with verses such as Isaiah 3:9, which invokes the sin of Sodom, and Ephesians 5:12, which is used to argue against gay men and lesbians being open about their sexual orientation.

4. See, for instance, Boswell (1980, 1994), Countryman (1988), Scanzoni and Mollenkott (1994), and Scroggs (1983). Other gay Christian theology includes Alexander and Preston (1996), Comstock (1993), Edwards (1984), Goss (1993), Heyward (1984, 1989), Horner (1978), and some of the papers in Comstock and Henking (1999), Geis and Messer (1994), and Olyan and Nussbaum (1998).

5. Most Christians read Jesus' admonishment "If your right eye causes you to sin, tear it out and throw it away" (Matthew 5:29) as a metaphoric remark, and similarly, most agree that commandments such as "You shall love God with all your heart, and with all your mind, and with all your soul, and with all your strength" (Mark 12:30) and "You shall love your neighbor as yourself" (Mark 12:31) are literally true as a general rule.

6. See, for instance, Ephesians 6:5, Colossians 3:22, Titus 2:9–10, Genesis 9:24–27, Genesis 16:1–9, Leviticus 25:44–46, Exodus 21:2–4, and Exodus 21:20–21 and 26–27.

7. See Swartley (1983) for reviews and analyses of debates about scriptural teachings on slavery and women.

Tina Harrison provided a similar account as to why the church today did not need to follow Paul's exhortation for women not to speak in church or teach men (I Corinthians 14:34–36, I Timothy 2:11–15), pointing out that within Scripture itself there are exceptions, such as the teacher Priscilla, to whom Paul himself wrote. She also made the case that in the historical period in which Paul wrote those letters, women were causing specific distractions during worship.

8. Ephesians 4:11–16: "The gifts he gave were that some would be apostles, some prophets, some evangelists, some pastors and teachers, to equip the saints for the work of ministry, for building up the body of Christ, until all of us come to the unity of the faith and the knowledge of the Son of God, to maturity, to the measure of the full stature of Christ. We must no longer be children, tossed to and fro' and blown about by every wind of doctrine, by people's trickery, by their craftiness in deceitful scheming. But speaking the truth in love, we must grow up in every way into him who is the head, into Christ, from whom the whole body, joined and knit together by every ligament with which it is equipped, as each part is working properly, promotes the body's growth in building itself up in love."

9. See, for instance, Skolnick (1991) and D'Emilio and Freedman (1988).

10.   See, for instance, Gifford (1987), Norwood ([1923] 1976), and Swartley (1983).

11.   See, for instance, Blee (1991) and MacLean (1991).

12.   John 3:16–21 says, "For God so loved the world that he gave his only Son, so that everyone who believes in him may not perish but may have eternal life. Indeed, God did not send the Son into the world to condemn the world, but in order that the world might be saved through him. Those who believe in him are not condemned; but those who do not believe are condemned already, because they have not believed in the name of the only Son of God. And this is the judgment, that the light has come into the world, and people loved darkness rather than light because their deeds were evil. For all who do evil hate the light and do not come to the light, so that their deeds may be exposed. But those who do what is true come to the light, so that it may be clearly seen that their deeds have been done in God."

13.   Matthew 28:19–20: "Go therefore and make disciples of all nations, baptizing them in the name of the Father and of the Son and of the Holy Spirit, and teaching them to obey everything that I have commanded you. And remember, I am with you always, to the end of the age."

14.   Even though in these two congregations there is considerable overlap between those who believe that homosexuality is sinful and those who consider themselves evangelical, it is important to point out that not all of those who consider themselves "evangelicals" believe that homosexuality is sinful. For instance, the United Fellowship of Metropolitan Community Churches upholds the belief that God ordains a variety of sexual orientations, while also upholding a number of tenets of evangelism (Warner 1995, Comstock 1996). Similarly, some pro-gay Christians I met both within and beyond these two congregations tended to support some aspects of evangelical belief, including a suspicion of heavy liturgy, and have had "born again" experiences. However, among the members of these two congregations, those who believed that a personal relationship with Jesus Christ is necessary for individual salvation also tended to believe in the sinfulness of homosexuality.

15.   A thread runs throughout this discussion of people dealing with the debates about whether people are born gay or whether it is a choice to be gay. Stein (2001) discusses the concepts of choice and innate sexuality in religiously infused secular debates, while I explore the effects of the antigay language of choice and the liberal language that posits that gay people are "born gay" (Moon 2001).

16.   In part, these views may make sense because members have built their lives around them and have had no reason to doubt them.

17.   Her analogy between sin and disability, drawing from her definitions of both sin and handicaps as "imperfection," has led her to this implication.

18.   For instance, in the Letter of Paul to the Ephesians (5:21–30):

Be subject to one another out of reverence for Christ. Wives, be subject to your husbands as you are to the Lord. For the husband is the head of the wife just as Christ is the head of the church, the body of which he is the Savior. Just as the church is subject to Christ, so also wives ought to be, in everything, to their husbands.

Husbands, love your wives, just as Christ loved the church and gave

himself up for her, in order to make her holy by cleansing her with the wash-
ing of water by the word, so as to present the church to himself in splendor,
without a spot or wrinkle or anything of the kind—yes, so that she may be
holy and without blemish. In the same way, husbands should love their wives
as they do their own bodies. He who loves his wife loves himself. For no one
ever hates his own body, but he nourishes and tenderly cares for it, just as
Christ does for the church, because we are members of his body.

19.   Recall that Ron Wilson, too, saw homosexuals as children; this view will be
further explored in chapter 8.

20.   This view of God's family ideal generally pays little regard to the wide variety
of family patterns that have existed throughout even Judeo-Christian history. In their
understandings of a timeless heterosexual ideal, Carol, Maureen, and Andy all ignored
Old Testament polygamy and would not be able to account for the variety of family
patterns historian John Boswell (1994) found in his research on premodern Christianity.
Rather, their view of God's original intent, God's plan dating back to time immemorial,
echoes Berger's (1969) understanding of transcendence, as we saw in chapter 2.

21.   ¶65D of the *Discipline* reads: "When a married couple is estranged beyond
reconciliation, even after thoughtful consideration and counsel, divorce is a regrettable
alternative in the midst of brokenness. . . . Divorce does not preclude a new marriage."

22.   See, for instance, Countryman (1988).

23.   This case is made in most pro-gay Christian theology (see note 4 in this
chapter), as well as Boswell's (1980, 1994) historical analyses.

24.   Micah 6:8: "He has told you, O mortal, what is good; and what does the Lord
require of you but to do justice, and to love kindness, and to walk humbly with your
God?"

25.   For this view, see Nelson (1978, 1994) and Scanzoni and Mollenkott (1994).

26.   Marsden (1980) shows how liberal theology, with its belief in science as one
of God's methods of ongoing revelation, came out of the crisis sparked by evolutionary
theory in the late nineteenth century.

27.   Ruthie Shafer called our attention to another possible response, making
an argument many pro-gay liberals made in these congregations, that gay people
are born gay, that God makes them genetically gay. This argument brings us back to
the argument our speakers in the first section made again and again, that an innate
predisposition—such as to alcoholism—does not make a characteristic good. These
members argue that we are all born with a "downward tendency." The argument that
gay people are born gay does nothing to counter that argument.

28.   In this respect, the contemporary divide in congregations mirrors the original
split between modernism and fundamentalism. (See, for instance, Marsden 1980.)

Chapter Four

Special thanks are due to Michael Burawoy for helping me to conceptualize this
chapter.

1.   The Gospels are the first four books of the New Testament, which chronicle
Jesus' life and teachings. These books do not mention homosexuality directly; however,

Jan's way of understanding Scripture is shaped by the central idea that God's message is singular and timeless. See Berger (1969) on timelessness.

2. Examples include Elisha (I Kings 19:19–21) and Jesus' disciples (Matthew 4:18–22, Mark 1:16–20).

3. In this sense, Mary Ann and her husband Ernie typified those who seek the stability of Wuthnow's spirituality of place. In other ways, however, they idealized the spirituality of the quest, for instance, in their focus on the Holy Spirit and in searching for a congregation that was "spirit led." This blending of purposes reflects what I found among many members of both congregations, the idealization of both forms of spirituality that Wuthnow describes, which he also portrays as opposed to each other.

4. It struck me as strange at first that Pete associated the Reconciling movement with the goddess Sophia, since no one had mentioned Sophia, either at City Church or from any of the participants in the national movement or at the national RCP Convocation. When I asked around, I learned about another movement, which includes United Methodists, based around the academic Protestant feminist theological discussions of the Re-Imagining conferences, which take place once every several years. As some United Methodist theologians had participated in these conferences, they drew a great deal of attention and heavy criticism from the Confessing Movement.

On the matter of Sophia in particular, I heard two versions from RCP supporters. One seminarian told me that *sophia*, the Greek word for wisdom, was present throughout accounts of life before Jesus in the Old Testament, as an indicator of the presence of God. Then, when God became incarnate as Jesus Christ, there was a change, and the indicator of God's presence became "the Word" rather than "wisdom"; feminist theologians have thus posed the question of why God must become incarnate in "the Word," which is gendered masculine in Greek, rather than "wisdom," which is gendered feminine. This seminarian saw God as something more omnipresent than a personality.

The other version I heard is more in line with the version Pete Vogel described in the meeting at Missionary Church. A student from a second seminary told me that Sophia was the original mother-creator, who was supplanted by the patriarchal God, and that Sophia, rather than being simply the word for wisdom, is a personality, like God, who can be invoked and worshipped in Christian theology. This version, like the first version, sees the imagery of "God the Father" as sexist but redresses that sexism with a more woman-centered imagery, rather than a more gender-neutral one.

5. In the UMC, each congregation pays an amount of money, proportional to its membership, into the Annual Conference budget for clergy support, administration, and benevolence programs (*Discipline*, ¶612).

6. This formulation was, in fact, made explicit at the 1996 RCP biannual convocation in a homily by the Reverend Sally Dyck (her real name) in Atlanta.

7. It is interesting to note that Ruthie responded with pity to those with whom she disagreed theologically. We will see how many members avoid anger and impatience with others by instead feeling compassion (which can resemble pity) for their pain, which Ruthie suggests here.

8. Fish (1997) discusses this paradox confronting those who see themselves as embracing diversity.

9. The classes were based on a book edited by Geis and Messer (1994) that assembled writings by various religious experts from both sides of the homosexuality debate.

10. *COPS* was a television program that videotaped police officers and their interactions with people engaged in sensational criminal activities.

11. Because the question of membership in the national Reconciling Congregations Program was so contentious, spelling the phrase "reconciling congregation" with lowercase letters was a heavily guarded practice, and to spell it with capital letters, even for typographical reasons (as in a list of church committees), would anger certain members. Thus, the committee that worked on gay and lesbian concerns in the congregation was known as the "reconciling congregation Committee."

12. Jack Katz (1999) explores how emotions link the physical world to the psyche. See also Rosaldo (1984).

13. The group assembled consisted of about fifteen men and women ranging in age from their early thirties to late sixties; three people in attendance were African American, the other twelve were white. The four reconciliation meetings ranged from having one dozen to two dozen participants. Participants ranged in age from their thirties to their seventies, and were all, like this one, predominantly white with 10 to 30 percent being African American, Asian, and Latino.

14. The sociologist Penny Becker (1997, 1998, 1999) examines the conflicts in a number of congregations, showing how these events provide an opportunity for a community to articulate its core moral principles, or to avoid doing so. Chaves (1997) and Eiesland (2000) also examine congregational conflicts in depth.

15. See also Foucault (1980) and Rabinow (1984).

16. Fish (1997) describes this radical incompatibility of different worldviews and, thus, sees true multiculturalism as impossible.

Chapter Five

1. For more on these movements, see Marsden (1980) and Swartley (1983).

2. The anthropologist Claude Lévi-Strauss (1966) expanded on this definition in his attempt to understand common ways of thinking across all human societies.

3. For more sociological uses of post-structuralism, see Nicholson and Seidman (1995).

4. Dick Featherstone seems to have been referring to Matthew 28:18–20: "And Jesus came and said to them, 'All authority in heaven and on earth has been given to me. Go therefore and make disciples of all nations, baptizing them in the name of the Father and of the Son and of the Holy Spirit, and teaching them to obey everything that I have commanded you. And remember, I am with you always, to the end of the age.' "

5. For more analysis of the Promise Keepers, see Kintz (1997) and Minkowitz (1998).

6. The understanding that the Promise Keepers are a political organization is also supported by the personal ties between Promise Keepers leaders and religious right political groups, such as Coloradans for Family Values and Focus on the Family

Institute, and supporters who make explicitly antigay and antifeminist statements, such as Pat Buchanan.

7. "It appears that America's anti-Biblical feminist movement is dying, thank God, and is possibly being replaced by a Christ-centered men's movement" (Jerry Falwell, quoted in Neiberger 1996).

8. Both IATC and "The More Excellent Way" are reprinted in *Transforming Congregations*, April–June 1997.

9. Patton (1995) shows how this language of the violence of overt homosexuality ("forcing it down people's throats") has helped the religious right to gain strength by portraying the gay movement as violent and its supporters as victims.

10. Literary critic Lauren Berlant points out that when radicals of the 1960s exposed the failings of public debate, they demonstrated that the comfortable life of Middle America existed *because* it excluded and brutalized some people. Because they were the bearers of this bad news, others could accuse them of having "damaged and abandoned the core of U.S. society" (1997, 3). That core is, in some sense, the belief that Americans can, under the current economic and governmental arrangements, be free from participation in politics. Of course, those whose interests are served by social arrangements can refrain from discussing them more easily than those with demands to make.

11. I borrow the concept of unmarkedness from Peggy Phelan (1993) to refer to the power and privilege accorded those deemed "neutral" human beings, unmarked by race, gender, class, age, ability, sexual orientation, and the like.

12. This case is made by both sociologists and church "insiders." See, for instance, Vance (1999), Gray and Thumma (1997), and Alexander and Preston (1996).

13. This tendency has, it is true, led to a certain level of instability on the left, where such definitions reign. The solution may be to make strategic choices about what battles to fight, to be self-consciously political. Indeed, it is when we forget that what we are doing is not about timeless truths but about situated power, that we find and fight power everywhere we see it, which precludes the possibility of organizing for political change.

Chapter Six

1. See, for instance, Galatians 5:16–17: "Live by the Spirit, I say, and do not gratify the desires of the flesh. For what the flesh desires is opposed to the Spirit, and what the Spirit desires is opposed to the flesh; for these are opposed to each other, to prevent you from doing what you want." Also see Augustine (1998).

2. Thus, to claim to be "apolitical" while casting some members as more spiritual and others as more "embodied" ignores the power and authority it takes to be able to make such a claim, and the power that claim reproduces.

The literature on the body/spirit distinction is extensive and well-documented throughout Christian and Western colonial history, but some examples relevant to gender and sexuality include Angelides (2001), Bordo (1993), Jordanova (1989), McClintock (1995), Pateman (1988), Riley (1988), Sánchez-Eppler (1992), and Scarry (1985).

3. Sedgwick (1990) provides an example of how to analyze such hierarchical oppositions, or binarisms, to examine how they facilitate power.

4. Members rarely expressed their own sexual anxiety as forthrightly as Jerome Washington; usually people invoked concerns about the anxieties they observed in *other* people. Although it is beyond the scope of this project, psychoanalytic theory best explains the anxiety he seems to describe, as the detrimental result of people's constant enforcement of particular sexual norms. See, for instance, Bersani (1987), Butler (1990, 1993), Mercer (1992), Rose (1986), and Watney (1993).

5. I use the word "normative" to refer to the power of what seems "normal" to force itself on people and to police those who fail to meet its standards. What counts as "normal" or "normative" changes throughout history and must be negotiated constantly by those with a stake in maintaining a category of normalcy and those who fail to meet its standards. Queer theorists have done a great deal to understand the workings of normativity. See, for instance, Berlant and Warner (1998), Butler (1993), Halley (1993), and Warner (1993).

6. Angelides (2001) details the roots of this anxiety about sexual fluidity, seeing it as a recurrent threat throughout the history of modern sexuality.

7. The *Discipline* has endorsed legalized abortion since 1972 (the first General Conference after its founding) and takes no position on prophylactic methods of birth control.

8. Unlike the UMC, I use the word "sexuality" to refer to a particular social arrangement of sex into the rest of life, a particular set of social patterns relating to sexuality or way of organizing sex into life.

9. Of course, the UMC does not prohibit a gay man or lesbian from marrying someone of a different sex and having sex with this spouse, but this situation could well go against the ideal that marriage be passionate, loving, fulfilling, and honest.

10. The 1996 *Discipline* says: "When a married couple is estranged beyond reconciliation, even after thoughtful consideration and counsel, divorce is a regrettable alternative in the midst of brokenness. . . . Divorce does not preclude a new marriage" (¶65D). The *Discipline* does not explain how the policy's writers reconcile this principle with Jesus' apparent teachings against divorce and remarriage in Matthew 19 and Mark 10.

In both congregations, members' views on divorce lined up with the *Discipline*, yet they nonetheless looked at the subject from slightly different perspectives. Missionary Church focused on working through the problems in a marriage as a means to avoid divorce, while allowing parenthetically that abusive or otherwise irresolvable situations should not be allowed to continue. The congregation had some members who had been divorced and who were able to speak about their experiences without apparent judgment from the congregation or its leaders.

11. This view of the godly as nurturing and loving—that God is about love rather than law and that personal feelings have a central role in a person's spiritual experience—figures prominently in contemporary theologies, for evangelicals only somewhat less frequently than liberals. Chapter 7 looks at these ideas in more depth.

12. Other versions of this view appear in the theologies put forth by Comstock (1993), Heyward (1984, 1989), and Rogers (1998).

13. This becomes even more evident when we consider that nonreproductive married couples draw far less furor than same-sex or other more visibly nonnormative

sexual relationships. The UMC does not require sex to be reproductive—it allows contraception and abortion, as well as sex for infertile and postmenopausal married couples. Yet one of the most prominent arguments in the world against same-sex marriage, aside from homosexuality being sinful, is that it is not reproductive and therefore not "natural." Here, the physical realm is equated with the spiritual realm, to the extent that it serves to reproduce the hierarchy of hetero- over homo-. See Olyan and Nussbaum (1998) and the "Sexual Orientation" (1995) for more on the natural law argument. See Sedgwick (1990) for more on how binarisms can be deployed in contradictory ways to serve the purposes of those in power.

14. We will examine the implications of this assertion, and its detractors' responses, in chapter 8.

Proponents of the born-gay argument base their claims on the tentative findings of such scientists as Dean Hamer and Simon LeVay, which suggest to some people a correlation between genetic makeup and homosexuality. Their faith in science draws from liberal Christianity's modernist optimism that the progress of science and culture, along with people's work for social justice, help to bring about the ever-unfolding kingdom of God (Marsden 1980). The specific studies are reported in LeVay and Hamer (1994). See also Hamer (1993) and LeVay (1991). For more on the usefulness and limitations of this argument, see Stein (2001).

15. As Michael Warner points out, "Being queer means fighting about these [endemic social] issues all the time, locally and piecemeal but always with consequences. It means being able, more or less articulately, to challenge the common understanding of what gender difference means, or what the state is for, or what 'health' entails, or what would define fairness, or what a good relation to the planet's environment would be. Queers do a kind of practical social reflection just in finding ways of being queer" (1993, xiii). By *queer* he means self-avowedly nonheterosexual.

16. The alternative to dispensing rights on the basis of group membership would be to grant rights as a function of simply being human, which leads us to the political question of who is defined as fully human.

17. It may be argued, however, that by creating the category of unrepentant sinners to account for those gay people who do not themselves see their sexual practices as sinful, religious conservatives create an out-group, albeit one constructed differently from the category of "homosexuals" in civil society.

18. The category of sexually marked may include transgendered people, divorced people, people who have been "caught" (by those who disapprove) having nonmarital or extramarital or interracial or intergenerational sex, young people, promiscuous people (however defined), and the like—anyone whose sex is not seen as conforming to church sexual norms and is made into a public issue.

19. The anthropologist Gayle Rubin (1993) addresses this point, attributing this elision of sex and violence to a dominant Western antisex ideology.

20. See Patton (1993) for a critique of the gay movement's invocation of duty, an invocation to which this member seemed to respond. In Patton's view, invoking the duty to "come out" enlists people in a certain program, which may only partially be in their interests, as we see here.

21. The political scientist Deborah Gould (2001) analyzes such lesbian and gay

ambivalence in depth, arguing that simultaneously belonging to and being shunned by social groups such as families (and, we might add, religious groups) produces a particular ambivalence.

22. Such an action on the part of this usher was seen as wholly inappropriate and unchristian by most of the congregation, and the usher was chastised by a member of the clergy. Such an incident is illustrative only in that it shows how easy it can be for members of a church to slip into a boundary-maintenance model of community. They also show that gay people are hardly the only ones causing problems for church communitas.

23. See Becker (1997, 1999).

Chapter Seven

1. See Nolan (1998).

2. Rosaldo (1984), Lutz (1986), and Jaggar (1989) examine Western construction of the category of emotion, and Swidler (2001), along with anthropologists such as Abu-Lughod (1986), Kulick (1998), Kondo (1990), Lutz (1988), and Lutz and Abu-Lughod (1990), explore the relationships among emotion, culture, and language. Hochschild (1990) points out how emotions seem "natural" because of the physical cues we interpret in our naming of them and describes how people can manage emotions (1983). Nolan (1998) and Berlant (1999) discuss the strategic implications of this understanding of emotions in politics.

3. This is an interesting development, in that feelings have traditionally had less of a legitimate place in the religious experiences of liberals and evangelicals, distinguishing these groups from the more feeling-based charismatic movements in Christianity (see Marsden 1980).

4. With regard to pain and its ability to shatter language, see Scarry (1985). I do not dispute that some feelings, such as physical pain, are impossible to communicate. I mean to say, however, that there is an extent to which feelings can be articulated, and sometimes our failure at articulation is not simply because feelings cannot be described.

5. Charismatic religious experience is that where the divine is experienced as both directly intervening in people's lives and as nonrational, felt and expressed through emotions. The larger part of mainline denominations is not charismatic, and many mainline Protestants are somewhat suspicious of charismatic religious practices. See, for instance, Marsden (1980), Minkowitz (1998), and Riesebrodt (1990).

6. See Kant (1987).

7. A similar view appears in Maitland (1995), which Fred Hershey cited in several sermons during my time at City Church.

8. Betsy's analysis of Scripture is not unlike that which Roland Barthes described in his essay "Operation: Margarine" (1972). There, he describes the mechanism whereby people reinforce an ideology by first producing a litany of its failings, and then save it in the end by those failings. For instance, people often represent the army as narrow-minded, unfair, and undemocratic, among other things, only to save it in the end with the feeling of glory and safety the army can produce. Similarly, Betsy produced a wide range of reasons not to interpret Scripture literally, only to, in the

end, affirm that a literal reading is ultimately the best and most comforting reading of Scripture.

9. Members often point out that there are scriptural examples of God calling people to break one rule in the name of a higher one, such as to spread his message. On the other hand, members tended not to think God might call people to be gay. Some more radical pro-gay Christians might respond that God's message might be, in fact, that conventional nuclear family and heterosexual marriage patterns have distracted people from God's message of love, but that argument was not made in these two congregations.

10. Romans 1:25–27: "Because they exchanged the truth of God for a lie, and worshiped and served the creature rather than the Creator, who is blessed forever. Amen! For this reason God gave them up to degrading passions. Their women exchanged natural intercourse for unnatural, and in the same way also the men, giving up natural intercourse with women, were consumed with passion for one another. Men committed shameless acts with men and received in their own persons the due penalty for their error."

11. In the book of Ruth, the man who was Ruth's husband and Naomi's son died, so Naomi, left with no man to take care of her or her daughter-in-law Ruth, ordered Ruth to go back to her own people, which would have been the standard and right thing to do. Ruth refused to leave Naomi, saying, "Do not press me to leave you or to turn back from following you! Where you go, I will go; where you lodge, I will lodge; your people shall be my people, and your God my God. Where you die, I will die—there I will be buried. May the Lord do thus and so to me, and more as well, if even death parts me from you!" The two returned to Naomi's home in Bethlehem, where Naomi instructed Ruth in how to entice Boaz into marrying her, thus preserving her late husband's lineage, which eventually produced Jesus. Some interpreters see this, along with the story of Jonathan and David, as a scriptural example of a covenant between two people of the same sex, blessed by God. (See, for instance, Comstock 1993, Horner 1978, Scanzoni and Mollenkott 1994, and Scroggs, 1983.)

12. For a similar understanding of God's love, see Rogers (1998).

13. The sociologist Arlie Russell Hochschild (1983) describes this management of emotions taking place at two levels, in what she calls "surface acting" and "deep acting." While a major trend among sociologists of emotion is to look at how people manage the emotions they have, another set of scholars, especially anthropologists, draw from their experiences with different societies' understandings of emotions and see emotions not as given, natural responses to situations but as themselves produced and understood within discourse/languages. (See, for instance: Abu-Lughod and Lutz 1990, Abu-Lughod 1986, Jaggar 1989, Kulick 1998, R. Rosaldo 1983, M. Rosaldo 1984, and Scott 1991.) This view has the advantage of accounting for the wide differences in the ways people experience and understand emotions, while not implicitly comparing different cultures to an implicit standard based on our own assumptions (Lutz 1986). Furthermore, by viewing emotions the way we view language and power, we avoid trying to make an untenable distinction between those ways of knowing we see as rational or unemotional and those ways of knowing we see as emotional (Rosaldo 1984, Jaggar 1989).

Chapter Eight

1. *The Adventures of Priscilla, Queen of the Desert* (directed by Stephen Elliott, 1994) is about three performers (two drag queens and a male-to-female transsexual) traveling in their bus *(Priscilla)* from Sydney into the Australian outback.

2. Family dysfunction is a major theme of ex-gay discourse. However, ex-gay proponents can account for the possibility of gay people coming from apparently functional families as well. In his book addressed to the "Fighter" who fights his or her homosexual desire, Joe Dallas (1991, 98–99) explains why "most homosexually inclined adults" had problems in their relationships with their parents:

> First, let's remember that sin manifests itself in any number of ways, yet sin is still the root problem. So a boy who is unloved by his father will develop some type of problem later in his life. Drugs, violent behavior, or antisocial tendencies might all be traced back to this root. Homosexuality is only one of many possible manifestations of poor family relationships.
> But let me take this point even further. It was not what *actually happened* between you and your parents that contributed to your homosexuality. Instead, it was the way you *perceived* your relationship with them, and the way you emotionally *responded* to that perception. (This may explain why your sexual development took a different turn from your brother's or sister's. You responded in one way, they responded in another.)
> . . . You may have perceived your father to be disinterested in you, when in fact he cared very much about every part of your life. Still, you didn't respond emotionally to what really was—only to what you *thought* was reality. . . . And that emotional response was probably the beginning of strong, unfulfilled needs contributing to erotic same-sex attractions [emphasis in original].

3. See, for instance, sociologist Barrie Thorne's (1993) account of elementary school socialization processes. Sedgwick (1993) and Halley (1993) also examine the production of heterosexuality.

4. Pete's understanding of science seemed to flow directly from the traditional evangelical view that science can help to explain God's truth as it empirically observes and explains how the physical world works. This view of science does not give credence to theories and hypotheses but defines scientific facts as readily observable phenomena (see Marsden 1980). For Pete, the fact that some gay people could change was readily observable through his experience with ex-gays. If other gay people could not change, Pete had not observed this, nor had gay "gene theory" proven it to him.

5. See Berlant (1999) and Scarry (1985).

6. He referred to a statement issued in April 1996, which read, in part, "We the undersigned bishops wish to affirm the commitment made at our consecration to the vows to uphold the *Discipline* of the church. However, we must confess the pain we feel over our personal convictions that are contradicted by the proscriptions in the *Discipline* against gay and lesbian persons within our church and within our ordained and diaconal ministers" (McAnally 1996).

7. Alex conceded that having multiple sex partners in and of itself does not cause AIDS, while he made clear that this was the story of specific people he was thinking of.

8. The anthropologist William Reddy (1997) demonstrates how language limits and shapes emotions; this example brings out the political context in which that shaping happens.

9. For instance, Matthew 5:1–11 and Matthew 19:23–24.

10. This view of homosexuals as immature can be traced at least as far back to Freud ([1962] 2000), even though Freud also argued for greater social acceptance of sexual variation.

11. For Berlant (1999) this "social deathmaking" takes place in secular liberal politics, for instance, where she observes that, even as they decry sweatshop labor, liberals feel more comfortable "mourning" sweatshop workers as unfortunates than engaging them as equals.

12. In this respect, gay church members were placed in a bind similar to that of Aborigines in the Australian land claims cases Povinelli (1997) writes about, where they had to demonstrate their "authenticity" by mirroring liberal whites' ideas of what an authentic Aborigine is.

Conclusion

1. Penny Edgell Becker (1998) sees very similar things happening in the congregations she examined. Where politics were seen as "hurtful" or "divisive" congregation leaders were most effective when they could deal with problems such as racism in ways that seemed "apolitical." Becker found this with many issues, including homosexuality, when a gay man's songs about the pain of being gay were warmly received but his suggestion that the congregation have a group for gay men and lesbians was seen by the pastor as too potentially divisive.

2. "Search for the Truth Regarding Enron," *Los Angeles Times,* 15 January 2002, pt. 2, editorial section, 12.

3. Tina Daunt and Matea Gold, "Chief, Charging Conspiracy, Berates Mayor, Police Union," *Los Angeles Times,* 17 April 2002, A-1.

4. No member that I met would say that the church has the authority to determine what happens between an individual and God; however, if members do not believe that God can say or do "such-and-such," and a member testifies that God says or does "such-and-such" in his life, members must each decide how to treat that person and how much authority to give his or her claims. In some cases, this can amount to deciding whether this member is a prophet or a lunatic. Lawson (1997) describes what can happen under such circumstances in a charismatic group, where such testimonies are perhaps more frequent.

5. For more on the limits of this move in liberal politics, see Berlant (1999), Fish (1997), and Povinelli (2000).

6. Identity politics are those that attempt to mobilize people based on their identities, on what they supposedly are, rather than their goals—such as equal rights legislation or stricter regulation of the police force to prevent police brutality. Discussions of

such politics appear in Halley (1993), Nicholson and Seidman (1995), Patton (1993), and Rajchman (1995).

7. Even abolitionist uses of the language of pain were not without some politically conflicting side-effects, as white women abolitionists and suffragists sometimes abandoned the cause to pursue their own advancement. Karen Sánchez-Eppler (1992) explores how abolitionist speakers and writers invoked both the pain and the "indelicacy" of slavery to invoke their audiences' identification with slaves and, thus, inspire them to work toward ending slavery. This method was useful to some extent, she points out, even though female abolitionists' own pursuit of political equality often depended on the existence of slavery as a foil for the unfreedom of womanhood. This history helps to explain the legacy of tensions between the white women's movement and movements for the liberation of people of color, tensions that have impeded the success of both movements and led to failures to understand the positions of those whose lived experience falls between such movements' ideal-typical beneficiaries. Also see the papers in Samuels (1992).

8. See Brown (1995), Samuels (1992), and Berlant (1997, 1999) for a discussion of the place of wounding in American politics. Stein (2001) and Patton (1993, 1995) show how this strategy has worked for the religious right as well.

9. I do not mean to imply that members do not also experience church as other things—a place of worship, a place to address the world's evils, a place to come together with others in goodwill, and the like. Becker (1999) describes various reasons people belong to congregations and how these purposes give congregations different identities.

10. Nolan (1998, 14) points out, "The concern about whether one is happy or healthy now challenges in import whether one is good or bad or even right or wrong."

11. Bellah et al. make this point with respect to institutions—family, government, economic, educational, and religious—stating that they "live and die by ideas of right and wrong and conceptions of the good" (1991, 11–12).

12. Butler (1993) explores what happens when people cite authoritative languages in nonauthoritative ways. My question is this: What happens when we cite authoritative, naturalized, moral languages in different ways, ever aware that to denaturalize one set of assumptions we must be standing on some other naturalized foundation?

13. Minkowitz (1998) makes a similar set of observations about direct-action leftist politics and the Other.

14. See Reagon (1983) for an eloquent statement of the balance between retreat and struggle.

15. Bellah et al. (1991) and Demerath and Williams (1992).

References

Abelove, Henry, Michèle Aina Barale, and David M. Halperin. 1993. *The Lesbian and Gay Studies Reader.* New York: Routledge.

Abu-Lughod, Lila. 1986. *Veiled Sentiments: Honor and Poetry in Bedouin Society.* Berkeley: University of California Press.

Alexander, Jeffrey C., and Philip Smith. 1993. "The Discourse of American Civil Society: A New Proposal for Cultural Studies." *Theory and Society* 22: 151–207.

Alexander, Marilyn Bennett, and James Preston. 1996. *We Were Baptized Too: Claiming God's Grace for Lesbians and Gays.* Louisville, Ky.: Westminster John Knox Press.

Ammerman, Nancy Tatom. 1987. *Bible Believers: Fundamentalists in the Modern World.* New Brunswick, N.J.: Rutgers University Press.

———. 1997. *Congregation and Community.* New Brunswick, N.J.: Rutgers University Press.

Angelides, Steven. 2001. *A History of Bisexuality.* Chicago: University of Chicago Press.

Augustine. 1998. *The Confessions.* Translated by Maria Boulding, with a preface by Patricia Hampl. New York: Vintage.

Barthes, Roland. 1972. "Operation: Margarine." In his *Mythologies,* 41–42. New York: Hill and Wang.

Becker, Penny Edgell. 1997. "What Is Right? What Is Caring? Moral Logics in Local Religious Life." In *Contemporary American Religion: An Ethnographic Reader,* edited by Penny Edgell Becker and Nancy L. Eiesland, 121–45. Walnut Creek, Calif.: AltaMira Press.

———. 1998. "Making Inclusive Communities: Congregations and the 'Problem' of Race." *Social Problems* 45, no. 4: 451–72.

———. 1999. *Congregations in Conflict: Cultural Models of Local Religious Life.* New York: Cambridge University Press.

Becker, Penny Edgell, and Nancy L. Eiesland, eds. 1997. *Contemporary*

American Religion: An Ethnographic Reader. Walnut Creek, Calif.: AltaMira Press.

Bellah, Robert N. 1970. *Beyond Belief: Essays on Religion in a Post-Traditionalist World.* Berkeley: University of California Press.

———. 1992. *The Broken Covenant: American Civil Religion in Time of Trial.* Chicago: University of Chicago Press.

Bellah, Robert N., Richard Madsen, William M. Sullivan, Ann Swidler, and Steven M. Tipton. 1985. *Habits of the Heart: Individualism and Commitment in American Life.* New York: Harper and Row.

———. 1991. *The Good Society.* New York: Vintage.

Benford, Robert D., and David A. Snow. 2000. "Framing Processes and Social Movements: An Overview and Assessment." *Annual Review of Sociology* 26: 611–39.

Berger, Peter L. 1969. *The Sacred Canopy: Elements of a Sociological Theory of Religion.* New York: Anchor.

Berlant, Lauren. 1997. *The Queen of America Goes to Washington City: Essays on Sex and Citizenship.* Durham: Duke University Press.

———. 1999. "The Subject of True Feeling: Pain, Privacy, and Politics." In *Cultural Pluralism, Identity Politics, and the Law,* edited by Austin Sarat and Thomas R. Kearns, 49–84. Ann Arbor: University of Michigan Press.

Berlant, Lauren, and Michael Warner. 1998. "Sex in Public." *Critical Inquiry* 24: 547–66.

Bersani, Leo. 1987. "Is the Rectum a Grave? AIDS and Anal Intercourse." *October* 43: 197–222.

Blee, Kathleen M. 1991. *Women of the Klan: Racism and Gender in the 1920s.* Berkeley: University of California Press.

Bordo, Susan. 1993. *Unbearable Weight: Feminism, Western Culture, and the Body.* Berkeley: University of California Press.

Boswell, John. 1980. *Christianity, Social Tolerance, and Homosexuality: Gay People in Western Europe from the Beginning of the Christian Era to the Fourteenth Century.* Chicago: University of Chicago Press.

———. 1994. *Same-Sex Unions in Premodern Europe.* New York: Random House.

Brown, Wendy. 1995. *States of Injury: Power and Freedom in Late Modernity.* Princeton, N.J.: Princeton University Press.

Burawoy, Michael, ed. 1991. *Ethnography Unbound: Power and Resistance in the Modern Metropolis.* Berkeley: University of California Press.

———. 1998. "The Extended Case Method." *Sociological Theory* 16, no. 1 (March): 4–33.

Butler, Judith. 1990. *Gender Trouble: Feminism and the Subversion of Identity.* New York: Routledge.

———. 1993. *Bodies That Matter: On the Discursive Limits of "Sex."* New York: Routledge.

Calhoun, Craig, ed. 1992. *Habermas and the Public Sphere.* Cambridge: MIT Press.

Chaves, Mark. 1997. *Ordaining Women: Culture and Conflict in Religious Organizations.* Cambridge: Harvard University Press.

Church, F. Forrester. 1987. *The Essential Tillich: An Anthology of the Writings of Paul Tillich.* Chicago: University of Chicago Press.

Clifford, James, and George E. Marcus, eds. 1986. *Writing Culture: The Poetics and Politics of Ethnography.* Berkeley: University of California Press.

Collins, Patricia Hill. 1989. "The Social Construction of Black Feminist Thought." *Signs* 14, no. 4: 745–73.

Comstock, Gary David. 1993. *Gay Theology without Apology*. Cleveland: Pilgrim Press.

———. 1996. *Unrepentant, Self-Affirming, Practicing: Lesbian/Bisexual/Gay People within Organized Religion*. New York: Continuum.

Comstock, Gary David, and Susan E. Henking. 1999. *Que(e)rying Religion: A Critical Anthology*. New York: Continuum.

Coontz, Stephanie. 1988. *The Social Origins of Private Life: A History of American Families, 1600–1900*. New York: Verso.

Countryman, William. 1988. *Dirt, Greed, and Sex: Sexual Ethics in the New Testament and their Implications for Today*. Philadelphia: Fortress Press.

Crowder, Carla. 1998. "Funeral to Draw Large Crowd; Casper Situation Uneasy as Gay, Anti-Gay Groups Plan to Attend Services." *Rocky Mountain News* (Denver), 16 October 1998, 7A.

Dallas, Joe. 1991. *Desires in Conflict: Answering the Struggle for Sexual Identity*. Eugene, Ore.: Harvest House.

———. 1998. "Consequences of Homosexuality." Transcript by author of talk presented at Hope and Help for the Homosexual Struggler, North Clairemont United Methodist Church, San Diego, 24 January.

Demerath, N. J., and Rhys Williams. 1992. *A Bridging of Faiths: Religion and Politics in a New England City*. Princeton, N.J.: Princeton University Press.

D'Emilio, John. 1983. "Capitalism and Gay Identity." In *Powers of Desire: The Politics of Sexuality*, edited by Ann Snitow, Christine Stansell, and Sharon Thompson, 100–13. New York: Monthly Review Press.

D'Emilio, John, and Estelle B. Freedman. 1988. *Intimate Matters: A History of Sexuality in America*. New York: Harper and Row.

Diamond, Irene, and Lee Quinby, eds. 1988. *Feminism and Foucault: Reflections on Resistance*. Boston: Northeastern University Press.

Dillon, Michele. 1999. *Catholic Identity: Balancing Reason, Faith, and Power*. New York: Cambridge University Press.

———. 2001. "Pierre Bourdieu, Religion, and Cultural Production." *Critical Studies ⇔ Critical Methodologies* 1, no. 4: 411–29.

Durkheim, Emile. [1912] 1965. *The Elementary Forms of the Religious Life*. New York: Free Press.

Edwards, George R. 1984. *Gay/Lesbian Liberation: A Biblical Perspective*. New York: Pilgrim Press.

Eiesland, Nancy L. 2000. *A Particular Place: Urban Restructuring and Religious Ecology in a Southern Exurb*. New Brunswick, N.J.: Rutgers University Press.

Eliasoph, Nina. 1998. *Avoiding Politics: How Americans Produce Apathy in Everyday Life*. New York: Cambridge University Press.

———. 1999. " 'Everyday Racism' in a Culture of Political Avoidance: Civil Society, Speech, and Taboo." *Social Problems* 46, no. 4: 479–502.

Ellingson, Stephen. 1995. "Understanding the Dialectic of Discourse and Collective Action: Public Debate and Rioting in Antebellum Cincinnati." *American Journal of Sociology* 101, no. 1: 100–44.

England, Paula, and George Farkas. 1986. *Households, Employment, and Gender: A Social, Economic, and Demographic View*. New York: Aldine de Gruyter.

Epstein, Steven. 1994. "A Queer Encounter: Sociology and the Study of Sexuality."
    Sociological Theory 12, no. 2: 188–202.

Erikson, Kai. 1966. *Wayward Puritans: A Study in the Sociology of Deviance.* New
    York: John Wiley and Sons.

Finke, Roger, and Rodney Stark. 1992. *The Churching of America, 1776–1990: Winners
    and Losers in Our Religious Economy.* New Brunswick, N.J.: Rutgers University
    Press.

Fish, Stanley. 1997. "Boutique Multiculturalism, or Why Liberals Are Incapable of
    Thinking about Hate Speech." *Critical Inquiry* 23: 378–95.

Foucault, Michel. 1977. *Discipline and Punish: The Birth of the Prison.* New York:
    Vintage Books.

———. 1978. *The History of Sexuality.* Vol. 1, *An Introduction.* New York: Vintage
    Books.

———. 1980. *Power/Knowledge: Selected Interviews and Other Writings, 1972–1977.*
    Edited by Colin Gordon. New York: Pantheon.

———. [1965] 1988. *Madness and Civilization: A History of Insanity in the Age of
    Reason.* New York: Vintage Books.

Fox, Kathryn J. 1999a. "Changing Violent Minds: Discursive Correction and Resistance
    in the Cognitive Treatment of Violent Offenders in Prison." *Social Problems* 46,
    no. 1 (February 1999): 88–103.

———. 1999b. "Reproducing Criminal Types: Cognitive Treatment for Violent Of-
    fenders in Prison." *Sociological Quarterly* 40, no. 3 (summer 1999): 435–53.

Fraser, Nancy. 1989. *Unruly Practices: Power, Discourse, and Gender in Contemporary
    Social Theory.* Minneapolis: University of Minnesota Press.

Freud, Sigmund. [1962] 2000. *Three Essays on the Theory of Sexuality.* Freud's 1925
    essay translated by James Strachey, with a new foreword by Nancy J. Chodorow
    and an introductory essay by Steven Marcus. New York: Basic Books.

Gagnon, John, and William Simon. 1973. *Sexual Conduct: The Social Sources of Hu-
    man Sexuality.* Chicago: Aldine de Gruyter.

Gamson, Joshua. 2001. "Normal Sins: Sex Scandal Narratives as Institutional Morality
    Tales." *Social Problems* 48, no. 2: 185–205.

Geertz, Clifford. 1973. *The Interpretation of Cultures.* New York: Basic Books.

Geis, Sally B., and Donald E. Messer, eds. 1994. *Caught in the Crossfire: Helping Chris-
    tians Debate Homosexuality.* Nashville, Tenn.: Abingdon Press.

Gifford, Carolyn de Swarte, ed. 1987. *The Defense of Women's Right to Ordination in
    the Methodist Episcopal Church.* New York: Garland Publishing.

Gilroy, Paul. 1991. *"There Ain't No Black in the Union Jack": The Cultural Politics of
    Race and Nation.* Chicago: University of Chicago Press.

Glaser, Barney G., and Anselm L. Strauss. 1967. *The Discovery of Grounded Theory.*
    Chicago: Aldine Publishing.

Goffman, Erving. 1986. Reprint. *Frame Analysis: An Essay on the Organization of
    Experience.* Boston: Northeastern University Press. Original edition, New York:
    Harper and Row, 1974.

Gordon, Linda, ed. 1990. *Women, the State, and Welfare.* Madison: University of
    Wisconsin Press.

Goss, Robert. 1993. *Jesus Acted Up: A Gay and Lesbian Manifesto.* San Francisco:
    Harper San Francisco.

Gould, Deborah. 2001. "Rock the Boat, Don't Rock the Boat, Baby: Ambivalence and the Emergence of Militant AIDS Activism." In *Passionate Politics: Emotions and Social Movements*, edited by Jeff Goodwin, James M. Jasper, and Francesca Polletta, 135–57. Chicago: University of Chicago Press.

Gray, Edward R., and Scott L. Thumma. 1997. "The Gospel Hour: Liminality, Identity, and Religion in a Gay Bar." In *Contemporary American Religion: An Ethnographic Reader*, edited by Penny Edgell Becker and Nancy L. Eiesland, 79–98. Walnut Creek, Calif.: AltaMira Press.

Habermas, Jürgen. 1984. *The Theory of Communicative Action.* Vol. 1, *Reason and the Rationalization of Society.* Boston: Beacon Press.

———. 1987. *The Theory of Communicative Action.* Vol. 2, *Lifeworld and System: A Critique of Functionalist Reason.* Boston: Beacon Press.

Halley, Janet. 1993. "The Construction of Heterosexuality." In *Fear of a Queer Planet*, edited by Michael Warner, 82–102. Minneapolis: University of Minnesota Press.

Hamer, Dean H., et al. 1993. "A Linkage between DNA markers on the X Chromosome and Sexual Orientation." *Science* 261 (July 16): 321–27.

Hartsock, Nancy. 1990. "Foucault on Power: A Theory for Women?" In *Feminism/Postmodernism*, edited by Linda J. Nicholson, 157–75. New York: Routledge.

Heyward, Carter. 1984. *Our Passion for Justice: Images of Power, Sexuality, and Liberation.* Cleveland, Ohio: Pilgrim Press.

———. 1989. *Touching Our Strength: The Erotic as Power and the Love of God.* New York: Harper Collins.

Hochschild, Arlie Russell. 1983. *The Managed Heart: Commercialization of Human Feeling.* Berkeley: University of California Press.

———. 1989. *The Second Shift.* New York: Avon.

———. 1990. "Ideology and Emotion Management: A Perspective and Path for Future Research." In *Research Agendas in the Sociology of Emotion*, edited by Theodore Kemper, 117–42. Albany: State University of New York Press.

———. 1997. *The Time Bind: When Work Becomes Home and Home Becomes Work.* New York: Henry Holt.

Horner, Tom. 1978. *Jonathan Loved David: Homosexuality in Biblical Times.* Philadelphia: Westminster Press.

Hout, Michael, and Claude S. Fischer. 2002. "Why More Americans Have No Religious Preference: Politics and Generations." *American Sociological Review* 67: 165–90.

Hunt, Lynn. 1992. "Foucault's Subject in *The History of Sexuality.*" In *Discourses of Sexuality: From Aristotle to AIDS*, edited by Domna Stanton. Ann Arbor: University of Michigan Press.

Hunter, James Davison. 1991. *Culture Wars: The Struggle to Define America.* New York: Basic Books.

Hybels, Bill. 1990. *Honest to God? Becoming an Authentic Christian.* Grand Rapids, Mich.: Zondervan.

Ireland, Patricia. "Beware of 'Feel-Good Male Supremacy.' " *Washington Post*, 7 September 1997, C-3.

Jacobs, Ronald N. 1996. "Civil Society and Crisis: Culture, Discourse, and the Rodney King Beating." *American Journal of Sociology* 101, no. 5: 1238–72.

Jaggar, Alison M. 1989. "Love and Knowledge: Emotion in Feminist Epistemology." In *Gender/Body/Knowledge: Feminist Reconstructions of Being and Knowing*, edited by Alison M. Jaggar and Susan R. Bordo, 145–71. New Brunswick, N.J.: Rutgers University Press.

JanMohamed, Abdul. 1992. "Sexuality on/of the Racial Border: Foucault, Wright, and the Articulation of 'Racialized Sexuality'." In *Discourses of Sexuality: From Aristotle to AIDS,* edited by Domna Stanton. Ann Arbor: University of Michigan Press.

Jordanova, Ludmilla. 1989. *Sexual Visions: Images of Gender in Science and Medicine between the Eighteenth and Twentieth Centuries.* Madison: University of Wisconsin Press.

Kant, Immanuel. 1987. *Critique of Judgment.* Translated and with an introduction by Werner S. Pluhar. Indianapolis: Hackett Publishing.

Katz, Jack. 1999. *How Emotions Work.* Chicago: University of Chicago Press.

Kintz, Linda. 1997. *Between Jesus and the Market: The Emotions That Matter in Right-Wing America.* Durham, N.C.: Duke University Press.

Kondo, Dorinne K. 1990. *Crafting Selves: Power, Gender, and Discourses of Identity in a Japanese Workplace.* Chicago: University of Chicago Press.

Kulick, Don. 1998. "Anger, Gender, Language Shift, and the Politics of Revelation in a Papua New Guinean Village." In *Language Ideologies: Practice and Theory,* edited by Bambi B. Schieffelin, Kathryn A Woollard, and Paul V. Kroskrity, 87–102. New York: Oxford University Press.

Kurson, Bob. "No Warm Welcome for Anti-Gay Reverend." *Chicago Sun-Times,* 22 November 1998, final ed., 6.

Lamont, Michèle. 1992. *Money, Morals, and Manners: The Culture of the French and the American Upper-Middle Classes.* Chicago: University of Chicago Press.

Lancaster, Roger, and Micaela di Leonardo. 1997. *The Gender/Sexuality Reader.* New York: Routledge.

Landes, Joan, ed. 1998. *Feminism, the Public, and the Private.* New York: Oxford University Press.

Lawson, Matthew P. 1997. "Struggles for Mutual Reverence: Social Strategies and Religious Stories." In *Contemporary American Religion: An Ethnographic Reader,* edited by Penny Edgell Becker and Nancy L. Eiesland, 51–78. Walnut Creek, Calif.: AltaMira Press.

Lee, Orville. 1998. "Culture and Democratic Theory: Toward a Theory of Symbolic Democracy." *Constellations* 5, no. 4: 433–55.

LeVay, Simon. 1991. "A Difference in Hypothalamic Structure between Heterosexual and Homosexual Men." *Science* 253 (August 30): 1034–37.

LeVay, Simon, and Dean H. Hamer. 1994. "Evidence for a Biological Influence in Male Homosexuality." *Scientific American* 270, no. 5 (May): 44–49.

Lévi-Strauss, Claude. 1966. *The Savage Mind.* Chicago: University of Chicago Press.

Lukács, Georg. [1922] 1971. *History and Class Consciousness: Studies in Marxist Dialectics.* Cambridge: MIT Press.

Luker, Kristen. 1984. *Abortion and the Politics of Motherhood.* California: University of California Press.

Lutz, Catherine. 1986. "Emotion, Thought, and Estrangement: Emotion as a Cultural Category." *Cultural Anthropology* 1, no. 3: 287–309.

———. 1988. *Unnatural Emotions: Everyday Sentiments on a Micronesian Atoll and Their Challenge to Western Theory.* Chicago: University of Chicago Press.

Lutz, Catherine, and Abu-Lughod, Lila. 1990. *Language and the Politics of Emotion.* New York: Cambridge University Press.

MacLean, Nancy. 1991. "The Leo Frank Case Reconsidered: Gender and Sexual Politics in the Making of Reactionary Populism." *Journal of American History* 78, no. 3 (December): 917–48.

Maitland, Sara. 1995. *A Big-Enough God: A Feminist's Search for a Joyful Theology.* New York: Riverhead Books.

Marcuse, Herbert. 1966. *Eros and Civilization.* Boston: Beacon Press.

Marsden, George M. 1980. *Fundamentalism and American Culture: The Shaping of Twentieth-Century Evangelicalism, 1870–1925.* New York: Oxford University Press.

Maxwell, John C. 1996. *Making the Most of Your Marriage.* Student workbook. Waco, Texas: Word Ministry Resources.

McAnally, Tom. "Bishops Express 'Pain' over Church Policy on Gay, Lesbian Issues." United Methodist Release #010 (2974), 18 April 1996.

McClintock, Anne. 1995. *Imperial Leather: Race, Gender, and Sexuality in the Colonial Conquest.* New York: Routledge.

McIntosh, Mary. 1968. "The Homosexual Role." *Social Problems* 16, no. 2: 182–92.

Mercer, Kobena, with Isaac Julien. 1992. "Black Masculinity and the Sexual Politics of Race." In Mercer's *Welcome to the Jungle: New Positions in Black Cultural Studies,* 131–70. London: Routledge.

Mills, C. Wright. 1959. *The Sociological Imagination.* New York: Oxford University Press.

Minkowitz, Donna. 1998. *Ferocious Romance: What My Encounters with the Right Taught Me about Sex, God, and Fury.* New York: Free Press.

Mintz, Steven, and Susan Kellogg. 1988. *Domestic Revolutions: A Social History of American Family Life.* New York: Free Press.

Moon, Dawne. 2001. "How Ex-Gay and Pro-Gay Discourse Are Really the Same: Discourse and the Unthinkable." Paper presented at the annual meeting of the American Sociological Association, Anaheim, Calif., August.

———. 2002. "Religious Views of Homosexuality." In *Handbook of Lesbian and Gay Studies,* edited by Diane Richardson and Steven Seidman. London: Sage Publications.

———. 2003. "Gay Pain in Church." *Contexts: Understanding People in Their Social Worlds* 2, no. 1: 58–59.

"The Most Potentially Divisive Issue Today." *United Methodist Reporter,* Northern Illinois Conference Edition, 27 March 1998.

Nardi, Peter M. 1999. *Gay Men's Friendships: Invincible Communities.* Chicago: University of Chicago Press.

National Organization for Women, Promise Keepers Mobilization Project. [n.d.] "Promises of the Patriarchy." National Organization for Women Web site: <http://www.now.org/issues/right/promises/quote/html>

Neiberger, Ami. "Promise Keepers: Seven Reasons to Watch Out." <www.FAS/FreedomWriter/September1996/promise.html>

Neitz, Mary Jo. 1987. *Charisma and Community: A Study of Religious Commitment with the Charismatic Renewal.* New Brunswick, N.J.: Transaction Books.

Neitz, Mary Jo, and James V. Spickard. 1990. "Steps toward a Sociology of Religious

Experience: The Theories of Mihaly Csikszentmihalyi and Alfred Schutz." *Sociological Analysis* 51, no. 1: 15–33.

Nelson, James B. 1978. *Embodiment: An Approach to Sexuality and Christian Theology.* Minneapolis: Augsburg.

————. 1994. "Are Christianity and Homosexuality Incompatible?" In *Caught in the Crossfire: Helping Christians Debate Homosexuality,* edited by Sally B. Geis and Donald E. Messer, 99–109. Nashville, Tenn.: Abingdon Press.

Nicholson, Linda, and Steven Seidman, eds. 1995. *Social Postmodernism: Beyond Identity Politics.* New York: Cambridge University Press.

Nolan, James L., Jr. 1998. *The Therapeutic State: Justifying Government at Century's End.* New York: New York University Press.

Norwood, John Nelson. [1923] 1976. *The Schism in the Methodist Episcopal Church 1844: A Study of Slavery and Ecclesiastical Politics.* Philadelphia: Porcupine Press.

Olyan, Saul M., and Martha C. Nussbaum. 1998. *Sexual Orientation and Human Rights in American Religious Discourse.* New York: Oxford University Press.

Osterman, Mary Jo. 1997. *Claiming the Promise: An Ecumenical Welcoming Bible Study Resource on Homosexuality.* Chicago: Reconciling Congregations Program.

Pateman, Carole. 1988. *The Sexual Contract.* Stanford: Stanford University Press.

Patton, Cindy. 1993. "Tremble, Hetero Swine!" In *Fear of a Queer Planet,* edited by Michael Warner, 143–77. Minneapolis: University of Minnesota Press.

————. 1995. "Refiguring Social Space." In *Social Postmodernism: Beyond Identity Politics,* edited by Linda Nicholson and Steven Seidman, 216–49. New York: Cambridge University Press.

————. 1997. "From Nation to Family: Containing African AIDS." In *The Gender/Sexuality Reader,* edited by Roger N. Lancaster and Micaela di Leonardo, 279–90. New York: Routledge.

Pertman, Adam. "Democrats Lambaste GOP Attitude on Women's Rights." *Boston Globe,* 27 August 1992, city ed., 22.

Phelan, Peggy. 1993. *Unmarked: The Politics of Performance.* New York: Routledge.

Plummer, Kenneth. 1975. *Sexual Stigma: An Interactionist Account.* New York: Routledge and Kegan Paul.

————, ed. 1981. *The Making of the Modern Homosexual.* London: Hutchinson.

Povinelli, Elizabeth A. 1997. "Sex Acts and Sovereignty: Race and Sexuality in the Constitution of the Australian Nation." In *The Gender/Sexuality Reader,* edited by Roger N. Lancaster and Micaela di Leonardo, 513–28. New York: Routledge.

————. 2000. "The State of Shame: Australian Multiculturalism and the Crisis of Indigenous Citizenship." In *Intimacy,* edited by Lauren Berlant, 253–88. Chicago: University of Chicago Press.

Puri, Jyoti. 1999. *Woman, Body, Desire in Postcolonial India: Narratives of Gender and Sexuality.* New York: Routledge.

Putnam, Robert D. 2000. *Bowling Alone: The Collapse and Revival of American Community.* New York: Touchstone.

Rabinow, Paul, ed. 1984. *The Foucault Reader.* New York: Pantheon Books.

Rajchman, John, ed. 1995. *The Identity in Question.* New York: Routledge.

Reagon, Bernice Johnson. 1983. "Coalition Politics: Turning the Century." In *Home Girls: A Black Feminist Anthology,* edited by Barbara Smith, 356–68. New York: Kitchen Table: Women of Color Press.

Reddy, William M. 1997. "Against Constructionism: The Historical Ethnography of Emotions." *Current Anthropology* 38, no. 3: 327–51.

Riesebrodt, Martin. 1990. *Pious Passion: The Emergence of Modern Fundamentalism in the United States and Iran.* Translated by Don Reneau. Berkeley: University of California Press.

Riley, Denise. 1988. *"Am I That Name?" Feminism and the Category of "Women" in History.* Minneapolis: University of Minnesota Press.

Rogers, Eugene F. 1998. "Sanctification, Homosexuality, and God's Triune Life." In *Sexual Orientation and Human Rights in American Religious Discourse,* edited by Saul M. Olyan and Martha C. Nussbaum, 134–60. New York: Oxford University Press.

Rosaldo, Michelle Z. 1984. "Toward an Anthropology of Self and Feeling." In *Culture Theory: Essays on Mind, Self, and Emotion,* edited by Richard A. Shweder and Robert A. LeVine, 137–57. New York: Cambridge University Press.

Rosaldo, Renato I. 1983. "Grief and a Headhunter's Rage: On the Cultural Force of Emotions." In *Text, Play, and Story: The Construction and Reconstruction of Self and Society,* edited by Edward M. Bruner, 178–95. Washington, D.C.: American Ethnological Society.

Rose, Jacqueline. 1986. *Sexuality in the Field of Vision.* London: Verso.

Rubin, Gayle. 1993. "Thinking Sex: Notes for a Radical Theory of the Politics of Sexuality." In *The Lesbian and Gay Studies Reader,* edited by Henry Abelove, Michèle Aina Barale, and David M. Halperin, 3–44. New York: Routledge. (First published in Carol S. Vance, ed., *Pleasure and Danger: Exploring Female Sexuality* [Boston: Routledge and Kegan Paul, 1984]).

———. 2002. "Studying Sexual Subcultures: Excavating the Ethnography of Gay Communities in Urban North America." In *Out in Theory: The Emergence of Lesbian and Gay Anthropology,* edited by Ellen Lewin and William L. Leap, 17–68. Urbana: University of Illinois Press.

Samuels, Shirley, ed. 1992. *The Culture of Sentiment: Race, Gender, and Sentimentality in Nineteenth-Century America.* New York: Oxford University Press.

Sánchez-Eppler, Karen. 1992. "Bodily Bonds: The Intersecting Rhetorics of Feminism and Abolition." In *The Culture of Sentiment: Race, Gender, and Sentimentality in Nineteenth-Century America,* edited by Shirley Samuels, 92–114. New York: Oxford University Press.

Saussure, Ferdinand de. [1915] 1983. *Course in General Linguistics.* Translated, with an introduction and notes, by Wade Baskin. New York: McGraw-Hill.

Scanzoni, Letha, and Virginia Ramsey Mollenkott. 1994. *Is the Homosexual My Neighbor? A Positive Christian Response.* San Francisco: Harper.

Scarry, Elaine. 1985. *The Body in Pain: The Making and Unmaking of the World.* New York: Oxford University Press.

Scott, Joan Wallach. 1991. "The Evidence of Experience." *Critical Inquiry* 17: 773–97.

———. 1999. *Gender and the Politics of History.* Rev. ed. New York: Columbia University Press.

Scroggs, Robin. 1983. *The New Testament and Homosexuality: Contextual Background for Contemporary Debate.* Philadelphia: Fortress Press.

Sedgwick, Eve Kosofsky. 1990. *Epistemology of the Closet.* Berkeley: University of California Press.

———. 1993. "How to Bring Your Kids Up Gay." In *Fear of a Queer Planet: Queer Politics and Social Theory*, edited by Michael Warner, 69–81. Minneapolis: University of Minnesota Press.

Seidman, Steven. 1996. *Queer Theory/Sociology*. Malden, Mass.: Blackwell.

"Sexual Orientation." 1995. Special issue, *Notre Dame Journal of Law, Ethics and Public Policy* 9, no. 1.

Skolnick, Arlene. 1991. *Embattled Paradise: The American Family in an Age of Uncertainty*. New York: Basic Books.

Smith, Christian. 1998. *American Evangelicalism: Embattled and Thriving*. Chicago: University of Chicago Press.

Smith, Dorothy E. 1987. *The Everyday World as Problematic: A Feminist Sociology*. Boston: Northeastern University Press.

Snow, David A., et al. 1986. "Frame Alignment Processes, Micromobilization, and Movement Participation." *American Sociological Review* 51, no. 4: 464–81.

Spender, Stephen. 1988. *The Temple*. New York: Grove Press.

Stacey, Judith. 1991. *Brave New Families: Stories of Domestic Upheaval in Late Twentieth-Century America*. New York: Basic Books.

Stanley, Charles. 1992. *The Wonderful Spirit-Filled Life*. Nashville, Tenn.: Thomas Nelson.

Stein, Arlene. 2001. *The Stranger Next Door: The Story of a Small Community's Battle over Sex, Faith, and Civil Rights*. Boston: Beacon Press.

Steinberg, Marc. 1999. "The Talk and Back-Talk of Collective Action: A Dialogic Analysis of Repertoires of Discourse among Nineteenth-Century English Cotton Spinners." *American Journal of Sociology* 105, no. 3: 736–80.

Swartley, Willard. 1983. *Slavery, Sabbath, War, and Women: Case Issues in Biblical Interpretation*. Scottsdale, Penn.: Herald Press.

Swidler, Ann. 1986. "Culture in Action: Symbols and Strategies." *American Sociological Review* 51, no. 2: 273–86.

———. 2001. *Talk of Love: How Culture Matters*. Chicago: University of Chicago Press.

Swidler, Arlene, ed. 1993. *Homosexuality and World Religions*. Harrisburg, Penn.: Trinity Press International.

Thorne, Barrie, ed. 1992. *Rethinking the Family: Some Feminist Questions*. Boston: Northeastern University Press.

———. 1993. *Gender Play: Girls and Boys in School*. New Brunswick, N.J.: Rutgers University Press.

Tillich, Paul. 1948. "You Are Accepted." In his *The Shaking of the Foundations*, 153–63. New York: Charles Scribner's Sons.

Tipton, Steven M. 1982. *Getting Saved from the Sixties: Moral Meaning in Conversion and Cultural Change*. Berkeley: University of California Press.

Transforming Congregations. 1997. *Transforming Congregations* (newsletter). April–June. 724 Niles Street, Bakersfield, Calif. 93305.

Turner, Victor. 1969. *The Ritual Process: Structure and Anti-Structure*. Hawthorne, N.Y.: Aldine de Gruyter.

———. 1974. *Dramas, Fields and Metaphors: Symbolic Action in Human Society*. Ithaca: Cornell University Press.

United Methodist Church. 1991. *United Methodist Hymnal*. Nashville, Tenn.: Abing-
    don Press.
————. 1996. *Book of Discipline*. Nashville, Tenn.: United Methodist Publishing.
Vance, Laura L. 1999. *Seventh Day Adventism in Crisis: Gender and Sectarian Change*.
    Urbana: University of Illinois Press.
Warner, Michael, ed. 1993. *Fear of a Queer Planet: Queer Politics and Social Theory*.
    Minneapolis: University of Minnesota Press.
Warner, R. Stephen. 1988. *New Wine in Old Wineskins: Evangelicals and Liberals in a
    Small-Town Church*. Berkeley: University of California Press.
————. 1995. "The Metropolitan Community Churches and the Gay Agenda: The
    Power of Pentacostalism and Essentialism." In *Religion and the Social Order*,
    edited by Mary Jo Neitz and Marion S. Goldman. Vol. 5, *Sex, Lies, and Sanctity:
    Religion and Deviance in Contemporary North America*, 81–106. Greenwich,
    Conn.: JAI.
Watney, Simon. 1989. *Policing Desire: Pornography, AIDS, and the Media*. 2d ed.
    Minneapolis: University of Minnesota Press.
Weeks, Jeffrey. 1977. *Coming Out: Homosexual Politics in Britain, from the Nine-
    teenth Century to the Present*. London: Quartet.
————. 1986. *Sexuality*. Chichester, England: Ellis Horwood/Tavistock.
————. 1989. *Sex, Politics, and Society: The Regulation of Sexuality since 1800*. 2d ed.
    New York: Longman.
————. 2000. "The 'Homosexual Role' after 30 Years: An Appreciation of the Work of
    Mary McIntosh." *Sexualities* 1, no. 2: 131–52.
Weston, Kath. 1991. *Families We Choose: Lesbians, Gays, Kinship*. New York:
    Columbia University Press.
Wilde, Melissa J. 2004. *Reconstructing Catholicism: A Sociological Analysis of Vatican
    II*. Princeton: Princeton University Press.
Williams, Patricia. 1988. "On Being the Object of Property." *Signs* 14, no. 1: 5–24.
Williams, Rhys H., and N. J. Demerath. 1991. "Religion and Political Process in an
    American City." *American Sociological Review* 56 (August): 417–43.
Willimon, William H. 1990. *Why I Am a United Methodist*. Nashville, Tenn.: Abing-
    don Press.
Wood, James R., and Jon P. Bloch. 1995. "The Role of Church Assemblies in Building a
    Civil Society: The Case of the United Methodist General Conference's Debate on
    Homosexuality." *Sociology of Religion* 56, no. 2: 121–36.
Wuthnow, Robert. 1988. *The Restructuring of American Religion*. Princeton: Princeton
    University Press.
————. 1998. *After Heaven: Spirituality in America since the 1950s*. Berkeley: Uni-
    versity of California Press.
Žižek, Slavoj. 1989. *The Sublime Object of Ideology*. New York: Verso.
————. 1994. *Mapping Ideology*. New York: Verso.
Zuckerman, Phil. 1999. *Strife in the Sanctuary: Religious Schism in a Jewish Commu-
    nity*. Walnut Creek, Calif.: AltaMira Press.

Index